Hacking the Iron Curtain

Hacking the Iron Curtain

A Media Archaeology of the Russian Internet

Natalia Konradova

THE UNIVERSITY OF WISCONSIN PRESS

The University of Wisconsin Press
728 State Street, Suite 443
Madison, Wisconsin 53706
uwpress.wisc.edu

Printed in the United States of America
This book may be available in a digital edition.

Library of Congress Cataloging-in-Publication Data

Names: Konradova, Natal'i͡a, author.
Title: Hacking the Iron Curtain : a media archaeology of the Russian internet / Natalia Konradova.
Description: Madison, Wisconsin : University of Wisconsin Press, 2025. | Includes bibliographical references and index.
Identifiers: LCCN 2025016653 | ISBN 9780299354008 (hardcover)
Subjects: LCSH: Internet—Soviet Union—History. | Internet—Russia (Federation)—History. | Internet—Social aspects—Soviet Union. | Cold War—Social aspects—Soviet Union.
Classification: LCC HM851 .K6664 2025
LC record available at https://lccn.loc.gov/2025016653

CONTENTS

A NOTE ON TRANSLITERATION, PLACE-NAMES, AND TERMS

This book follows the Library of Congress transliteration system without diacritical marks to transliterate Russian personal names, place-names, and words. To avoid confusion and in recognition of the historical context, this book refers to locations as they appear either in the documents or the secondary sources being cited, except in the case of cities such as Kyiv.

The book also includes Russian names that have previously appeared in English-language publications in their established versions. To avoid confusion, they are presented in this book without transliteration, in their standardized English forms.

Hacking the Iron Curtain

INTRODUCTION

"It's wooden. It's round at one end. And it has something like a moveable nose dropper." This is how Karl Nikolaev described an image transmitted to him telepathically from San Francisco to Moscow (Kripal 2008, 322). It was the fall of 1971. Nikolaev was sitting in the basement of the Popov Society, at the Bioinformatics Section, founded a couple of years earlier with the specific aim of conducting research into telepathy. Michael Murphy, one of the founders of the Esalen Institute, was in San Francisco at that moment: he was transmitting to Nikolaev an image from an illustrated dictionary. The picture showed a wooden elephant with a moveable trunk and a rounded rump. Although Nikolaev did not guess any of the remaining four images, the elephant that he guessed impressed the participants in the experiment so much that the transatlantic telepathy session was declared a success.

There is nothing unusual about telepathic experiments in the 1960s and 1970s, which were popular leisure activities and, in many cases, jobs. This particular 1971 event, however, was an essential episode in the history of Cold War techno-utopias. Murphy and Nikolaev were representatives of the two officially warring poles of the bipolar world, desperate to connect. While not affecting science and technology, their transatlantic telepathy session is a pivotal moment in the story I am about to tell in this book.

The research behind the book began as a study of the history of the Russian internet. The 1990s was the time when a noticeable number of Russian-speaking users gained access to computer networks. Given the historical lack of other means of grassroots communication—as well as of freedom of speech in general—and the significant number of emigrants who needed contact with their homeland and each other, the internet became an essential communications medium for post-Soviet society. However, it rather quickly turned from a way to communicate with people from different cultures into a medium of literature experiments and Russian-speaking get-togethers. That is, the *runet*.

When researching the *runet* of the 1990s, you soon find out that the first online contact with Western users occurred in the Soviet period. You wonder where access to the internet could have come from in the USSR, and then quickly fall back first into the 1980s, then into the 1970s and 1960s. The possibility of using e-mail and social networks resulted from the efforts of very different people. They were not only engineers and programmers but also diplomats, anti-war activists, and parapsychology enthusiasts. In turn, their actions would have been impossible if the previous generation had not prepared the ground for them. First and foremost, there were visions of future communication technologies and, in general, the future of humanity, or techno-utopias. As a result, in my research, the internet has become historically and conceptually closely related to studies in alternative media in the context of the Cold War. That is, telepathy.

The internet and other computer networks are very often studied by the social sciences. Even media history, when dealing with the subject, considers it in the context of computer-mediated communication (Winston 1998, Ryan 2010, Naughton 2016, Driscoll 2022). An offspring of the Cold War and the arms race, computer science was also on the agenda at another geopolitical pole: the USSR. A significant number of seminal works have been written about the history of Soviet science and technology (Gerovitch 2002, Peters 2016, Rindzevičiūtė 2016, Tatarchenko 2024). As expected, these works deal with conventional, officially recognized sciences—even those striving to be something more, such as cybernetics.

However, suppose we approach computer networks not as a present-day reality but as one of the possible means of remote communication in the past, specifically in the 1960s. In that case, a very different historical and methodological context emerges. Potential alternatives to the internet, both realized and imagined, such as radio, teleconferencing, and telepathy, present themselves as valid research subjects. When mentioning telepathy, it is necessary to clarify that this refers specifically to its scientific interpretation, which was plausible 50 years ago but is no longer considered so today. Attention to telepathy and other forms of ESP in Soviet and post-Soviet culture has garnered significant interest from researchers over the past 15 years (Menzel et al. 2012, Golubev 2020). However, these studies do not address the comparison of ESP research with other "genuinely" scientific disciplines.

Meanwhile, the exploration of new contexts is the actual task of historical science, if we follow Michel Foucault's classic thesis:

> In fact, in its traditional form, history proper was concerned to define relations (of simple causality, of circular determination, of antagonism, of expression) between facts or dated events: the series being known, it was simply a question of defining the position of each element in relation to the other elements in the series. The problem now is to constitute series. (Foucault 1972, 7)

Out of a desire to see known history as having new contexts or series, I came to media archaeology, a relatively new field in media history. Media archaeology, traditionally represented mainly by European studies, has until recently refused to be labeled an academic discipline and saw itself at the intersection of academic research and practice, artistic or educational. Disciplinary uncertainty allowed a free choice of methods and objects, which is why the studies include such different areas as, for example, the history of cinema, electricity, radio, telegraph, and multimedia.

However, as Simone Natale notes in his review essay *Understanding Media Archaeology*, there are certainly features common to the various studies that allow us to outline the field and approaches of media archaeology in the broadest approximation (Natale 2012). First of all, it is "the refusal of the notion of linear progress." As one of the founders of media archaeology, Siegfried Zielinski, puts it, "the history of the media is not the product of a predictable and necessary advance from primitive to complex apparatus. The current state of the art does not necessarily represent the best possible state" (Zielinski 2006, 7). Secondly, it's "the emphasis given to recovering the meaning of episodes and facts in the history of media that are usually disregarded" (Natale 2012). In this sense, there are no "dead ends" in media history, and the history of unrealized ideas or failed inventions is no less important than the history of winners, which are existing media. Thirdly and finally, there is "a substantial methodological anarchy," which I would rephrase as open-mindedness. In my case, work with online archives is combined with an anthropological approach (eyewitness interviews) as well as with the analysis of literary sources (science fiction utopias and historical fantasy). The diversity of the sources is due to the fact that, as in other media archaeological studies, for me the most important concept in media history is the imaginary, which anticipates the medium, often co-exists with it, and sometimes desperately fantasizes about it.

The history of electronic media and their relationship to "beliefs in the supernatural" became part of media archaeology after the publication of works by Jeffrey Sconce on the history of the invention of the telegraph (Sconce 2000) and John Durham Peters about utopias of immediate communication in different times (Peters 1999). Moreover, this approach has already been practiced in studying the history of computer networks and digital media as well (Natale and Pasulka 2019). These studies, however, are mainly concerned with irrational representations, that is, the actual beliefs that precede or accompany digital media. Finally, there are researchers who incorporate telepathy into the history of science and thus advocate an approach close to my own:

> Though most modern thinkers no longer believe in outright telepathy, I argue that dreams of thought transmission and other mental miracles subtly persist—not in obscure and occult circles, but at the forefront of technoscience. (Shure 2018, 3)

The idea that research into telepathy may be—or once was—part of the same science that made other discoveries accepted as scientific today is key to my research. The second point I want to make in this book is that two modern societies, American and Soviet, were protagonists of the same techno-utopia during the Cold War. Its concept is unlimited communication: with the people of the neighboring city, another country, another continent, and, ultimately, the other side of the Iron Curtain. Alaina Lemon discusses this subject in her study of the extraordinary enthusiasm for telepathy in American and late and post-Soviet societies precisely in the context of the desire to communicate with each other (Lemon 2017). However, Lemon only deals with telepathy and other forms of alternative communication but does not consider communication technologies such as computer networks.

For the first time, the close connection between telepathy research as an alternative form of communication and computer networks in the context of the Cold War was explored in my Russian-language book *Arkheologiia russkogo interneta: Telepatiia, telemosty i drugie tekhnoutopii kholodnoi voiny* (2021). It is partially based on the same research as this book but differs significantly in content, being intended for a Russian-speaking audience.

For example, it includes much more material on the history of American communication technologies and far less on those in post-Soviet Russia in the 1990s.

In recent years, there has been a great discussion about whether the USSR and the United States can be compared and viewed as two versions of a modern society. In fact, modernity has many competing definitions, and a substantial part of the ongoing debate is devoted to figuring out which one works best. In the context of the history of media and communication technologies during the Cold War, the most important aspect of modernity that seems to converge across the different strands is the reliance on rational change in the world and the belief in scientific and technological progress. In general, the very idea of a better future in which social justice prevails, disease and suffering are reduced, knowledge is universally available, and the economy is efficient is a key feature of modern society.

The word "belief" in this case should be explained: it is not a religious feeling but the confidence that science will never cease improving the quality of life. In Soviet postwar society—against the background of the scientific and technological revolution of the 1960s and especially the first human space flight—such techno-optimism supported by state money led to the rapid development of a particular field of research. This was the study of "human reserve capabilities" (human potential in the US), which included telepathy and other types of extrasensory perception (ESP). There was such a huge number of ESP research projects in the 1960s and 1970s in the USSR, mostly classified but also amateur and non-academic, that mainstream academic scientists organized a special commission on pseudoscience in the 1990s. For more than a decade, the commission issued bulletins exposing the methodological failures of alternative research.

It is still common in the Russian-speaking intellectual environment to accuse the technical intelligentsia of a tendency to esotericism. There are quite easy explanations for this: the deficit of social knowledge, which was supplanted by primitive Soviet Marxism; the overproduction of technical professions premised on the high status of scientists and engineers, and so on. On their own, these explanations look credible. Especially since in post-Soviet societies, particularly in Russia, there is, indeed, a problem of trust in scientific knowledge. This is also partly due to the current search for a new spirituality coupled with the gradual isolation of Russian science.

However, my challenge is temporarily to step outside the current scientific frame where computer networks and artificial intelligence are the everyday reality and telepathy is pseudoscience or esotericism. My aim here is to pull alternative research out of the New Age and esotericism, to examine it in detachment from current judgment (as an archaeologist, according to Foucault, examines an object taken out of context), to place it in a series of other scientific trends of the 1960s and 1970s, and to eventually come back to the modern scientific worldview. I will not consider modern techno-utopias and new information-transfer technologies, such as computer-mediated brain-to-brain impulse transfer, direct control of devices, and other topics of the NBIC-convergence era, characterized by expectations of a synthesis of nanotech, biotech, infotech, and cognitive science. My interest concerns the twentieth century.

After the end of World War II and the beginning of the Cold War, the United States and the USSR closely monitored the technical achievements of the enemy while simultaneously leaking fake news about their own successes; invested in high tech and raised generations of highly professional, informed and loyal scientists. However, the Cold War had a reverse side: the mutual interests of the two societies. The Iron Curtain had significant holes but did not allow the free exchange of information, so it was up to ordinary people to establish contacts. Beginning in the early 1970s, there was a movement of citizen diplomats, American activists who traveled to the USSR under the guise of tourists to establish contacts with Soviet citizens and try to prevent the next war, a nuclear one. Not only did they succeed but managed to do even the unexpected: the citizen-diplomat movement started the thrilling story of connecting Soviet users to the internet.

The role of media and communication became crucial during the Cold War, and large government budgets were allocated to this field. Of course, not all investments yielded discoveries. For media archaeology, the dead ends that are failed discoveries and missed inventions are the best means to find out what scientists, engineers, philosophers, and users have dreamed of and what alternatives they have faced. In this way, computer science, which gave birth to the global network, the internet, has had alternatives. For example, these include experiments to discover patterns of telepathic communication, or a system of worldwide teleconferences linking peoples of different continents.

The collapse of the USSR and the end of the bipolar world was followed by a post-Soviet crisis of the future—the most fundamental utopia of modernity, which gave way to fantasies about the past. It is open to debate how specific this process was to post-Soviet countries and how much it was, conversely, part of a global trend. One thing is certain—the utopia of an interconnected global community was replaced by ethno-national projects rooted in superiority and exclusion.

The frustration and profound identity crisis of the 1990s proved to be, in a certain sense, fruitful: the internet, already accessible to the first generation of Russian-speaking users, became a tool for constructing a new public sphere and a new literary discourse (Schmidt et al. 2006; Schmidt 2011), as well as for exploring a new national idea, this time network-based (Laruelle 2015). For quite some time, attempts to reconstruct a "great Russia" remained a marginal pastime, something akin to an online game. In 2014, ideas and programs to reclaim the past ceased to be exclusively verbal: Russia attacked Ukraine. A new epoch had arrived, which had not yet found its name but had already characterized itself by a full-scale war.

The Outline of the Book

A strict chronological order of narration is impossible when it comes to the development not of a single concept, technology, or phenomenon, but of several, either connected or entangled with each other. Therefore, although this book is organized mainly chronologically, within each chapter this principle is sometimes violated.

The first chapter, "Soviet Power Plus the Digitalization of the Entire Country," is devoted to the techno-fantasies that followed the Soviet computer industry and cybernetics. The science of control, cybernetics, was ideally suited to the ground prepared by the Russian Revolution and became a kind of upgrade of the ideas of the 1920s.

In chapter 2, "The Technology of the Future Is Telepathy," I discuss a little-studied aspect of the history of cybernetics, that is, its role in the institutionalization of Soviet parapsychology. Among the various extrasensory phenomena that parapsychologists investigated—telekinesis, clairvoyance, and so on—I am most interested in experiments with telepathy. This direction appeared to be the most developed and it was here that the next scientific and technical breakthrough was expected. Furthermore, telepathy, if its existence could be proved, and if it could become a technology, would be the most obvious alternative to computer networks: it would be the same global communication network, only based on other principles.

Chapter 3, "Telepathy—Spacebridge—Internet," discusses how American and Soviet parapsychologists, beginning in the 1970s with transatlantic telepathy sessions, switched in the 1980s to more conventional (from a modern point of view) types of contact, such as teleconferences. In the end, it was parapsychologists who played one of the key roles in the USSR's access to the internet, not yet mainstream but still available to scientists, teachers, environmentalists, and other activists.

In chapter 4, "User Revolution," I turn to the user history of communication technologies, and the history of communities that existed long before the internet and which have shaped the internet subculture in the 1980s. It reaches from the radio amateurs and telephone hackers who created virtual communities, to the early 1980s, when they were replaced by graduate students and young university employees who embraced new technologies and effectively turned the internet into a social network.

The culmination of the grassroots contact between American and Soviet users was their first online meeting, which is discussed in chapter 5, "The USSR Is Connected to the Usenet." This took place in the late 1980s and early 1990s on different platforms and networks. A well-preserved archive makes it possible to trace it back to Usenet. Not only the end of the Cold War but of the USSR itself are virtually broadcast live, with Soviet subscribers to Usenet proving to be the main source of information about the 1991 August putsch for the world's media. And as soon as this happens, the net already has hundreds and then thousands of Russian-speaking subscribers.

The sixth and final chapter, "The Russian Colonization of the American Internet," focuses on the emergence of the Russian-speaking user community in the late 1990s and the process of its separation from the American segment of the web. What is the "Russian internet" and who are the Russian-speaking users? In the early years, they were mostly young people who had emigrated to the United States, Israel, and Europe and joined the internet from the universities where they studied or worked. The internet was an unprecedented medium that allowed them to stay in touch with their homeland and each other but also to create a new identity based on a common language and cultural background. The sense of borderlessness of the virtual Russian-speaking space that the internet had provided gave rise to the latest iteration of *runet*: the concept of the Russian World as a network community of Russian language speakers, a pillar of future Russian statehood and a new form of the nation's existence.

1

Soviet Power Plus the Digitalization of the Entire Country

"Everyone has probably read in science fiction novels about tiny transceivers that allow people of the future to talk to each other at any moment. Millions of radio stations working simultaneously!" This is how Academician Vladimir Kotelnikov, a radiophysicist and cryptographer, and one of the fathers of Soviet secret communications technology, described the near future in an interview for the book *Reporting from the XXI Century* (Vasil'ev and Gushchev 1963, 335). The first edition came out in 1958, a year after the launch of the Soviet satellite, and the second was published in 1963, two years after Yuri Gagarin's flight. The book collected conversations between journalists and leading Soviet scientists, mostly full members of the Academy of Sciences, about discoveries and inventions they expected in the following fifty years.

The late 1950s–early 1960s were the years when the future in the USSR seemed truly bright. The country had survived World War II and Stalinism, the success of the Soviet space program was obvious to the whole world, and this was only the beginning of a promising scientific and technological revolution: industrial process automation was underway, the first computer networks had been created, and there were already projects to computerize the entire country. In other words, technological optimism was reaching its peak, and, as a consequence, the genre of popular futurology was experiencing unprecedented blossoming. In this sense, *Reporting from the XXI Century* was a very typical product of the era.

The academicians' predictions in the book covered all the key areas of science and technology at the time. Some of them, such as the construction of nuclear power plants, the launching of spaceships to the moon and Mars, flat-panel TVs, artificial fabrics, moving sidewalks, or housekeeping cybernetic automata—became a reality in the following decades. Others, such as triumph over cancer or contactless energy transfer, humankind is still trying hard to make reality. Meanwhile, such ideas as full weather control will, probably, forever remain science fiction. The same applies to the predictions of human improvement: a future human will need less time to sleep and to work as a result of the nascent "intensification of higher nervous activity" (Academician Alexander Nesmeyanov) and, finally, will become immortal as soon as scientists find a way "to turn off the mechanism that makes cells age" (Academician Vasily Kuprevich).[1]

It would seem that there can be nothing more visionary than the idea of immortality, which still provides multimillion-dollar budgets to researchers. And yet, the most radical prediction in the book is the suggestion of Academician Kotelnikov, cited above, about future communication via miniature transmitters. The idea of improving the human body belongs completely to the natural sciences while any new concept of communication is strictly related to social changes.

Most importantly and yet surprisingly, the academician left behind what seemed then to be the only possible model of communication—the centralized one—that assumes a single source of information (the Soviet state) and, therefore, full control over information flows—to prefer instead that of grassroots information exchange and networking. In fact, Kotelnikov outlined a postmodern model of social communication that presumes the distribution of information flows not from the center to the periphery, but throughout the entire network structure. His was the very model that early internet communities used to self-describe in the 1980s, and which, no doubt, corresponded exactly to the reality of mobile telephony that emerged in the 1990s. We will return to this phenomenon to compare it with what another academician, Sergei Lebedev, designer of the first Soviet computers and computer networks, has suggested.

By 1960, Lebedev, who at the time headed the Institute of Precise Mechanics and Computer Engineering, a part of the USSR Academy of Sciences, had already successfully connected three machines into a single system. Of course, it was a military computer network commissioned by the Soviet Ministry of Defense and created by Lebedev's team in order to increase computer power and the speed of data processing of a missile defense system. The U.S. military computer network ARPANET was developed with roughly the same tasks, and as a result has radically changed the world by becoming a technology provider for the internet. Theoretically, the author of such an important and advanced project could have made a bold prediction about how machines would change society and mankind. However, a computer network is still not the internet, which we think represents a social phenomenon. So, in his interview Lebedev talked to the journalists about prospects for computer management of production, construction, aircraft design, and other fields of the Soviet economy, including its planning. Toward the end of the interview, he did turn to the everyday life of an average user but considered library lecture broadcasts as the greatest achievement of future computer networking. In other words, he focused on how easy it would be to get the information you needed from the center, anywhere in the USSR. Lebedev says:

> Somewhere in Transcarpathia, in the heart of a tidy Ukrainian village, there's a sign on one of the houses: "Biblio-broadcasting." Boys and girls enter the house, one could tell they are students at high schools and technical colleges located in the village. Each of them comes exactly at the appointed hour. One cannot be late: in the booths, like those designed for international telephone conversations, the bluish screens of TV sets are already lit . . . It turns out that biblio-broadcasting is the transmission of literary, historical, or scientific reference data by individual orders through television devices.

So, according to Lebedev, the computer networks of the future will allow a better distribution of knowledge, such as lectures and bibliography references from information centers. This description of knowledge spreading from large cities to villages has deep roots and reproduces the early Soviet, and to a broader extent, modernist model of mass education, whether it be the dissemination of hygiene rules, the campaign against illiteracy (*likbez*), or the fight against religion. Around the time that the *likbez* began in Soviet Russia, in 1921, the avant-garde poet Velimir Khlebnikov revealed to the world his utopian vision of the instantaneous propagation of knowledge through radio:

> Radio has solved a problem that the church itself was unable to solve and has thus become as necessary to each settlement as a school is, or a library.

> The problem of celebrating the communion of humanity's one soul, one daily spiritual wave that washes over the entire country every twenty-four hours, saturating it with a flood of scientific and artistic news—that problem has been solved by Radio using lighting as its tool . . . Everyone can read whatever he chooses. This one book, identical across the entire country, stands in the center of every small town, always surrounded by a ring of readers, a carefully composed silent Reading Wall in every settlement. (Douglas 1987, 395)

Khlebnikov's medium is the "lighting" while Lebedev's is the "bluish screens of TV sets"; Khlebnikov appoints the "radio-reading wall" as the main institution, Lebedev uses "biblio-broadcasting," and for both of them, the measure of the project's success is the spread of knowledge to small towns and villages. However, Khlebnikov was writing in the 1920s, a period of bold visions, when the first broadcast by the central radio station was still a year away. Lebedev, on the other hand, gave his interview 40 years later, when radio had long become an everyday part of life and the first computer networks had already been built. In his time, social projection was fully appropriated by the state: there was no question of what the society would be like: it would be the communist one. *Reporting from the XXI Century* does not include any predictions related to social sciences or the humanities, except maybe the forecasted ability of cybernetic automata to recognize speech and to edit texts. The scientists celebrate scientific progress per se, while its goal, communism, is obvious to readers and journalists alike. In the disclaimer, the latter specify: powered by the virtues of the socialist system, it is the Soviet scientists who will build a radiant future for the whole Earth.

From the very beginning of his professional activity, engineer Lebedev faced purely pragmatic tasks, as we can conclude by reading the minutes of the meeting on the design of computers at the USSR Academy of Sciences in 1951:

> I have information about 18 machines designed by the Americans, this information is of advertising nature and doesn't contain any data on how the machines are arranged. We must catch up with abroad in the construction of calculating machines, and we must do it quickly. (Khodakov 2010; 68)

In other words, Lebedev's mission was very specific: to build a machine with the same parameters as in the United States but in two years instead of five. The goal wasn't to achieve a technological breakthrough; moreover, in the situation of the postwar shortages this "catching up with America" was already a rather fantastic project.

The question that remains is why, against the background of modernist utopia's complete victory, does Academician Kotelnikov suddenly describe grassroots communication: that is, a postmodern network model of society? In his vision of the future, people communicate directly and privately, beyond institutions and state-controlled channels. They are connected through pocket radio sets, which people today will easily recognize as cell phones. This is no longer the utopia of enlightenment, which means improving society from above, but the utopia of a user, more typical of the next generation.

According to media historians Simone Natale and Gabriele Balbi, accurate predictions about the development of technologies are always based on the present experience, that is, they are extrapolations of an already existing order of things (Simone and Balbi 2014). The authors give the examples of photography and artificial intelligence, which had been described long before they were developed. What experience might Kotelnikov have had by the early 1960s?

Known as a developer of secret government communications and a cryptographer, twice the Stalin Prize winner, Kotelnikov had never once shown himself to be a dissident and, on the contrary, was loyal to the system to the core; during the Stalinist repressions, although he was not directly in charge of special prisons for scientists and engineers (the so-called *sharashki* described by Solzhenitsyn in his novel *In the First Circle*), but worked side by side with them; in 1962, he supervised the work to establish radio communication through the planet Venus (the words "Peace," "Lenin," "USSR" were transmitted); in 1973, he signed a letter against Academician Sakharov. In the mind of a man with this biography, there should be no place for any user-to-user concept, only there was one: Kotelnikov was a radio amateur.

The future academician became interested in radio as a teenager, in the early 1920s, when the first state radio station in Soviet Russia had just started broadcasting. He subscribed to the *Radiolyubitel* magazine (*Radio Enthusiast*, later *Radio* magazine, with a peak circulation of 1.4 million), built his own radio receivers and transmitters, and, according to his son's memoirs, dreamed of working in radio (Kotel'nikov 2011). More than thirty years later, in 1957, Kotelnikov participated in the launch of the first Sputnik.

According to his memoirs, published by his daughter, one of the important tasks in the design was to track the satellite from Earth using a radio signal:

> A theory was just a theory, but no one knew how it would actually work out. It was unclear where it would fly and whether it would be possible to bring it to the planned orbit at all. And then, it was unclear whether the radio equipment would work after such overloads. If the equipment was all right, it was unknown how the radio signal would pass through the ionosphere . . . First of all, it was necessary not to miss it and catch the signal. Then, it was necessary to control its trajectory reliably, to follow its changes, by which it would be possible to judge what was happening to it there. . . . We could not involve specialists from other countries in this case, as launches . . . were kept in the strictest secrecy: it was the time of the Cold War, there was an arms race. . . . I suggested that we involve our radio amateurs. They are active, enthusiastic people. To publish such articles in the magazine *Radio*, which would talk about the possibility of launching a satellite . . . and the help that radio amateurs could provide in this endeavor. This is a popular magazine, not the kind of magazine whose materials are followed by serious scientists and all kinds of "special services." (Kotel'nikov 2011, 206)

That is, despite the strict secrecy and the generally tense military and political situation, Kotelnikov came up with an idea of mobilizing radio enthusiasts, which he successfully realized. The articles were published (Kazantsev 1957; Vakhnin 1957), radio amateurs responded, and the Institute of Radioengineering and Electronics, where Kotelnikov was working at the time, received, in his words, "a trunk of letters" with data on satellite radiolocation.

In the 1920s, radio was, and in many ways still is, the most democratic of all communication technologies. Without a major investment and advanced high-tech manufacturing, you can't build your own computer, much less a computer network. In the meantime, to become an amateur radio operator you need knowledge of how a radio receiver and transmitter work and their basic parts, which were already available to teenagers in the 1920s. Unlike an internet user, an amateur radio operator never knows in advance who he will meet on the air. At the same time, he doesn't depend on existing networks. That is why, despite the government's attempts to manage their activities, radio amateurs were never entirely under state control, neither in the United States nor in the USSR. It is fairly safe to assume that it was the radio that gave birth to the techno-utopia of global communication, which returned decades later in the shape of the internet-utopia.

What did these scientists, who in the late 1950s and early 1960s were charting the future development of communication technology, display? We see two mindsets and two visions representing two different approaches: that of a pathfinder, with a designer or an engineer making the key contribution to the level of technological progress; and that of a user, who does not necessarily need paternalistic care, but, instead, may at some point even appropriate the state-developed technologies for his or her own needs. These two types of imagined future don't exist separately: they depend on each other, switch places from time to time, and in this dialectical interaction bring the history of communication to what was called *the Net* in the 1980s: the global connectivity space.

In the next parts of this chapter, we will examine how the Soviet computer industry responded to political demands, why it did not produce an original techno-utopia, and how cybernetics, on the contrary, became the ideal environment for scientific and technological fantasy.

Soviet EVMs:
From a Homemade Hi-Tech to a Copying Mode

Soviet engineers were aware that an electronic computer had been launched in the United States but couldn't get any detailed information about it owing to international restrictions on the export of sensitive technologies (The Coordinating Committee for Multilateral Export Control, or CoCom). As Boris Malinovskij writes in his book *History of Information Technology in Personalities*,[2] Bashir Rameyev, who in 1947 was working as a technician at the Central Scientific Research Institute of Communications in Moscow, heard the news about ENIAC in a BBC broadcast and initiated the first EVM (Electronnaya Vychislitelnaya Mashina—Electronic Computing Machine) project in the USSR (Malinovskii 1995, 239). Although the project remained on paper for some time, four years later the first two Soviet computers became operational, almost simultaneously: Sergey Lebedev's MESM (Small Electronic Computing Machine) in Kyiv, and Isaac Bruk's M-1 in Moscow.

The Soviet industry wasn't producing high-tech components, and components that *were* available belonged to a prewar generation of technologies. Hence, both teams were faced with the same task: to duplicate the U.S.

achievement, but without the same materials, in complete isolation from the West, and under the rigidly state-managed science-based industry that could not cope with the nonstandard needs of the new branch. In these circumstances, the chief designers had to find unique solutions. These involved personal connections and access to scarce materials, parts accidentally found in a warehouse, advertising brochures for American computers, scraps of information from Western radio programs, and so on.

A good example of the above situation is the discrepancy between the first two Soviet computer projects and their chief designers, Sergei Lebedev and Isaac Bruk, in spite of their almost identical biographies and similar achievements. Both were born in 1902 and died in 1974, graduated from the Moscow Power Engineering Institute in the 1920s, worked on military projects during World War II, and presented the first two Soviet computers a mere couple of weeks apart in 1951. However, Sergei Lebedev was well integrated into the Soviet scientific and industrial infrastructure, enabling him to design and order new components. Unlike Lebedev, Isaak Bruk had to make do with an academic budget and a small team of Moscow Power Engineering Institute graduates. As a military engineer, however, Bruk also had access to so-called trophy resources, that is, booty plundered from Germany during World War II. This allowed him to incorporate German semiconductors (cuprox rectifiers) into the design of his M-1 model, which would otherwise have remained an exclusively vacuum tube–based machine. Mikhail Kartsev, one of Bruk's engineers, recalls these circumstances:

> In early 1950, an odd component was discovered among the stuff brought in from the booty warehouse. . . . For a long time, nobody could understand its purpose or figure out its origin, but eventually it became clear what it was—a miniature cuprox rectifier. . . . . The M-1 became the world's first computer whose logic circuits were all semiconductor-based. (Malinovskii 1995, 182)

Such homemade machines could exist only as the first generation of computers, when it was necessary to prove that the Soviet Union could invent a computer from scratch. However, for the second generation, which moved from a vacuum-tube base to a semiconductor one, and even more so for the third generation, personal ingenuity was not enough. It was necessary to have full information about world developments and an appropriate high-tech industry. This did not appear in the USSR until its very end.[3]

The gap between Soviet and Western IT developments widened. The 1964 launch of IBM's first integrated-circuit machine, the IBM/System 360, prompted a major discussion in the Soviet Union around the possibility of creating a Unified System of Electronic Computers (acronymized in Russian as ES EVM). Until then, all Soviet machines were unique, which required equally unique software and made it hard, or impossible, to connect them to each other. This, among other things, complicated the construction of computer networks.

Participants in the discussion, organized by the Ministry of Radio Industry, included the first- and second-generation computer designers Lebedev, Bruk, Rameyev, and Viktor Glushkov, as well as some officials from the State Planning Committee and the Ministry itself. The real issue under discussion was not whether local developments must all be integrated into a single system, but which Western computer ought to be taken as a model for the ES EVM.

The choice was between three manufacturers: America's IBM, West Germany's Siemens, and Britain's ICL. IBM expressed interest in collaborating but wasn't greenlighted to do so by the American government, and could not, therefore, dispatch their machine or its documentation to the USSR. Rameyev began negotiations with ICL. Unexpectedly enthusiastic about the idea, the British firm agreed to sell the Soviets several machines, provide them with relevant documentation, and even train Soviet specialists to operate the computer. ICL were willing to violate the CoCom restrictions because they could see serious advantages in such a move: capturing a major Eastern European market might subsequently help them triumph over IBM in the global competition for IT dominance.

ICL's System 4 mainframe, however, was derived from the Radio Corporation of America's Spectra 70, itself a clone of the IBM/System 360 (Lavington 2011, 457). In fact, Soviet developers were faced with a choice: they could either copy the machine in collaboration with the manufacturer—or do so unilaterally. Given that American technology had been used in System 4, ICL asked the United States to greenlight the mainframe's sale to the USSR. A 1971 CIA memo reports that, though the green light was not given, ICL pressed on regardless (CIA 1971).

The ES EVM project involved all Warsaw Pact countries. The USSR's most important partner in this area was East Germany, where direct cloning of the IBM/System 360 was already underway by the time the discussion began. It was therefore decided in 1969 to create a single series of computers based on IBM 360 architecture—this despite a lack of documentation, components, or assistance from the manufacturer. Over the course of the next few years, funding for proprietary development projects in the USSR was sharply curtailed, with financial resources redirected toward the establishment of the ES EVM (Malinovskii 1995). The first ES EVM computer was launched in 1971, the last in 1998. According to people with firsthand experience of these machines, they were vastly inferior not only to the American originals, but also to Soviet-produced computers such as Lebedev's BESM-6. The course of action decided upon in 1969 prompted Rameyev, an advocate of Soviet IT integration and collaboration with Great Britain, to resign from his post as deputy chief engineer of the ES EVM project. Lebedev, for his part, succeeded in maintaining the independence of his Institute of Computer Engineering and continued to produce the BESM.

If the switch to compatible computers could theoretically lead to a Soviet version of the internet, it was unlikely to give rise to any network-related techno-utopia. The engineers had to catch up with an already existing technological breakthrough, not to create a new one.

Utopia of Command and Control

Unlike the Soviet computer industry, Soviet cybernetics proved to be fertile ground for a vigorous techno-utopia. Paradoxically, it took the import of a theory from America and the computers from the Soviet Union to produce the original ideas.

A key figure in the development of computer networks was Anatoly Kitov, an engineer with the military rank of colonel. His story is detailed in the book *How Not to Network a Nation* by Benjamin Peters (2016) and publications by Kitov's son Vladimir (Kitov 2020). In a nutshell, in the early 1950s, Kitov discovered a copy of Norbert Wiener's *Cybernetics* in the Special Design Bureau's *spetskhran* (a library of classified information materials with highly restricted use). It made him interested in the idea of control automation, which he began to popularize despite the fact that cybernetics had been officially branded a "bourgeois pseudoscience." In 1955, Kitov and two mathematicians, Sergei Sobolev and Alexandr Lyapunov, co-authored an article entitled "The Main Features of Cybernetics" for the *Voprosy filosofii* [*Problems of Philosophy*] journal (Sobolev et al. 1955), the following year saw the release of Kitov's book *Electronic Digital Machines* (Kitov 1956), and in

1959 Kitov sent a letter to the Soviet leader Nikita Khrushchev proposing to construct a computer network in order to improve the management of the national economy.

According to historians of Soviet computers, this letter influenced the subsequent decisions by the Central Committee of the Communist Party, specifically "on the introduction of electronic equipment in all sectors of the economy" (Kuteynikov and Shilov, 48–49). However, Kitov was not satisfied with the results and sent the second letter six months after the first one. It outlined a detailed program for the construction of a comprehensive network. But because, in the very same letter, Kitov criticized the Ministry of Defense, of which he himself was an employee, his program did not find support. Officials of the Ministry of Defense were offended by his criticism, and Kitov was dismissed.

Nevertheless, in the late 1950s, Kitov's project—and cybernetics in general, which after Stalin's death was fully embraced by the Soviet Academy of Sciences—came to be the subject of energetic discussions. A report co-presented by Kitov, Axel Berg, and Lyapunov at a meeting of the Academy's Presidium in 1959 accelerated the establishment of a Scientific Council for Cybernetics, with Berg becoming its chair. Already in 1962, the idea of an all-union computer network became officially recognized: *Priroda* magazine published an article *The Science with the Greatest Potential* in which Berg described it as follows:

> The country is planning to establish a unified system of control over the entire national economy, doing so with the help of specially created, powerful computing centres kitted out with modern ultra-high-speed electronic computers and connected to planning, financing, transport and industrial organizations by means of a so-called single technological automatic connection system. This will ensure that our governing bodies receive timely, comprehensive information regarding the course and development of economic activity across the country, as well as allowing them to manage it expeditiously, uninterruptedly and in the most optimum manner possible . . . no capitalist system can compete with such a system of control, founded as it invariably is on the contradictory, antagonistic interests of different segments of the population. (Berg 1962)

By the early 1960s, cybernetics laboratories, institutes, and departments began to materialize throughout the USSR, as did an entire generation of cyberneticists—theorists, practitioners and administrators, engineers, physicists, and mathematicians. Gerovitch defined cybernetics as a mathematical substitute for all scientific disciplines and pointed out that cybernetics was considered "a panacea for the Soviet economic woes" due to its "aura of objectivity and truth" (Gerovitch 2008, 337). Several departments featuring the word "cybernetics" in their names now materialized within the Soviet Academy of Sciences, essentially duplicating the traditional sciences with their modern—that is, cybernetic—versions. This turn to cybernetization can be considered a paradigm shift: mathematicians came to the support of engineers in information technology. Cybernetics was originally, going back to Wiener's version, a bridge between mathematical theory and the material world. Not only did it enable the solution of specific problems, but it also fired up the imagination about solving global issues. Its super-disciplinary nature was perfectly suited to its main function of renewal—not only of science itself, but also of society—based on scientific findings.

Of course, the first-generation designers had to possess the mathematical tools to build their unique computers. Cyberneticians of the 1960s were engaged not only in theorizing, but also in developing new machine models. However, it was cybernetics that became the new utopia of technology.

In the early 1960s, Kitov's idea found resonance with mathematician Glushkov, who replaced electrical engineer Lebedev as the head of the computer lab at the Institute of Mathematics in Kiev (from 1961, the Institute of Cybernetics). The potential of cybernetics to improve control systems across the country preoccupied him far more than computer production and he invited Kitov to develop a new version of the project. The updated project was called the Unified State Network of Computer Centers but in the early 1970s changed its name to the All-State Automated System of Accounting and Information Processing, or OGAS. It also involved the creation and centralization of automated control systems (ACS) designed to connect all the production facilities of the Soviet Union. Responsibility for control over the work of every factory and plant—and, in future, over that of other organizations as well—was to be entrusted to a specially designed inter-agency computing center that would receive and process field data. Doing his utmost to secure funding for the project, Glushkov explained its relevance to officials by referring to the needs of the planned socialist economy and the concomitant challenges of communism-building. The electronic socialism proposed by Glushkov even entailed a rejection of money—one version of the project featured electronic payments,[4] a logical corollary of the system of automatic links between industries and the administration.

An attempt to adopt the project as a state program was made in early 1960s, when Deputy Chairman of the USSR Council of Ministers Alexei Kosygin was implementing economic reforms. He considered a nationwide information system as one of the possible options to improve the functionality of the planned economy. In 1962, Glushkov enlisted his support; in 1963, a scientific council for the introduction of mathematical methods and computer technology into the national economy was founded by the State Committee for Science; in 1964, the council presented a pre-design project to the Presidium of the Council of Ministers, but this was returned for revision (Kutejnikov and Shilov 2011).

Eventually, Kosygin chose not to make planning more efficient with a computer network but to reduce the degree to which the economy was planned. He preferred the ideas of "liberal economists," led by the reform-minded economist Evsei Liberman. They were based on a partial democratization and liberalization of the economic system and were ideologically opposed to OGAS, a project founded on the idea of total centralization and control.

According to the version told by the economists themselves, Glushkov personally was not the problem, nor was it his information system project, but rather the low level of planning itself, which was the basis of the Soviet economy. Victor Belkin and Igor Birman, two of the economists behind the Liberman reforms, regarded the expenditure required by the OGAS project as senseless—at least until more basic problems could be solved, arguing that "one can establish computer centers, and conceive superb algorithms, but nothing will come of it as long as the transport organizations reckon plan fulfillment in ton-kilometers." (Belkin and Birman 1964; quoted in Ellman 1973, 10)

Nevertheless, Glushkov highly resented the authors of the reforms and took their criticism of his project very personally. In a memoir recorded by Glushkov's daughter in 1982, shortly before his death, he said that the liberal economists deceived Kosygin. He also emphasized their biographies: "Beginning in 1964, the academic economists Lieberman, Belkin, Birman, and others, many of whom later went to the United States and Israel, began to openly oppose me" (Malinovskii 1995, 160). In the Soviet context, naming recognizably Jewish surnames and mentioning their departure "to the United

States and Israel" was an explicitly anti-Semitic statement. In Glushkov's case, this made clear how highly personally he took the failure of his OGAS project.

Despite the fact that the project of Glushkov and Kitov was not adopted on a national scale, they managed in the 1970s to install its basic element, the automated control system, at a large number of enterprises and institutions, including the military. The implementation of this model ceased only by the mid-1980s, when the USSR witnessed a new wave of economic reforms, the gradual disintegration of the Iron Curtain—and, ultimately, a transition to American network technologies.

For a media archaeologist, it is more important to analyze the ideas that have been expressed than the projects that have been realized. It is the former that give a glimpse of the imaginary of an era. In this sense, OGAS, as an unfulfilled cybernetic fantasy of integrating all production facilities into a single information system, can be seen as a utopia of command and control—the ultimate centralization and homogenization of economic and, in perspective, social processes, with cybernetics serving as an objective, progressive, and infallible agent of modernization.

Automated systems were believed to be capable of making control exerted over the entire Soviet territory possible, regardless of the scale of the facilities or their remoteness from Moscow. Although the concept of centralization and homogenization itself was not unique, the idea of machine perfection underpinning it was a novel creation of the age of cybernetics. Gerovitch and Peters attribute this fact to a trauma of the post-Stalin period, with its unpredictable repressions and erratic governance (Gerovitch 2001; Gerovitch 2002; Peters 2016). Peters articulates it as follows:

> There was an unusual contender for filling the political vacuum left by Stalin's passing. To the scientists under study here, Stalin's best replacement was no person at all but rather a technocratic conviction that computer-aided governance could avoid the past abuses of its strongman state. (2016, 201)

Khrushchev-era scientists regarded information-oriented systems as a benchmark of order, certainty, and rationality, and the computer as an agent of progress and an ideal means of rational, disciplined management. Manageability had been an important therapeutic concept throughout the 1960s and 1970s—a fact that informs Ilya Kukulin's investigations of the popularity of science fiction and other types of "alternative social design" during those decades (Kukulin 2007).

Today, there is a well-established tradition of critiquing the cybernetic worldview, or the *cybernetic episteme*, as an integral part of modernity. It is often seen as synonymous with authoritarianism, built on the total rationalization of all processes, alienating corporeality and sensibility, and acting as an agent of colonialism in the broadest sense (Emmelhainz 2023, Pfohl 2010). Undoubtedly, the utopia of command and control contains within it the dystopia of uniformity, which excludes individual differences. Returning to the historical context of Soviet cybernetics, it should be noted that it largely continued the revolutionary era's concepts of machinocracy and technocracy.

Before and during the Russian October 1917 Revolution, radical utopians dreamed of modernizing the country based on the same two principles: centralization and scientific and technological progress. And Soviet cybernetic philosophy directly succeeded the early Soviet utopian visions of an ideally constructed new society.

Cybernetics as Tektology

Most relevant of all the visions of the Russian Revolutionary era to the ideas of Kitov and Glushkov were works by Alexander Bogdanov (real last name Malinovsky) on the universal organization science *tektology*, best described in *Red Star*, a science fiction novel published in 1908 (Bogdanov 1984). It begins with a description of Menni the Martian who looks almost like a human being. Russian political émigrés whose community Menni has infiltrated have been organizing demonstrations and discussing the future of socialism, unaware that said future has already been built—on Mars. And it is to Mars that the novel's protagonist sets out, intent on seeing how this future society functions and bringing this knowledge back to Earth, to his comrades in arms.

Martian socialism isn't merely a fair system of dividing labor and distributing goods: it's also a complex of eminently rational, high-tech solutions geared toward the implementation of an error-free labor-and-production statistics system. The author describes this system in detail:

> the engineer took us to a small cubical building between the central factory and one of the corner edifices. There were three more such structures, all of

> them arranged in the same way. Their black walls were covered with rows of shiny white signs showing tables of production statistics. I knew the Martian language well enough to be able to decipher them. On the first of them, which was marked with the number one, was the following: "The machine-building industry has a surplus of 968,757 man-hours daily, of which 11,325 hours are of skilled labor." . . . There were similar figures on the third and fourth tables, which covered occupations such as preschool education, primary and secondary education, medicine in rural areas, and medicine in urban areas. (Bogdanov 1984, 65)

This Martian computing center, known as the Institute of Statistics, has "agencies everywhere which keep track of the flow of goods into and out of the stockpiles and monitor the productivity of all enterprises and the changes in their work forces," allowing it to calculate any disparities between production output and demand. It is obvious that Bodganov's detailed description of a labor-and-production computation system uncannily anticipates the OGAS. Only there was no mystery in Bogdanov's "prophecy"; instead, the cybernetic theories of the 1960s revealed the profound relations with the early socialist techno-utopia.

Following Bogdanov's conflict with Lenin, his name would not be publicly mentioned until the late 1960s and his works would be kept in *spetskhrans*. However, Soviet cybernetic scientists read Bogdanov's texts and knew about his ideas.

The most important source of spreading Bogdanov's ideas among Soviet cyberneticians was his son Alexander Malinovsky, a biologist, a member of the Scientific Council on Cybernetics at the Presidium of the USSR Academy of Sciences, and professionally associated with Glushkov, Igor Poletaev,[5] Berg, Lyapunov, and other notable figures in the field. Alexander Malinovsky Jr. made serious efforts to popularize his father's ideas among his colleagues. Two of his letters have been preserved in Lyapunov's collection. In the first one, dated 1961, Malinovsky promises to send Lyapunov "some materials about Tektology," apparently already discussed earlier (Malinovsky 1961). In the second letter, dated 1965, Malinovsky reports his participation in the preparation of the reprinting of Bogdanov's *Tektologiya*:

> Besides, two other things have appeared which I cannot evade, both concerning my father. One is that they want to publish [Alexei] Gastev and other

> classics on organizational issues (Section of Organization of the Council on Cybernetics), including my father's *Tektologiya* ("Universal Organization Science"). I was drawn into the work of the section. I've only been there twice, will probably give a talk in February (although here people don't want to let me go). But the main thing is to help with the preparation of the publication. The second thing is that they wanted to make a movie ("Through the Icy Mist") about 1906–1907, where they completely pervert Lenin's attitude to Bogdanov (which was really very good until 1908). I had to intervene, but it seems that even without my intervention everything will be sorted out here now. (Malinovskii 1965)

There are earlier indications that Bogdanov's texts were known to Soviet writers and scientists. As biologist, philosopher, and popularizer of cybernetics, Viktor Yagodinsky writes in his book *The Martian Abandoned on Earth: About A. Bogdanov (1873–1928) and His Utopias*, Alexander Malinovsky talked in the mid-1950s to paleontologist and science fiction writer Ivan Efremov, who admitted that he knew and appreciated his father's work. Apart from the fact that this admission was recorded and published already in the 1990s (Yagodinskii 1989, 31), the fiction writer was not directly involved in the theory of management and computer network design. He was, though, a prominent figure in the era of cybernetics directly working with the imaginary behind the communication technologies, and continued Bogdanov's ideas of information society in his novels about other planets. In his 1957 socialist utopia *Andromeda Nebula*, Efremov describes a communication system considered very similar to the internet as we know it now (Chugunov 2007). His 1963 novel *Razor's Edge* deals with new approaches to managing a socialist society and creating a new man. Among other things, one of the protagonists examines the hidden potential of the human mind (see chapter 2).

In the late 1960s and early 1970s, for the first time since Bogdanov's death, his "universal organization science" tektology and his novel *Red Star* were discussed publicly. In 1971, a popular scientific journal *Khimiya i Zhizn'* (*Chemistry and Life*), which often published excerpts and reviews of science fiction, a short review of the novel appeared. Its author Vsevolod Revich, a science fiction writer and one of the first literary critics to write about science fiction, brought Bogdanov back to the Soviet reader. Revich focused on Bogdanov's scientific foresight in his descriptions of Martian life: in addition to blood transfusions, nuclear-powered engines, and synthetic tissues, Revich was fascinated by the "calculating machines" that Martians used for labor statistics. He writes:

> Computing machines in 1908! I do not undertake to assert that the apparatuses described by Bogdanov were electronic-computing machines, but it is most likely the first [book] in the world literature to foresee the age of cybernetics—the "invention" of a device that instantly processes a huge amount of continuously incoming information and just as continuously gives out information about, say, the surplus or shortage of labor in certain branches of industry. (Revich 1971, 42)

This is a description of the very system of labor and production accounting developed by Bogdanov and fantastically similar to the already existing 1971 project of the OGAS.

A little earlier, in connection with the publication of Wiener's works in Russian, several mentions of Bogdanov's universal organization science appeared in the Soviet scientific literature. This moment marks the beginning of a growing wave of interest in Bogdanov. At first, researchers working at the time saw Bogdanov's concept as a precursor to Ludwig von Bertalanffy's theory of systems and Wiener's cybernetics. Then, they began to wonder whether Bertalanffy and Wiener were familiar with Bogdanov's works and whether there was a direct link between their texts (Setrov 1967, Povarov 1968, Takhtadzhjan 1971, Gorelik 1975). For example, biologist Armen Takhtadzhjan gives a definite positive answer, referring to his personal correspondence with Bertalanffy: in one of his letters, the latter admitted that he had read Bogdanov's works published in Germany. Like other authors of the late 1960s and early 1970s, Takhtadzhjan fantasizes about a possible movement of ideas: from Bogdanov through Bertalanffy to Wiener and back to Soviet cybernetics.

A different version, that Bogdanov's concept was unconsciously assimilated by later authors, was defended by the American researcher who had discovered Bogdanov in the West:

> Since tektological laws are scientific in nature, a number of Bogdanov's ideas on science, economic planning, and ideology have also been quietly absorbed by orthodox Marxists without, of course, any acknowledgement of the source. (Gorelik 1983)

So, we know that Kitov and Glushkov could have known about Bogdanov's texts, which his son Malinovsky made serious efforts to popularize. And that all three of them—Kitov and Glushkov and Bogdanov—had the same idea: centralized organization of production and labor based on a nationwide information system. However, a direct borrowing of ideas from the early twentieth century would be too simple, constituting a conspiracy-like explanation of what was happening in the 1960s. The restoration of the early socialist utopia could hardly be reduced to a literal reading of a text or to a revision of an idea. In fact, for media archaeology, it doesn't really matter whether Kitov and Glushkov read *Red Star* or *Tektologia*, whether they received this information indirectly through Wiener's *Cybernetics* and Bertalanffy's *General System Theory*, or whether their computer networking projects "quoted" Bogdanov unintentionally, without familiarity with the original texts. What is important is that it is one and the same: namely, the modern myth about the ability of machines to control social processes and the need for technology to organize life at any level, a myth that was reproduced by authors living in different times and even on different sides of the Atlantic Ocean. Russia in the first quarter of the twentieth century was not a unique producer of this myth, but it became a phenomenally fertile environment where it was formulated in its most radical form. That is why the control systems theory formulated by Wiener became so easily a part of the postwar socialist order.

This striking similarity between Soviet and American ideas of the second half of the twentieth century and early socialist ideas is not limited to tektology. It also applies, for example, to rejuvenation through blood transfusion, another idea of Bogdanov that was nearly realized by the contemporary Californian startup Ambrosia.[6] It is also relevant to the idea of digital immortality, which will be discussed next.

From Electricity to Electronics: Upgrade of the Revolutionary Techno-Utopia

The two projects, the cybernetics of the 1960s and Lenin's electrification plan of the 1920s, are connected both technically and ideologically. The designers of the first-generation computers, including Lebedev and Bruk, were trained in the 1920s as electrical engineers. They studied at the Power Engineering Institute in Moscow in the initial postrevolutionary years, when the institute became a design center of electrification in Soviet Russia and contributed to the realization of the GOELRO plan (of electrification of the Soviet economy).

They obviously caught the incredible techno-optimism for electricity: their contemporaries considered it to be the gateway for future breakthroughs and a vehicle for the construction of communism.

Herbert George Wells described Lenin as "a good orthodox Marxist" who "denounces all 'Utopians'" but has himself "succumbed at last to a Utopia, the Utopia of the electricians" (Wells 1921). When the science fiction writer came to Moscow in 1920, it was hard to imagine the GOELRO project being realized: it required too many resources. Still, Lenin was above all a pragmatist, and there were concrete economic objectives behind his statement. The electrification plan not only involved the construction of thirty large power stations but also the development of industry, making it the beginning of industrialization in Soviet Russia. The most remarkable aspect was that the plan was exceeded: by 1935, forty power stations had been built, and the country started its transition to electric power.

It's clear that such results would have been impossible if the project relied solely on economic mechanisms. Its implementation was driven by enthusiasts who saw electricity as a force capable not only of lighting and heating but also of radically changing the order of things in the universe, its physical nature. Thousands of people participated in electrification, from the deputies of the VIII All-Russian Congress of Soviets in December 1920, where the GOELRO plan was adopted, to builders, engineers, and local managers, not to mention writers and artists. At the very end of his novel *The Road to Calvary* Alexei N. Tolstoy describes the incredible optimism with which the deputies listened to the speaker during the Congress of Soviets in 1920:

> Vladimir Ilyich Lenin, who is sitting among you and who inspired the report I am giving here to-day, has indicated the main lines of a creative revolution. He said: Communism is Soviet power plus electrification . . . Wherever in the age-old silence of Russia billions of tons of peat lie hidden; wherever a waterfall rushes down or a mighty river rolls its waters, there shall we build electric power stations, true lighthouses of socialized labor.
>
> Russia has freed herself for ever from the yoke of the exploiters—our task now is to light her way by an unquenchable glow of electric fires. What was the curse of labor shall now become its blessing . . . The audience, the men, in

> the pockets of whose military great-coats there was a handful of oats issued on today's ration cards in the place of bread, listened with bated breath to the staggering but entirely practicable prospects of a revolution now embarking on a course of creative effort. (Tolstoy 1945, 679)

The researcher Dmitry Lavrov finds a visual reflection of the same enthusiasm of the Russian revolution's contemporaries, close to religious ecstasy, in the miniature paintings by Palekh artists in the 1920s–1960s, where electric light is drawn in the same technique as icon painters used to depict divine light—thin golden lines and strokes called "assist" (from Latin *assisto*, to stand by, to be present), "transmitting rays of light emanating from the deity":

> In numerous lacquer miniatures from Palekh (as well as Kholuy to no lesser extent), depicting the "arrival" of the "Ilyich lamp" in the Soviet village, one can observe this truly iconographic technique: people, raising their hands to the "new" light, "bathe" (sometimes literally) in the glow, visually conveyed by delicate golden droplets stretching from the bulb located in the heavens (K. M. Melnikov's miniature "Ilyich Lamp" from 1970, held in the collection of the State Museum of Palekh Art; P. I. Ivakin's "Light to the Village" casket from the 1960s in the State Kholuy Museum, among many others). The glow, or assist, as an iconographic technique, generally speaks to the presence of the supernatural in the artistic space of the miniature. (Lavrov 2014, 111)

Though Lenin's formula of "Communism is Soviet power plus the electrification of the whole country" seemed to H. G. Wells more like literature than reality, Lenin himself consistently and harshly criticized the romantic sentiments about the future of Russia, as well as the "idealism" of his fellow revolutionaries, above all Alexander Bogdanov, who saw in matter a much greater potential than Lenin's version of materialism permitted.[7]

At the same time, as the literature and fine art of the 1920s shows, not only the revolutionaries themselves, but also the majority of electrification activists were on the side of romanticism. Lenin's contemporary, the writer and electrical engineer Andrei Platonov, unlike Lenin, knew not only the theory but also how to handle electricity, participated in the implementation of the GOELRO plan, and was the author of several inventions related to alternating current technology. However, in Platonov's texts, electricity appears as a great power of unknown origin, perhaps even alive. It is a substance destined to provide communism to an entire country, to defeat materiality, to make things obey human thoughts, and ultimately to raise the dead. "At the end of time, matter will all be electricity," Platonov writes in his pamphlet *The Culture of the Proletariat*, "Electrification is the realization of communism in matter" (Platonov 2004; Kaminskii 2020). Matter, according to Platonov, is an inconvenience and causes suffering; in the future, a remedy must be invented for it—"electric medicine" that will manage to restore the body and allow man to live forever, avoiding decay and "the deadly excitement of nature." "We shall soon organize socialism and defeat the very essence of matter!"—says one of the protagonists of *A Technical Novel* (Platonov 1991).

The idea of electricity as a source of future vitalism didn't belong to Russian revolution alone: to begin with, the electric light bulb, known in Russia in the 1920s as the "Ilyich bulb," was invented by Thomas Edison, an American, while the German company Siemens started to produce its famous dynamo machines, something Lenin was well aware of, having spent time traveling in Germany in 1908 (Banerjee et al. 2011). Rather, the specificity of Russia at the time of the revolution was that the concept of future electric life was not just one of the popular ideas, but a kind of backbone of the new state.

Defeating "the very essence" was a relevant task not only for Platonov; it was also discussed by other revolutionary utopians. They pinned their hopes on the future development of medicine, not only electrical but also classical.[8] Either way, by the end of the 1930s, the topic of electricity as a tool in the struggle for immortality faded away, and it hardly arose again before the emergence of cybernetics. Accelerated industrialization and World War II stimulated the development of applied disciplines. Electricity was pragmatically mastered in a Leninist manner, without any romantic or idealistic excesses.

In the late 1940s, Soviet engineers such as Lebedev learned to turn an electrical signal into electronic information, but there were no longer any grand ideas behind it. As Gerovitch describes in detail, the scientists of the postwar Stalinist years devoted a great deal of effort to the de-ideologization of the radio-electronic sciences (Gerovitch 2002). The computer industry was successfully separated from ideologically dangerous "imperialistic pseudoscience," as cybernetics had come to be labeled. At least for the time being.

In the 1960s, Platonov's concept of electricity as the "matter of communism," which changes the order of things in the universe and overcomes materiality, became relevant again. Only now, electronics have taken the place of electricity. In 1975, when Glushkov was already a renowned scientist and academician, his interview about the future of cybernetics appeared in the almanac *Fantastika, 1972–1973*. In conversation with a journalist, Glushkov speculated about the possible future based on real achievements of cybernetics and computer engineering. At this time, the design of a unified information system was still developing. According to Glushkov, such a system should not only collect and process information but also become the infrastructure for artificial intelligence worthy of socialism:

> When all information systems merge into one Unified System, it will operate with the participation of people and for the sake of people. The enormous advantages of our most just social system, multiplied by the informational power of future electronic computing machines, will help create abundance of material and spiritual wealth.[9] (Maksimovich 1975)

Biological immortality, Glushkov insisted, wasn't around the corner—science in the twenty-first century would succeed in extending human life expectancy, but only to a ceiling of "some 150 to 200 years." However, much more than in biological capabilities, Glushkov was interested in information preservation—the ability to transmit it from humans to machines and in their symbiosis. Starting his reasoning with the possibility of directly transferring information from the brain to the computer using "special helmets that capture electrical impulses," Glushkov notes that computers will be able to store and transmit human personality and even consciousness. According to Glushkov, man is his thoughts—the body remains ultimately unimportant. Thus, he delved into the possibilities of a *digital* immortality, which, so he believed, could become a reality as a direct consequence of a future symbiosis of man and machine:

> Then, at some point during the final stages of transferring all my cerebral information to a computer, I suddenly begin feeling that I am at once myself and the machine. My consciousness splits, as it were, since I have fed to the "electronic brain" of the computer not only my cerebral information but also my sense of self-awareness. . . . Will this frighten me? Bearing in mind the

> formula you just quoted—"I think, therefore I am"—probably not all that much, because I'll remember that man is mortal. . . . The computer, on the other hand, is practically immortal. Furthermore, it is now endowed with our train of thought, our methods of reasoning. . . . But if by that time we've become capable of transferring our self-awareness to a computer, along with all our cerebral information, it is quite reasonable to assume that the said computer . . . would be no less adept at carrying out just such a transfer itself, with another machine as the recipient. And in this rather simple way, your own self-awareness—and therefore, to a certain extent, you yourself—will migrate into a new, even more perfect shell. Which, incidentally, will help make my "I," my sense of self-apprehension, practically immortal. (Maksimovich 1975)

In Maksimovich's book *Conversations with Academician V. Glushkov* (1978), which includes excerpts from the 1975 interview, Glushkov's thesis became more radical. With some caveats ("purely theoretically," "with a certain degree of fantasy"), he nevertheless asserted that with the help of cybernetics, one would be able to achieve "almost complete immortality."[10]

Glushkov's belief that consciousness and personality can be digitized and stored eternally essentially represented a continuation and development of the electric techno-utopia of the generation that lived during the post-revolution period. As in the 1920s, the discussion revolved then as now around immortality achieved through scientific progress. The most promising way to it was to get rid of bodily organics and to transform them into inorganic material. During that early period, the nature of electricity was not fully understood, and the concept of the "ether" was prevalent, leaving ample room for imagination in this area of research. Therefore, the problem of bodily transience was symbolically addressed, including through cremation as a progressive alternative to burial. In the era of the scientific and technological revolution of the 1960s, when electronics replaced electricity as the almighty technology, the same utopia was formulated as a technical task.

Now, scientists only needed to develop the technology to transform consciousness into an electronic signal and transmit it into a working model—and eternal digital life will replace cremation. Interestingly, in his interview with Maksimovich, Glushkov referred to Lenin's work, in which the theory of the ether was mentioned several times, and continued to debate with Bogdanov:

> The latest revolution in science, the exhaustive analysis of the causes and essence of which was provided by V. I. Lenin in his brilliant work "Materialism and Empirio-Criticism," served as a prelude to the scientific and technological revolution. (Maksimovich 1975, 14)

Predicting further progress in cybernetics and the potentially resulting digital immortality, Glushkov believed that scientists would achieve a symbiosis of humans and machines "somewhere around 2020, that is, in less than half a century." Glushkov died in 1982. Already in the late 1980s, the idea of transforming personality into an electronic signal and uploading brain data into computers—and computer networks!—emerged in California and became the foundation of extropianism, one of the directions of transhumanism (see chapter 4). And in the early 2000s, based on this same idea, several startups emerged in Silicon Valley, with the task of turning this philosophical thesis into reality. Theoretically, Glushkov's work could have been known in the U.S.; however, as with Bogdanov, this does not necessarily mean that his texts became a direct source for subsequent generations of philosophers and developers. Simply put, the same utopia of digital immortality proved to be relevant in different places and at different times, on both sides of the Iron Curtain, in two societies envisioning a better life based on scientific and technological progress.

This is how the designer of Soviet computer networks responded to the revolutionary generation who had hoped for immortality based on scientific progress. The problem of the body's temporality, which the utopianists of the first quarter of the twentieth century hoped to solve, became, in Glushkov's approach, a problem of the transformation of consciousness into an electronic signal and its consequent preservation.

While Glushkov's concept of eternal digital life was original, its central idea was rather global, or at least, common in modern societies. As early as the 1950s, Wiener discussed how travelling by telegraph in addition to travel by train and airplane would expand the possibilities of the human body (Wiener 1954, 103–4) and considered the problem of transmitting the body temporary and technically solvable (for more detailed analysis of virtuality and cybernetics, see Katherine Hayles's book *How We Became Posthuman*, 1999). A decade after Glushkov's insight, the same existential techno-utopian function came to be performed on the other side of the Iron Curtain. The idea of transforming brain data into an electronic signal excited Californian transhumanists and IT-dreamers. Enriched with the concept of social networks, it became the basis for the *extropian* movement (see chapter 4). "In fact, a defining characteristic of the present cultural moment is the belief that information can circulate unchanged among different material substrates," concluded Hayles.

This takes us to the question of how to explain this similarity between the techno-utopias of two different modern societies, the American and the Soviet. The two classic and contradictory answers are historical and structural. The first looks for ways in which one inherited from the other, the second sees similarities in the very character of modern societies. Keeping in mind the difficulties in defining modernity, I would still suggest that the methodological contradiction be removed. Yes, there is a possibility that inventors were also Kulturträgers and brought ideas from other cultures. But these ideas would hardly have found fertile ground if modern societies hadn't been so similar, at least in their pursuit of progress through scientific discoveries.

2

The Technology of the Future Is Telepathy

The funding of telepathy research in the USSR owes its beginnings to Poletayev, a military engineer and cyberneticist. His book *Signal* was published by Sovetskoe Radio Press at the suggestion of Berg in 1958.[1] It was the first book on cybernetics in Russian, and Poletaev was one of the first cyberneticists to actively seek recognition of the new scientific discipline. In March 1960, Poletayev penned a letter to the Soviet defense minister Rodion Malinovsky to inform him that the Americans had long been conducting successful experiments in telepathic information transmission: "Telepathy—the transmission of thoughts at a distance without recourse to technological aids—has been adopted by the U.S. Armed Forces as a means of communicating with submarines while they're out to sea" (Rubel et al. 2016, 95; Poletaev 1998). The letter was accompanied by the article *Telepathic Communication* written by Poletaev together with Leonid Vasiliev and Pavel Gulyaev (Vasiliev et al. 1995). Arguing for the need to "widely deploy scientific research on telepathy in the Soviet Union," they insisted on the possibility of a scientific explanation of the phenomenon:

> It is assumed that the telepathic carrier of information is a new natural reality, something like a new physical field. There is no mysticism in this assumption. Postulation of new physical fields is a common and fruitful technique of physicists. Recall the discovery of the meson field, which at first was postulated and only 10 years later was proven experimentally. (Poletayev 1960)

This letter was a pivotal moment in the history of Soviet science: the avant-garde research of the 1920s and 1930s was in demand by nascent cybernetics, and telepathy gained the status of a strategically promising communication technology. Vasiliev, who since 1921 had worked as a physiologist and at the Institute for the Study of the Brain and Mental Activity (later renamed the Institute of the Human Brain), became the main mediator between prewar Soviet science and biocybernetics.

Vasiliev's professional biography, from his first experiments under the patronage of his senior colleague and renowned neurologist Vladimir Bekhterev to his alliance with Soviet cyberneticians in the 1950s, represents how the subject has developed from revolutionary science to the Scientific and Technical Revolution. Bekhterev, a trailblazer in the study of psychophysiology, displayed considerable interest in telepathy himself. He spent a lot of time searching for scientific evidence of the existence of telepathy[2] and finally concluded that telepathy does not exist. In spite of this, Bekhterev supported research into the matter as the director of the Institute. In 1922, a Commission for the Study of Mental Suggestion was established, its membership comprising psychologists, doctors, physiologists, physicists, and philosophers. Representatives of the Commission discussed its research at events such as the Second All-Russian Psychoneurology Congress of 1924, and subsequently published the results. The author of a review of the congress made the following conclusion:

> The Leningrad Institute of the Human Brain managed to establish that in the so-called transmission of thoughts at a distance we deal . . . with a type of energy; one person's brain is an induction apparatus sending energy waves, and another person's brain receives these waves. (Stoyukhina, Mazilov 2014, 27)

In the 1920s, Russian science was an integral part of the European scientific tradition, within which scientists from different countries—Great Britain, Italy, and the United States—worked on the electromagnetic hypothesis of telepathy, which had appeared in the late nineteenth century.[3] The most sensational results were shown by Italian scientist Ferdinando Cazzamali, who claimed that he was able to measure the electromagnetic radiation of the brain during telepathy sessions. The announcement of Cazzamali's success inspired a number of scientific experiments in different countries, including Soviet Russia. The Institute of the Human Brain and Institute of Biophysics in Leningrad, the Durov Center for Zoopsychology in Moscow, and several other scientific and amateur organizations began to study telepathy.

In 1928, Vasiliyev was dispatched to France and Germany to firm up links with fellow telepathy researchers. Four years later—Bekhterev having passed away in the interim—he commenced his own research into the psychophysiology of telepathy, only to discontinue it in the late 1930s. Following the electromagnetic hypothesis of telepathy, Vasiliev studied the influence of various external and internal conditions on the process. He conducted sessions with shielded/unshielded rooms, with hypnosis, with mescaline (peyote), and compared the results. Despite the large number of experiments, no hypothesis was confirmed before parapsychology research was discontinued in 1938.[4]

After World War II, Vasiliyev re-established contacts with foreign colleagues who provided him with scientific literature and news of developments in telepathy research. In 1958, he received from his Parisian colleague Raphael Kherumian[5] issues of the popular-science magazines *Constellation* and *Science et Vie* which featured articles on the *Nautilus* telepathy experiment. According to the magazines, the telepathic experiment had taken place under conditions permissive of no means of communication known to physicists, with the submarine beneath a layer of Arctic ice at the time.

The telepathic communication method allegedly employed in the experiment had been developed by J. B. Rhine, founder of the parapsychology lab at Duke University. In the words of the journalist Martin Ebon, who discusses the affair in his 1983 book *Psychic Warfare: Threat or Illusion*, a controlled timing device shuffled one thousand ESP cards in a revolving drum in such a manner as to drop five cards on a table, one at a time, at one-minute intervals. Each card bore one of five symbols—a square, a cross, a star, wavy lines, and a circle. A Duke student named Smith would pick up "each card . . . as it came out of the drum" and, seeking "to memorize the image, . . . drew a picture of the symbol . . . on a piece of paper before him;" "each test" would therefore produce "a sheet with five symbols." Smith would then seal "each paper into an envelope," which he'd hand to "the person in charge," one Colonel William H. Bowers, who locked it in a safe. "At the same time," writes Ebon, "a Navy lieutenant, identified as 'Jones,' sat isolated in a stateroom on the *Nautilus*, functioning as the recipient of the images Smith sought to convey by telepathy." "Jones," too, "drew five symbols on a sheet of paper" before sealing the sheet in an envelope and "turn[ing] it over to his superior." The experiment went on for sixteen days, and the results were dispatched to Bowers' lab upon the submarine's return to its homeport.

According to the articles in *Constellation* and *Science et Vie*, "the figures tallied" over 70 percent of the time—a success rate that would have been impossible in the absence of effective telepathic communication (Ebon 1983).

As Ebon shows, however, the *Nautilus* affair, which catalyzed a major telepathy research drive in the USSR, turned out to be a disinformation setpiece. U.S. naval authorities denied that the experiment had ever taken place. Ebon then met with Gerald Messadie, editor of *Science et Vie*, in the summer of 1980, and discovered that, two decades later, the latter now believed "that the whole thing was probably a hoax."[6] He also took care to stress that the affair actually generated "a circle of doubt and counter-doubt," with "some Americans [entertaining] the hypothesis that the whole *Nautilus* story was a 'Soviet plant,' a piece of 'disinformation,' launched in France to provide a reason for a start-up of Soviet psychic studies" (Ebon 1983, 29).

Vasiliev was wary of the *Nautilus* story from the beginning but saw it as an opportunity to continue his own parapsychological research. Capitalizing on the fact that Soviet science had ceded leadership in telepathy research to the United States, Vasiliev began making presentations at scientific conferences and informal gatherings, and in 1959 he published a book *Mysterious Phenomena of the Human Psyche*, where he devoted one chapter to telepathy. Among those who discussed this topic with Vasiliev were important personalities in the developing field of cybernetics—military engineer Poletaev and physiologist Gulyaev. Eventually, inspired by Vasiliev's lectures, Poletaev wrote the letter to Marshal Malinovsky. And it worked: in 1960, the Laboratory of Electromagnetic Fields and Aeroions was founded at the Physiological Institute at Leningrad State University, which included a biotelecommunications group.

Vasiliev was not the only 1920s researcher who participated in the revival of telepathy research within the cybernetics of the 1960s. Another such mediator was Sergei Turlygin, a student of physiologist Petr Lazarev, who also had conducted experiments in the 1930s, had presented the results of his research to the Moscow Society of Naturalists in 1939, and had received a favorable reaction from his colleagues. In the 1930s, Turlygin was a supporter of the electromagnetic hypothesis of telepathy, which in Lazarev's scientific tradition was called the "wordless hypnosis." As a result of experiments, Turlygin determined the approximate wavelength emitted by the brain: about 2 mm.

In the early 1950s, Turlygin began to doubt the electromagnetic hypothesis and suggested that the nature of brain radiation wasn't yet known to science. Together with his student, psychiatrist Dmitry Mirza, Turlygin organized several separate telepathic experiments at the Institute of Biophysics of the USSR Academy of Sciences, and in 1955 he succeeded in establishing a separate laboratory there. However, almost immediately afterward, Turlygin died, the laboratory was closed, and the Institute of Biophysics abandoned this line of research. In 1958, Turlygin's work was continued by Dmitry Mirza, who was invited to head the laboratory at the "Electron" research institute. In this way Turlygin's research was continued.

There was one more mediator, engineer, and electricity specialist: Bernard Kazhinsky. In 1959, his article "Radio Transmission of Thoughts" was published in the newspaper *Komsomolskaya Pravda* and Kazhinsky was invited to Moscow State University to read a paper on the subject. The organizer was Igor Mirzalis (his literary pen-name: Igor Vinokurov), at that time a student of the Department of Physiology of Higher Nervous Activity at the university and chairman of the general biology study club. Mirzalis later recalled that not only biologists but also cyberneticians, such as Poletaev, spoke at faculty meetings. Poletaev invited Kazhinsky to read his paper *Electromagnetic Hypothesis of Thought Transmission at a Distance*. Kazhinsky agreed and, believing that "a great deal of good for the useful development in the USSR of the problem under consideration depends on it," asked Mirzalis to invite well-known scientists, including the cyberneticist Berg, to the presentation of his paper. Despite the fact that just before the start, the MSU administration decided to cancel the presentation, it still took place: while Mirzalis was communicating with his superiors, Kazhinsky gathered people in another auditorium (Vinokurov et al. 1993, 99–101).

The case of Kazhinsky is perhaps the most remarkable from the point of view of the history of telepathy research and its close connection with the history of cybernetics. First, Kazhinsky was not a physiologist, but an electrical engineer and inventor. In the 1920s, his main activity was electrification of agriculture: he headed a department of the *Narkomzem* (People's Commissariat of Agriculture), invented a wind farm, and looked for other electricity-related ways to improve agrarian performance.[7] That is, he belonged to the generation of electricity enthusiasts, considered to be the very "matter of communism" in the 1920s, which in the 1960s gave way to electronics and computer networks. As for many of his contemporaries such as Platonov (with whom he once corresponded[8]), for Kazhinsky the prospects of electricity were virtually limitless: with this magical substance it seemed possible not only to put the country, destroyed by the Civil War and famine, back on its feet, but also to bring natural phenomena under the will of human beings. At the same time, he conducted experiments on the transmission of thought at a distance, developing the electromagnetic hypothesis of telepathy.

In 1922, Kazhinsky made a report on telepathy at the All-Russian Congress of the Association of Naturalists (Assnat). This association of "inventors, amateurs, and self-taught scientists" had been founded a year earlier to introduce spontaneous scientific discoveries into various economic sectors. After a successful report at the congress, Kazhinsky was invited to give lectures, cooperate with various laboratories, and conduct experiments, which resulted in the book *The Transmission of Thoughts* published in 1923. The author envisioned the human body as a radio device that transmits and receives electromagnetic signals. In his lectures and publications, he constantly drew parallels between the body and a radio device: "human thought is electricity," the thinking brain produces a "biological oscillating circuit," the nervous system resembles a radio circuit, and so on.

Supported by academic scientists and Konstantin Tsiolkovsky, whom Kazhinsky had befriended after his sensational presentation at the congress, he became convinced of the validity of his theory of telepathy as a process of transmitting electromagnetic waves. His task now became to design an instrument, an "electromagnetic microscope," that could detect these waves. In 1922, Kazhinsky developed a schematic of the device and even took a job in the testing laboratory of the Radio hardware factory in Moscow to get the opportunity to design it (Kazhinsky 1962, 38).

In 1929, Alexander Belyaev's science fiction novel *The Ruler of the World,* about the invention of a device to control telepathy, was published. Berlin inventor Stirner uses it to achieve love, wealth and power, while Moscow scientist Kachinsky, whose prototype was the writer's friend Kazhinsky, saves the world from Stirner, who has already managed to unleash a world war. After his victory over Stirner, Kazhinskiy uses the same device himself to create a system of controlled telepathy, which becomes the main method of communication in socialist Moscow:

> The transmission of thought at a distance has indeed been widely used . . . Moscow has become a city of great silence. We hardly speak to each other since we learned to exchange thoughts directly. How cumbersome and slow

> the old way of speaking seems to us now! It is possible that as time goes on, we may even become unable to speak at all. Soon the post offices, the telegraph, and even the radio will be discarded. We have already learned to talk to each other at a distance. (Belyaev 1947, 156)

Telepathy in Belyaev's imaginary Moscow not only enables people to communicate with each other: it is also a way to compose and listen to music ("mentally improvise and radiate improvisation"), to play chess and follow the game ("chess players radiate the whole process of thinking over moves"), to transmit theatre and cinema, and most importantly to manage the organization of work ("mechanical coercion has been replaced by our thought transmission, which does not coerce, but helps workers to coordinate the work of their nervous system and muscles with the work of the collective"), as well as disarm criminals ("with the help of the super-powered amplifiers we give the criminal the appropriate 'suggestion' and he becomes safe forever").

Belyaev wrote his book as a result of long conversations with Kazhinsky and a detailed introduction to his engineering and theoretical works. And although the genre of the science fiction novel is meant to radicalize the imaginary, we can assume that this description of the future is very close to Kazhinsky's original ideas, which were quite radical even for the 1920s. As he wrote to Tsiolkovsky in 1922:

> Unlike Nobel who invented dynamite for engineering purposes (mining) and then learned to his horror that this invention brought more grief to mankind in wars than benefit, and therefore threw his enormous resources to promote peace, because he could not think of any other counteraction, I have a concept of a ready-made device that can isolate man from the undesirable influences of external currents. (Pis'ma inzhenera . . .)

By the early 1930s, Kazhinsky came to the conclusion that there were no technologies relevant to his complex task. He began searching for materials and conductors with zero electrical resistance—essentially, for superconductors—but, as he later recalled, "all my attempts to find something appropriate were unsuccessful. Such was the state of technology at that time" (Kazhinsky 1962, 42).

The electronic era, of course, promised his project a much more ambitious future. After the decisive actions by the Ministry of Defense, which responded to the 1960 letter of the cyberneticists, this line of research received a serious boost. In addition to Vasiliev's laboratory at the USSR Academy of Sciences, the Institute of Information Transmission Problems was founded in 1961, where Mirza's laboratory was transferred. According to telepathy enthusiast Eduard Naumov, who was a biologist, a participant in experiments and an active researcher in Soviet parapsychology, the activities of Mirza and his laboratory were discussed at a special meeting in 1961 with Academician Mstislav Keldysh, then the president of the USSR Academy of Sciences. The meeting's attendees included neurophysiologist Ezras Asratyan, radio physicists Yuri Kobzarev and Alexander Mints, theoretical physicist and Nobel laureate Igor Tamm, acoustic physicist Alexander Kharkevich, and the already mentioned Berg, one of the fathers of Soviet cybernetics. It was decided that Mirza's work would continue (Kernbach 2013, 6).

By the early 1970s, dozens of laboratories and departments had been established to research telepathy and other manifestations of psychic phenomena.[9] Judging by the publications in newspapers and popular science magazines, its public perception became much more friendly. According to Naumov's calculations, by 1966, 152 articles on various phenomena of parapsychology, including telepathy, had been published in the USSR, and only fifteen of them were critical. This was a remarkable result, considering that in 1957 there were only three publications and all of them were negative (Ostrander and Schroeder 1971, 141).

In the first stage of postwar telepathy research, when the main actors were mostly scientists who had started their work in the 1920s, cybernetics played the role of a flagship rather than a methodology. The experience of cybernetics in instantly transforming yesterday's pseudoscience into the most advanced scientific discipline gave telepathy researchers the hope to continue their previous experiments on a new level.

In the early 1960s, Vasiliev brought out two books dealing with the scientific underpinnings of telepathy: *Mysterious Phenomena of the Human Psyche* and *Experiments in Mental Suggestion*. These were based in part on new experiments conducted by his laboratory, and in part on old data that he'd accumulated at the Institute of the Human Brain. Insisting on a strictly scientific approach to the study of telepathy, Vasiliev saw a direct connection between parapsychology and cybernetics, which deal with problems of information transmission and control:

> It is not surprising that cyberneticians are now beginning to be interested in telepathic phenomena as a special type of information transmission. Thus, for example, the famous mathematician and cyberneticist A. Turing is concerned in his book with the question on how to reconcile some provisions of cybernetics with the recognition of the real existence of parapsychic phenomena, in particular telepathy. It can be assumed that a "telepathic pair" at the moment of transmission of mental suggestion at a distance represents a temporarily active cybernetic system, with all the consequences of such a concept. (Vasiliev 1963, 62)

The development of cybernetics, according to Vasiliev, brought scientists closer to understanding the nature of telepathy. In particular, one can say that it is not the thoughts that are transmitted—these are inseparable from the brain—but the information concerning thought, energetic signals. Vasiliev then resorts to a more general argument:

> Were not quantum and relativity theory, and the rejection of the absolute meaningfulness of the principle of the conservation of mass, volume and energy, at first "incompatible with the present theories of science"? . . . [T]hat which yesterday appeared "supernatural" is today accepted as "natural." (Vasiliev 1963, 152)

Frequent references to cybernetics, of course, did not yet make Vasiliev himself a cyberneticist. He continued to do the work he had begun in the 1920s and 1930s, hoping that he could pass on the results to a new generation of researchers. In contrast to Vasiliev, Kazhinsky was more involved in cybernetic approaches to information transfer. In 1962, his book *Biological Radio* was published, detailing his theory and the results of telepathic experiments in the 1920s. While Vasiliev began to doubt the electromagnetic hypothesis by the late 1950s, Kazhinsky not only insisted on it, but considered it proven:

> Now that experiments in the USSR and abroad have proven the possibility of transmitting preconceived mental information over distances as well as the electromagnetic and bio-radiation nature of this phenomenon and, finally, that we encounter incidents of thought transference in daily life with increasing frequency, the assertion that this phenomenon is supernatural sounds archaic. The more we study the nature of these phenomena the sooner will

> the cloak of mystery disappear and the problem itself will take its place in the field of exact sciences. (Kazhinsky 1971, 12)

However, Kazhinsky leaves the possibility open for the discovery of "new elementary particles with still unknown functions, including also the function of thought transference." And the discovery of specific mechanisms of this transmission, according to his plan, should be followed by the ability to control the process—a quality that "will be useful in the coming age of communism on Earth, in the age of development of space travel to other planets" (137). Finally, Kazhinsky draws analogies between the brain and "cybernetic machines," that is, computers, arguing that the processes they produce are similar, but the brain is a much more complex device than the most sophisticated machine (118–19).

So both Vasiliev and his contemporary Kazhinsky belonged to the previous generation of visionaries and conducted their major research on telepathy in the 1920s. In the 1960s, they adapted cybernetic language to lend more credibility to their earlier work. Cybernetics promised new precise methods and apparatuses, but the most crushing argument lay in its own history: like cybernetics, telepathy too had a chance to break out of the "pseudoscience" category into the mainstream.

The next step was made by physiologist Gulyaev, the third co-author with Poletaev and Vasiliev on the article "Telepathic Transmission," which was sent in 1960 to Marshal Malinovsky and opened new perspectives for telepathic research. For Gulyaev, the cybernetic system was not just a metaphor for telepathy, but the most accurate reflection of its essence.

Electric Fields and Information Theory: Modernizing Telepathy Studies

Work on modeling biological systems started almost simultaneously with the design of computer networks and the development of cybernetic theory. This may be due to the fact that Soviet scientists not only developed further the theory of American mathematicians Claude Shannon and Wiener but were also keenly interested in the experience of British cyberneticians. And for the British tradition, the mathematical analysis of living systems was a key topic, and telepathy was as much a topic for discussion as artificial intelligence.[10] In the computer age, not only were the methods of natural sciences changing but also the basic definitions. In this context, it is logical that

Soviet postwar research on telepathy, first organized by representatives of cybernetics, ended up becoming a part of it.

In 1961, when the organizational and methodological development of cybernetics was underway, Andrey Kolmogorov, known for his works on probability theory, topology, and a dozen other areas of theoretical mathematics, gave a talk on "Automata and Life" at Moscow State University. The first thesis of the paper, published later in *Tekhnika Molodezhi* (*Technology for the Young Generation*), questioned the relevance of Friedrich Engels's definition of life as "the mode of existence of protein bodies":

> This definition was progressive and correct as long as we dealt only with specific forms of life developed on Earth. In the age of cosmonautics there is a real possibility of meeting with "forms of matter in motion" (see the article "Life" in the Great Soviet Encyclopedia), who possess the key properties of living and even thinking beings that are important to us, but are organized differently. (Kolmogorov 1961, 16)

Proposing to find a more general and functional definition of the concept of life, Kolmogorov argues that in the long run cybernetics will be able to do it. Moreover, according to the author, once this definition appears, it will be possible to "artificially create living and thinking beings" (16).

It was not by accident that Kolmogorov's paper was published with the subtitle *Materialism Is Wonderful*. The main research question that Soviet cybernetics addressed in the early years of its existence was its relationship to Marxist-Leninist materialism. This began as early as 1955, in the very paper by Sobolev, Lyapunov, and Kitov that opened the way for cybernetics to enter Soviet science:

> Until now, physiology could only observe the work of the brain. Now there is an opportunity to experiment, to create models of even the crudest, most primitive thinking processes and, by studying the work of these models, to learn more deeply the principles of higher nervous activity. This represents further development of the objective method of studying higher nervous activity proposed by I. P. Pavlov. (Sobolev et al. 1955, 20)

Such passages were more than relevant: only thirteen years had passed after the defeat of genetics and ten years after the so-called Pavlovian session of the USSR Academy of Sciences, where Soviet biologists were criticized for their deviation from materialism and inconsistency with Pavlov's and Ivan Sechenov's approaches to physiology. At that time, in 1951, the use of cybernetic methods in biology was also considered a "deviation from materialism."

One of the first biocyberneticians to work directly on the problems of telepathy was the physiologist Gulyaev. He started to work on biological cybernetics in the mid-1950s, when it was not yet accepted, and was even dangerous. His first popular science article on biological systems was published in the journal *Science and Life* six months earlier than the first positive article on cybernetics in the USSR, published by Lyapunov, Kitov, and Sobolev in the journal *Voprosy Filosofii* (*Problems of Philosophy*).[11] Gulyaev can be regarded as having been involved in biocybernetics at a time when the discipline itself did not yet officially exist.

In 1960, when Gulyaev was heading the Laboratory of Physiological Cybernetics at Leningrad State University and collaborating with Vasiliev's newly opened laboratory, his book *Electrical Processes of the Human Cortex* was published. In the last chapter, he asserted that the phenomenon of thought transmission at a distance, without the mediation of sensory organs, was "now considered proven and will probably soon be practically applied. The telepathic carrier of information, apparently, is a new to science physical field produced by the brain" (Gulyaev 1960, 103).

That is, Gulyaev doubted the electromagnetic nature of this field, calling it "new to science." Telepathic experiments in this laboratory were conducted with various devices for measuring brain radiation. At first, they were ordinary electroencephalographs, but in the mid-1960s, Vladimir Zabotin, a graduate student of Gulyaev's laboratory, built a special device called an *auratron*. It measured not the electromagnetic field but its component, the electric field "generated by muscle, heart and nerve biocurrents" (Zabotin, Shlippenbakh 1968).

Being a consistent biocyberneticist, Gulyaev sought to integrate cybernetic methods into physiology and wrote extensively about modelling biological systems, including human thought processes. For him, experiments with telepathic transmission were aimed not only at proving the existence of the phenomenon but also at building its model and, in the long term, at learning how to control telepathy. Media historian Vladimir Velminsky believed that Gulyaev was driven by the idea of mass control over people's consciousness (Velminski 2017, 2). The concept of mind control was popular among customers of parapsychological research. There were rumors among scientists that the idea to use telepathy for defense purposes belonged to Khrushchev, who during a trip to India saw yogis and decided that mastering their abilities could be useful for the defense of the country. Moreover, this military task is often used to explain the foundation in 1960 of the Institute for Information Transmission Problems (IITP), whose employees were engaged in "the study of clairvoyance, telepathy, telekinesis" in order to develop a system of control over telepathy for defense purposes (Vilenskaia 1985, 262). However, Gulyaev's published scientific and popular science works are about possible mechanisms of telepathy, not about its controlling function in the future.

In 1967, Gulyaev and his colleagues presented their discovery of the electric fields of the human heart and frog nerve at a meeting of the Leningrad Society of Naturalists. That is why in 1968 there was a publication about their work in the popular science magazine *Tekhnika—molodezhi* (Zabotin, Shlippenbakh 1968), which included an interview with the scientists. It clearly sounds optimistic about the soon-to-be proven existence of telepathy, but in response to a question about its possible application, Gulyaev limits himself to describing the medical diagnostics of the future, in which the patient and the doctor will have to do almost nothing—devices registering electrical emissions will be enough. This lack of bold imagination is compensated by a journalist in this article: he draws a future where Gulyaev's new device monitors the "flow of collective thought": in public places, he writes, "it will be possible to install sensitive devices that will continuously register the state of people's minds. Then, say, a theatrical director will be able to "see" the mood of the audience and give instructions to the actors during the play."

It is difficult to say whether this picture of an immersive theater of the future belonged to the fantasies of the cyberneticists themselves. Rather, it was part of the science fiction discourse that had existed at least since the late 1920s, when Belyaev wrote his novel *The Ruler of the World*. It had no room for individual freedoms and unique feelings, but it did offer technological solutions to social problems, be they crime or aggression.

Meanwhile, Gulyaev and his colleagues were concerned with the problem of accurately measuring the electrical radiation of the brain. According to their hypothesis, the electric field emitted by each organ exists only for thousandths of a second while the impulse travels along a nerve. This, they argued, explains the complexity of its registration and, even more so, its modelling: "If we take into account that there are more than 4 million nerve channels in our body and the activity of impulses is constantly changing, we can understand how complex the general picture of the "nerve" field of Homo sapiens is" (14).

Thirteen years later, Glushkov, director of the Institute of Cybernetics in Kiev, chairman of the Scientific Council on Cybernetics at the Presidium of the Academy of Sciences of the Ukrainian SSR, editor-in-chief of the journal *Kibernetika* (1965–1982), and one of the main visionaries of scientific and technological development in the country, attempted to explain this complexity at the theoretical level.

While not an expert in biocybernetics, Glushkov was nevertheless interested in modeling thought processes and also believed in the existence of telepathy and in the possibility of controlling it. According to several sources,[12] in the late 1950s, Glushkov invited the already elderly Kazhinsky to work at the Institute of Cybernetics in order to develop this area of research. At the same time, a group studying biological cybernetics was established at the Institute under the direction of surgeon Nikolai Amosov.[13] However, most Soviet research on telepathy is classified, so it is still not known for sure whether Kazhinsky worked for Glushkov, and if so, whether he had time to contribute to biocybernetics.

In Vasili Zakharchenko's popular science book *Razgovor s ėlektricheskim mozgom* (*Talking to the Electric Brain*) published in 1975, Glushkov comments on the prospects of this field:

> The day will come when we will be able to build a model of the brain whose weight would be comparable to the weight of the brain of a living human being. Especially since the latest research suggests that the design of the brain cannot be infinitely complex. It must be much simpler than we have assumed so far. (Zakharchenko 1975)

As Glushkov explains further, the transmission of biocurrents at a distance will work for medicine:

> A doctor can not only listen to the cardiogram of a patient's heart by wire or radio, but also provide help to the injured person by transmitting the appropriate biocurrents. If necessary, a doctor can even help a cosmonaut in flight by transmitting to him a biotelegram: how to act in this or that case. (Zakharchenko 1975)

Based on conversations with Glushkov and other cyberneticians, Zakharchenko develops their fantasies about the future. According to the journalist, the discovery of biocurrents will be followed by the ability to control them, which means that it will be possible to quickly transfer professional skills to another person, avoiding the training stage:

> Imagine that the biocurrents of talented people of various professions are recorded on tape. They could be turners, milling machine operators, wood or bone carvers, in other words, those whom we call "the craftsmen with golden hands." With the assistance of such recordings it will be possible to train people to mastery, influencing their muscles with biocurrents of talented craftsmen. For example, you have terrible handwriting. Biocurrents taken from the hand of a calligraphy teacher will correct it. I would like to believe that someday you will be able to buy, for example, a self-tutorial of dancing in a bioelectro-recording store: a sophisticated bio-recording of an excellent dancer. It will be enough to "play" this recording several times on your nervous system to teach you how to dance. (Zakharchenko 1975, 160)

Judging by what Glushkov told Zakharchenko, he had been working on the problem of biocurrent transmission for quite a long time. However, his only article on the subject was published in the magazine *Kibernetika* in 1981, shortly before his death (Glushkov 1990, 196). It was called *On Possible Peculiarities of Physical Fields of Biosystems*. In this paper Glushkov recognized the possibility of telepathic signal transmission and created its cybernetic model. This was a delayed answer to the question posed in 1968 by Gulyaev, namely, how it would be possible to measure the human body's emissions (Glushkov calls them "fields"), if there are many organs producing waves of different lengths. Glushkov proposed a mathematical model of telepathic transmission, according to which another biosystem can receive signals due to the fact that both the "inductor" and "receiver" work in different phases and amplitudes, which makes it possible to isolate and amplify the signals. "These (well-known in technology) phenomena," Glushkov wrote, "can explain many mysterious phenomena of parapsychological nature, of course, only those that take place in nature and are not a work of imagination."

Although Soviet developments in this field are still classified and there are not enough credible sources available, it is still possible to get a general idea from the memoirs of eyewitnesses. Thus, according to the memoirs of

Leonid Plyushch, a Soviet dissident and employee of the Institute of Cybernetics in 1962–1968, the subject of telepathy fascinated not only the leading scientists of the institute, such as its director Glushkov or surgeon Amosov, but also most of the rank-and-file staff members (Plyusch 1979). Some were just "positive about the subject," others read and listened to presentations, and still others organized their own research groups. In order to do research as paid work, many, according to Plyushch, were commissioned by the state, and their projects quickly became classified. Plyushch himself also organized a group for telepathic experiments under hypnosis using the method of Czechoslovak researcher Milan Ryzl. He recalled that "several official research groups appeared in different cities of the Union, but soon all of them were classified. Initially, we also wanted to receive financial support from the state, but with time we began to realize the immorality of the state's goals in this field."

Analyzing interviews and memoirs of cyberneticists who wanted to investigate telepathy, we can conclude that the majority of scientists pursued exclusively scientific goals. It is another matter that for the sake of financing their research they were usually ready to promise the state to improve its defense potential, all the way up to impacting the citizens' consciousness. However, this relationship between scientists and the state was not specific to the USSR: the exact same pattern can be found in the history of the military computer network ARPANET, only in that case American computer scientists played the role of Soviet cyberneticians and the internet took the place of telepathy (see chapter 4). Critical opinions about the tasks of the state by scientists could arise if the latter had different life experiences, for example, that of a dissident, as was the case with Plyushch.

In 1968, after his harsh criticism of the dissident trial, Plyushch was dismissed from the institute, left science and focused entirely on writing and political activity. From 1973 to 1976 he was under compulsory treatment in a psychiatric hospital, and after his release he left for France. In his book of memoirs *Na Karnavale Istorii* (*At the Carnival of History*) published three years later, he described the extraordinary rise of biocybernetics in the 1960s, in which he himself had been directly involved. Plyusch then switched to his disillusionment with cybernetic approaches to biology. Biocybernetics, he said, depended entirely on the data that biology supplied to it. Biology, on the other hand, was just emerging as a science, and often its theories did not match reality. As a result, cybernetics turned into "mathematical idealism": formulas became self-sufficient, no matter what they represented, and instead of true science one got "mathematical-physical-technocratic" mythology and "cybernetic magic of formulas, machines and spells."

Disillusioned with cybernetics, Plyushch criticized biologists for their blind faith in formulas, telepathy researchers for their readiness to work for secret military projects, and Glushkov's All-Union Information System project for its attempt to substitute cybernetics for social and psychological processes. Relecting on his own involvement, Plyusch concluded that "one cannot run away to science: one is still involved either in lies or in the police-militaristic industry."

It can be debated to what extent a "police industry" can be considered a science. On the one hand, it employs the same scientists as universities and research institutes. On the other hand, the secrecy surrounding its research deprives it of a key characteristic of science, if we rely on the classic definitions of Thomas Kuhn and Karl Popper: transparency for the scientific community, including the ability to replicate experiments and achieve the same results.

One way or another, all witnesses noted that the intelligence services appropriated all alternative research. Therefore, even assuming the possibility of meaningful results, their secrecy undermined their potential value.

Parapsychologists Seeking Contact: An International Cooperation of Enthusiasts

Plyushch's case was rather an exception. At the time when he was critically thinking about biocybernetics, new laboratories for the study of telepathy and other parapsychic phenomena continued to be founded all over the USSR.[14] Scientific articles and collections were published in which the object of research was formulated, for example, as "the impact of magnetic fields on biological objects" or "electromagnetic fields in the biosphere." The main task was still to prove the existence of these fields and the possibility of telepathic transmission of information. Biologist Gennady Plekhanov recalled how a researcher at his bionics laboratory in Tomsk in 1967 defended his PhD thesis in biophysics *On human perception of intangible signals*: "I took a breather. This was an indirect recognition of a scientific approach to telepathy" (Plekhanov 2004).

Information about the successes of Soviet parapsychology was regularly received in the United States, where it was of interest not only to intelligence agencies but also to scientists and amateur parapsychologists. A key role in the contacts between American and Soviet parapsychologists was played by the Bioinformation Section of the Popov Society, organized in 1965 by Ippolit Kogan. A consistent and diligent experimenter, Kogan collected a wealth of data on telepathy under various conditions: under hypnosis and without, at distances of a few meters and hundreds of kilometers, using Morse code and visual images, between two people and as "mass" telepathy (inviting everyone to participate in the experiment through a newspaper ad). His approach was to combine the electromagnetic hypothesis of telepathy with information theory in order to create a mathematical model of telepathic transmission. Analyzing the results of successful experiments (105 correct answers out of 135), Kogan suggested that telepathic transmission works on extra-long electromagnetic waves, which allows the signal to reach very large distances, up to thousands of kilometers. Calculating the number of bits and the time to "receive" over long distances, he concludes that the speed of information transmission is 0.22 bits per second (Kogan 1967).

Kogan's main place of work was at the Bauman Moscow State Technical University, where he had been teaching since the mid-1950s. The Bioinformation Section he founded was a public organization, so his activity was not paid for. However, the results of the work were not classified, and one of the tasks of the laboratory staff was to popularize them. In 1969, Kogan even participated in the symposium *A New Look at Extrasensory Perception* at the University of California, Los Angeles, but in absentia. His paper was entitled *The Information Theory Aspect of Telepathy* and it attracted a lot of attention not only from fellow parapsychologists but also from the CIA, who copied it for internal use (Kogan 1969).

Kogan's close colleague was the biologist Naumov. Thanks to him, the Laboratory of Bioinformatics became a real hub of international parapsychology, uniting Soviet scientists and enthusiasts with American experts.

Naumov initiated the publication of Kazhinsky's book in 1962 and considered himself his student. In 1966, he founded a laboratory at the Bioinformation Section and worked closely with Kogan for two years. Together they organized telepathic sessions, as they described, between Moscow and Novosibirsk and Moscow and Leningrad, whose results Kogan later reported on at a congress organized by the University of California Los Angeles (UCLA). Naumov supplemented his ideas with the hypothesis that successful telepathic sessions are possible when the inductor and receiver were "harmonized" (that is, know and understand each other well) and the transmitted thought has emotional significance for the receiver (Dudlei 1974).

Both Naumov and Kogan wrote a lot about their experiments in popular science magazines and central newspapers. However, unlike Kogan, Naumov was not a part of the academic science community, but rather an enthusiast, whose biography was quite complicated. This was largely due to his active work in popularizing parapsychology. Ebon devoted a chapter to Naumov in his book *Psychic Warfare: Threat or Illusion*. In 1968, Naumov and Kogan disagreed in their understanding of the future of parapsychology, Naumov was expelled from the Bioinformation Section, and organized the Section of Technical Parapsychology at the All-Union Evening Institute of Mechanical Engineering. Naumov was more of an organizer than a scientist: he introduced psychics, telepaths, and researchers to each other, made films, promoted parapsychology in the Soviet press, and kept in constant touch with Western activists.

In 1968 Naumov organized the International Conference on Technical Parapsychology, to which British and American specialists, including Sheila Ostrander and Lynn Schroeder, were invited. Following their trip to the USSR, they wrote the book *Psychic Discoveries Behind the Iron Curtain*, which had a bombshell effect in the United States. Once in Moscow for the conference, Ostrander and Schroeder quickly realized that they were fortunate to be unique witnesses to Soviet parapsychology's development, so little known in the United States. They therefore not only described what happened at the conference but also gathered interviews with Soviet scientists and activists from various cities. Their book is full of names, facts, and bibliography: published in 1970, it is still the most important source on the history of Soviet parapsychology.

Comparing the situation in the United States with what they saw in the Soviet Union, the authors concluded that America lagged behind the USSR "by at least 50 years." Soviet parapsychologists impressed Ostrander and Schroeder, first by their awareness of Western research, and second by their scientific approach to the subject matter:

> Backed by sophisticated machinery and mathematical theories, the Soviets are trying to lay bare some of the strange powers of man that have often been whispered about but have never been tracked down under the bright lights of the laboratories. (Ostrander and Schroeder 1970, 27)

The main task of Soviet scientists, as Ostrander and Schroeder wrote, was to create a theory of telepathy analogous to the theory of electricity "to be able to use psi and not have to wait until it strikes like lightning" (134). While the Soviets were trying to figure out how to use this power and make it into a technology, "in America, ESP research as a whole only recently emerged from the basics of establishing statistical proof of psi's existence," the authors concluded (258).

One of Ostrander and Schroeder's major discoveries was the combination of cybernetics and parapsychology they found in the USSR:

> The combination of cybernetics and ESP is a new idea. The concept of telepathic people as transmitters and radio receivers has been replaced with a model of them as a cybernetic system. Soviets talk of cybernetic instruments that would imitate telepathy in people, and many parapsychology groups are attached to cybernetics and bionics labs. (143)

By the early 1970s, as Larisa Vilenskaya, a close colleague of Naumov who emigrated in 1980, writes, the authorities' policy toward parapsychology had changed. "The enthusiasm of the 1960s had long since been replaced by strict following of superiors' assignments," Vilenskaya writes, "and the Popov Society's Bioinformation Sector was effectively closed to free research, while new secret projects under the control of the military and KGB were opening in dozens of cities across the USSR" (Vilenskaia 1985, 264).

Naumov continued to correspond with American parapsychologists despite threats from the KGB. As a result, in 1974 he was found guilty of making illegal money from lectures on parapsychology and sentenced to two years in the camps. According to the U.S. intelligence profile on Naumov, all his positions in sections and laboratories on bioinformation and parapsychology were voluntary work, and he earned money by lecturing on parapsychology (*Paraphysics R&D* 1978, 118).

The parapsychology community in the USSR and beyond began a campaign to defend Naumov, and after a year he was released. Naumov's Western colleagues and the press were convinced that the real reason was his active relations with the West, mainly the United States. In 1974, an emigre magazine in Paraguay, *Occultism and Yoga*, wrote:

> It was Eduard Naumov who broke the iron curtain between East and West in the field of parapsychology, developing and strengthening friendly scientific

> contacts between Soviet and foreign researchers. He was the first to actively promote in our country the achievements of modern parapsychology, proving the validity of parapsychology as a science. (Dudlei 1974, 15)

Despite its esoteric name, this journal closely followed the latest research on human potential and the fates of its authors. If we accept this interpretation, we can conclude that Naumov paid the price for his willingness to cooperate, while the authorities decided to stop sharing Soviet research data.

≈

In the wake of the success of cybernetics, massive research into telepathy became a reality. Cybernetics stimulated much of this research and attempted to apply its theories to telepathy. This does not mean that only cyberneticians were concerned with telepathy, or that all Soviet cyberneticians were exclusively concerned with telepathy. Cybernetic enthusiasm worked and, amazingly, it brought the Soviet Union closer to being connected to the global community of scientists . . . but not, however, in the way that the cyberneticians and parapsychologists of the 1960s had in mind, with the hope to communicate telepathically with colleagues on the other side of the Atlantic Ocean. In reality, the activities of parapsychologists like Naumov helped establish grassroots communication between American and Soviet researchers and their efforts led to the creation of a kind of transatlantic social network. This soon evolved into a citizen diplomacy movement and eventually to the opening of access to the internet in the USSR.

3

Telepathy—Spacebridge—Internet

American parapsychology in the 1960s seemed to be a much less developed discipline than the Soviet one. First, there were very few centers that conducted research on telepathy and other forms of extrasensory perception. Second, parapsychology was part of psychology: this disciplinary affiliation did not involve representatives of natural and exact sciences in research, unlike in the USSR. American parapsychology did not have the strong support that cybernetics gave to Soviet parapsychology, and thus there was no government funding. The methodology and approaches remained roughly the same as they were in the 1920s, the time when parapsychology went beyond esoteric circles and began to claim the status of a scientific discipline.

One of the oldest parapsychological laboratories in the United States was founded in 1919 at Duke University, and its most famous employees were the couple Louise and Joseph Banks Rhyne. Botanists by training, they became interested in parapsychology thanks to a public lecture by Arthur Conan Doyle: the writer was very interested in parapsychology and in his lectures talked about cases of communication between living people and the dead. Self-funding his research, Dr. Joseph Rhyne wrote his first work on extrasensory perception in the early 1930s and became active in creating an institutional framework for parapsychology.

Another great authority in the field was the psychologist Gardner Murphy, who became interested in parapsychology in the 1920s.[1] Most other prominent American parapsychologists were followers of Rhyne and Murphy: psychologist Gertrude Schmeidler conducted extrasensoric experiments at the psychology department of the City College of New York, J. G. Pratt worked at Virginia University, Stanley Krippner led Dream Lab at the Maimonides Medical Center in New York. Individual scholars and units have also conducted research at the University of Pittsburgh, the University of California Los Angeles, and St. Joseph's College in Philadelphia (Van Dyke and Juncosa 1973).

All this time, the main task of parapsychologists was to prove the existence of extrasensory perception, in particular telepathy, and, therefore, the right of parapsychology to be considered a science. A definite breakthrough came in 1969 when, thanks to the efforts of the anthropologist Margaret Mead, the Parapsychological Association became affiliated with the American Association for the Advancement of Science (AAAS), thereby according to parapsychology the formal status of a science. However, it was not until the CIA took over that parapsychology received a serious infusion of resources to boost personnel and the use of methods of the natural and exact sciences.

CIA: Catching Up and Overtaking the Soviet Union

American intelligence agencies were very interested in Soviet parapsychology, perhaps even more than American scientists. In 1995, CIA materials related to Cold War parapsychology were declassified: reports on the MKultra projects and telepathic experiments at the Stanford Research Institute, as well as information about what was going on in the USSR at that time. These materials show the full range of emotions their authors felt about the successes of the Soviet experimenters.

Thus, for example, the 1972 report *Controlled Offensive Behavior* demonstrates its authors' serious concern regarding the Soviet successes in the field of parapsychology. According to the report, by 1972 the USSR had spent about 21 million dollars on parapsychological research (CIA 1972, 24). Citing an interview with parapsychologist Montague Ullman, who visited the USSR in 1970 (Vaughan 1971), and drawing on data taken from Kogan's report on telepathic experiments presented at a conference in Los Angeles and from Ostrander and Schroeder's book, the CIA paper describes Soviet experiments as "a synthesis of a basic pragmatic approach and modern and sophisticated technology" (CIA 1972, 27). The authors go on to explain the potential danger of these experiments, suggesting that "if any of this highly questionable material is true then it can be inferred that organic matter can be transformed into "ectoplasm," that this can be rendered invisible and impalpable and thus converted into something which, for all practical purposes, amounts to a force" (29).

The authors of the report also ask: assuming that this discovery is real and the process can be managed on its basis, what are "the possible foreign policy implications of this process":

> Referring to Edward J. Pullman, Director of the Southeast Hypnosis Research Center in Dallas, Texas, the authors of the report warn about the potential danger of development of Soviet ESP for the USA: ". . . before the end of the 1970s, Soviet diplomats will be able to sit in their foreign embassies and use ESP . . . to steal the secrets of their enemies." (30)

In 1973, several new reports were published at once. The authors of "Cryptologic Aspects of ESP" discussed the possible future of battlefield telepathy and emphasized a certain "unknown energy" in the existence of which serious scientists in the USSR believed. "They also feel that in the future, machines on the moon or in the ocean will be controlled by thought" (CIA 1973), which would certainly give the enemy a strategic advantage. A report from the same year, *Paranormal Phenomena: Briefing on a Net Assessment Study*, commissioned by DARPA, was devoted to a comparison of American and Soviet parapsychology. Its authors concluded that the most noticeable difference concerns disciplinary approaches to the phenomena of extrasensory perception: in particular, in the United States there were several specialized journals on parapsychology, while in the USSR there were no such journals, since research was conducted by representatives of natural and exact sciences. Actually, it was this fact that worried the American side the most: the problems of parapsychology were dealt with by serious scientists who used sophisticated laboratory instruments.

In 1972, the Electronics and Bioengineering Laboratory was founded at the Stanford Research Institute (SRI) in Menlo Park, California, and the Stargate Project, also known as SCANATE (scan by coordinates), was established as a research program. The program was dedicated to "remote viewing," that is, telepathic exploration of an area by its geographic coordinates. Harold Puthoff, an electrical engineer and parapsychologist, headed the laboratory. When the CIA archive was declassified, SCANATE Project Director Harold Puthoff published a comment on it. According to his comments, we can reconstruct the events of the early 1970s: receiving more and more information about the success of Soviet scientists in the study of extrasensory perception, the CIA, together with military intelligence, decided to finance their own program. The program was to involve representatives of natural and exact sciences, which was unusual for American parapsychology, and the research was to be classified:

> In a few short weeks, a pair of visitors showed up at SRI with the above report in hand. Their credentials showed them to be from the CIA. They knew of my previous background as a Naval Intelligence Officer and then a civilian employee at the National Security Agency (NSA) several years earlier and felt they could discuss their concerns with me openly. There was, they told me, increasing concern in the intelligence community about the level of effort in Soviet parapsychology being funded by the Soviet security services. (Puthoff 1996)[2]

Among the tasks that, according to Puthoff, the SCANATE project staff successfully solved were the recognition of an "unidentified research center at Semipalatinsk" where the Soviet nuclear test site was functioning from 1949 to 1991, as well as the "scanning" of a Soviet submarine being built near Murmansk.

Politicians had been waiting for a big breakthrough in this field. This is what Congressman Charles Rose, the Chairman of the Evaluation Subcommittee of the House Permanent Committee on Intelligence, told *Omni* magazine in 1979:

> Some of the intelligence people I've talked to know that remote viewing works, although they still block further research on it, since they claim it's not yet as accurate as satellite photography. But it seems to me that it would be a hell of a cheap radar system. And if the Russians have it and we don't, we are in serious trouble. (Stuckey 1979)

The SCANATE project was indeed a breakthrough for American parapsychological research, primarily because of the new personnel involved. In fact, the CIA and military intelligence reproduced the Soviet model, inviting physicists and electronics specialists to work on the problems of a new type of communication, telepathy. In 1967, Puthoff received his doctorate from Stanford University. Two years later, he co-authored a work entitled *Fundamentals of Quantum Electronics* (Pantell and Puthoff 1969) and began work on the SCANATE project the year after that. He and Russell Targ published a series of works that viewed the study of paranormal phenomena as integral to modern physics and, more broadly, to the "new natural sciences." 1974 saw the publication in *Nature* of an article on *Psychic Research and Modern Physics* (Puthoff and Targ 1974), with a raft of comments appearing in the Letters column of the *Proceedings of IEEE* magazine in 1976 (Puthoff and Targ 1976 1), this alongside a report on the SCANATE program entitled "Development of Techniques to Enhance Man/Machine Interactions" (Puthoff and Targ 1976 2).

The term "human-machine interaction" has direct relevance to the history of computer networks: it was used by computer science theorists and ARPANET designers, and it was around the late 1960s when machines became accessible to scientists, so expectations were high. Although Puthoff and Targ did not directly create the internet, it is clear that they saw their work as part of the larger field of computer science. All the more so, because at the same time and at the same Stanford Institute, literally in the rooms adjacent to the SCANATE project, intensive work was going on to develop other forms of human-machine interaction: researchers were creating ARPANET, inventing user interfaces, and making the first steps to bring about the birth of "virtual communities"—prototypes of today's social networks (more on this in chapter 4).

This doesn't imply, of course, that parapsychology had no opponents. The scientific mainstream in the United States, much like in the USSR and subsequently in Russia, was categorically opposed to the inclusion of extrasensory phenomena into the category of the natural, and to the classification of parapsychology as a natural science. After the Targ/Puthoff article appeared in *Nature* in 1974, critics were quick to point out the inadequacy of the authors' experiments—and the unsoundness of the entire epistemic framework within which they'd been conducted—in a host of articles and books (Targ, Puthoff 1974; Pinch and Collins 1984). In his commentary on the declassified archive of the SCANATE program, Puthoff writes that, owing to the generally negative attitude displayed by scientists toward parapsychology, the CIA was forced to look for practitioners "outside of academia who could handle a quiet, low-profile classified investigation, and SRI appeared to fit the bill" (Puthoff 1996). By way of response to this proliferation of research into paranormal phenomena, the Committee for the

Scientific Investigation of the Claims of the Paranormal (CSICOP), subsequently renamed the Committee for Skeptical Inquiry (CSI), was founded under the aegis of the American Humanist Association (AHA) in 1975. CSICOP members published articles criticizing the methods and conclusions of parapsychological research.

Nevertheless, projects like SCANATE went on for many years, and their financial support was extended many times, until it was finally discontinued: first, for lack of unambiguous, reproducible, and intelligence-useful results, and second, because the Cold War was obviously coming to an end. As early as 1977, analyzing the similarities between the American and Soviet intelligence services in their interest in parapsychology, the *Washington Post* concluded that "the only difference between the CIA and the KGB is that the former has given up its efforts, and the other is continuing them" (*The KGB . . .* 1977). To some extent, this remains true today.[3]

Telepathy Through the Iron Curtain: A Transatlantic Session

"The so-called Iron Curtain did not just divide and block communication and movement; it also motivated attempts to communicate, generated 'excess' communications, and shaped longings for more contact," said Alaina Lemon in her book *Technologies for Intuition: Cold War Circles and Telepathic Rays* (Lemon 2017, xvii). Lemon analyzed the mutual fear and yet intense desire for contact between Americans and Soviets during the Cold War. This, she wrote, largely explained their shared interest in telepathy and other types of extrasensory perception. Since ordinary communication was impossible, there was hope for telepathic communication.

Lemon showed how the combination of fear and the desire to know what lay on the other side of the Iron Curtain shaped mutual interest at all levels, from intelligence agencies to amateur parapsychologists. Telepathy, Lemon concluded, was all the more popular because it was seen by grassroots research participants as a possible channel for the uncontrolled dissemination of information, a sort of samizdat.

To have hope in telepathy as a new type of secure communication, another precondition was needed: the belief that the near future would bring great discoveries in the field of "human potential" and that these scientific discoveries would be directly followed by improvements in life. Faith in scientific and technological progress on both sides of the Atlantic allowed people to build relationships based on parapsychology. They represented very similar societies, built on techno-optimism, on the idea of improving man and social life through new technologies. Only against this background, the mutual fears and desire for communication that Lemon spoke of resulted in parapsychology enthusiasts making a breakthrough in the relationship between the two societies. Both sides needed new channels of communication because the usual ones no longer worked.

Initially, American parapsychologists had their own interest in Soviet research: it was important for them to prove the existence of extrasensory perception, and for this purpose they wanted to know what the real achievements in this field in the USSR were. As relations between researchers from different geopolitical camps developed, the task changed: it became clear to them that further development of their activities was impossible before the Iron Curtain collapsed. Connecting the USSR to the internet was not their goal, but it was one of the consequences.

It all started with the 1968 international conference organized by Naumov (see chapter 2). After the publication of the book by Ostrander and Schroeder, a wave of American parapsychologists flooded into the USSR. In 1970, Ullman, director of the Maimonides Medical Center, visited Moscow during his sabbatical. In 1971, Krippner, director of the Dream Research Laboratory at the same Maimonides Medical Center, a parapsychologist who became famous for his experiments in dream telepathy, and a group of parapsychologists from the Esalen Institute came to Moscow at different times. All of them spoke first of all with Naumov, a man who had made a lot of effort to establish contacts with his American colleagues.

The last delegation, however, differed from the previous ones: the Esalen representatives and their Soviet colleagues from the Popov Society's bioinformation section were brought together not only by their interest in human potential research but also by their similar situation. Although many of them had a scientific background, they did not belong to the academic establishment and were, in fact, amateurs. This allowed them to become the key players in the subsequent history of the internet in the USSR.

The Esalen Institute was founded in 1962 by Dick Price and Michael Murphy, two Stanford graduates, devotees of Aldous Huxley,[4] and practitioners of esotericism and parapsychology. When it came to formulating the institute's mission, they did so in neutral terms, maintaining that the organization was created "to support alternative methods for exploring human consciousness." Thanks to their extraordinary enthusiasm, friendly ties with financial and political elites, and the fact that Murphy had inherited land in Big Sur, the duo succeeded in turning the Esalen Institute into a "mother church of a new American religion" (Andersen 2017, 178). The hot springs opened on the institute's grounds transformed it into a spa center, expediting a synthesis of theory and practice in the domain of research into human potential. The mission of the institute was to support "alternative research."

Murphy was captivated by the subject of exceptional human abilities and developed a theory of ongoing human evolution. According to Murphy, the human organism has already developed new traits in the form of extrasensory capacities. If you "hear" sounds (the singing of flowers, for instance), "feel" that someone's in the house even though you can't see or hear them, sense that someone is looking at you, spontaneously perceive events occurring at a distance, or exhibit any other signs of extrasensory perception, you're a representative of an evolved type of human being, a phenomenon described by Murphy in a 1990 interview in the periodical *Magical Blend Monthly* entitled "Michael Murphy: A Natural History of the Future" (Langevin and Daab 1990, 110).

Remarkably enough, Price, Murphy, and their institute managed to steer a middle course between marginality and mainstream. It was this balancing act that ultimately propelled them to notable successes—successes that went beyond the advancement of New Age ideas. On the one hand, Esalen's pursuit of a highly pragmatic agenda allowed it to flourish: Price and Murphy's Stanford friends worked as diplomats and advisers to several American presidents, and the institute's activities were variously funded by the Rockefeller family, George Soros, and other philanthropists. On the other hand, Esalen's interests lay in fringe domains: Eastern medicine and religious practices; yoga and meditation; avant-garde psychiatric and psychotherapeutic methodologies (including consciousness expansion experiments and telepathy); and so forth. Its visitors included Timothy Leary, Stanislav Grof, Abraham Maslow, Erik Erikson, and The Nine—a group of people claiming to be extra-terrestrial beings from Sirius.

In the words of Kurt Anderson, the 1960s marked the "beginning of the end of reason" in America. Esalen's mission was precisely to destabilize the boundaries of reason and venture beyond its limits, and to do so not merely in keeping with the cultural-historical landscape but as a true trailblazer (Anderson 2017). Esalen in this context was a unique platform that brought together academic scholars with amateur practitioners. What we call today "the mainstream" may have once seemed like an outrageous fantasy. In the 1960s, when the sciences were undergoing a major shift and new disciplines were emerging, it was not obvious which direction would become the norm. The achievements of the scientific and technological revolution that had already taken place by then—space exploration, the development of the computer industry, breakthroughs in nuclear physics and molecular genetics—demonstrated the unlimited possibilities for future discoveries. And telepathy would top the list of communication technologies of the future, rather than computer networks.

Let's go back to an Esalen staff trip to Moscow in 1971. Murphy, like other parapsychologists before him, was motivated by Ostrander and Schroeder's book, which an Esalen employee had given him. In order to make the trip to Moscow, Murphy enlisted the support of both the Senate Foreign Relations Committee and President Jimmy Carter's secretary ("we were feeding the president items he'd put in his speeches" [Wood 2014]). Making use of the contacts made by their predecessors Schroeder and Ostrander, the Americans met with Moscow-based parapsychologists as well.

Their first contact was the above-mentioned Naumov:

> A lot is happening here, but it's hard to know how much of it is government-sponsored. . . . The person who seemed to be the impresario for parapsychologists, Edward Naumov, was pathetically eager to impress us and work with us, but also to find out everything we knew. We decided he must be some sort of agent, because he had freedom to travel anywhere—whenever we'd change our plans, he would be free to come with us, and he would insist on coming. ("Michael Murphy" 1976)

Knowing Naumov's biography, one can easily assume that his desire to communicate with American parapsychologists and his attempts "to find out everything they knew" were dictated, on the one hand, by information hunger and, on the other hand, by the desire for contacts. However, it is just as clear that Murphy and his colleagues were driven by the very fear that Lemon wrote about: they were sure that any suspiciously behaving person was a KGB agent.

Nevertheless, thanks to Naumov, the delegation from Esalen became acquainted with many Soviet parapsychologists. Their first Soviet-American project was a telepathic experiment conducted between Moscow and San Francisco in 1971. The roles of transmitter and receiver would be played, respectively, by Murphy and Karl Nikolayev—an actor and telepathy research enthusiast, Naumov's colleague in the bioinformatics section of the Popov Society, a participant in Kogan's telepathic experiments, and the character in Ostrander and Schroeder's book. Murphy attempted to transmit to Nikolayev a series of five randomly selected images. As far as the participants were concerned, the session reaped some interesting results: one of the transmission attempts resulted in a successful connection, with Nikolayev glimpsing the trunk of an elephant from an illustrated dictionary (Kripal, 322).

Nikolaev was well known in Moscow for his telepathic shows. In the 1970s and 1980s, he often performed them in clubs and at informal gatherings (Vilenskaia 1985, 253). Although he was an actor by profession, Nikolaev's performances were not the usual circus magic: they were accompanied by lectures and references to scientific research in which he participated as a telepath. Nikolaev, like Naumov, spent a lot of time with guests from the United States. However, unlike other enthusiasts, contacts with America were important to him not only professionally, but also as part of his family history: his father Nikolai Gurvich (Nicholas Hourwich[5]) was a co-founder of the U.S. Communist Party. Forced to emigrate from Russia in 1910, he returned to the country 10 years later as a member of the Comintern. However, having "aroused Lenin's ire," Gurvich was not only expelled from the Comintern but was also blocked from leaving Russia (Draper 2003, 280). He stayed in Moscow forever to teach political economy at the university. His son Karl knew his family history well and spoke freely about it to friends and colleagues.[6] So, his transatlantic telepathy session was not only a scientific experiment but also a symbolic reunion with the country that would become his homeland. For us, however, it is another connection from the 1960s–1970s to the 1920s, that is, to a time when everything seemed possible, from the transformation of matter into electricity to the Communist International.

For Esalen, in turn, telepathy through the Iron Curtain was the first step of a larger project to tear it down. The 1971 transatlantic telepathy session with Nikolaev was only the beginning, followed by more teleconferences, an extensive program of Soviet-American exchange, indirect assistance in the internetization of the Soviet Union, and finally the organization of Boris Yeltsin's first visit to the United States, which led to his resignation from the

Communist Party of the Soviet Union and hastened the political death of the USSR.

The Murphys were regular visitors to Moscow throughout the 1970s, taking full advantage of their connections at the president's administrative office. Like his predecessors, Murphy eventually wrote a book—*An End to Ordinary History*—based on these trips. It was a spy novel with elements of mysticism (Murphy 1982).[7] Actually the novel's most unembellished passages struck the novel's readers as complete fabrications—not least its claims that telepathy and other "hidden human reserves" were being studied in the USSR. No flight of fancy could ever have topped the Cold War reality of the 1970s: the arms race, confrontations between the American and Soviet special services, the two "superpowers" vying to outdo one another in the field of research into human consciousness potential.

A key event in the history of Esalen's communication with Soviet parapsychologists was the 1979 international symposium in Tbilisi on problems of the unconscious. In Soviet science, the term "unconscious" and psychoanalysis in general were under an ideological ban. In addition, any international event was of special interest to the KGB and carried great danger for the organizers. So, it was a fantastic thing by all accounts: three Soviet psychologists were able to hold a symposium in Tbilisi, which turned out to be a turning point in the fate of psychoanalysis in Russia and in the history of relations between Soviet and American parapsychologists.[8] One of the organizers of the symposium, Vadim Rotenberg, described in his memoirs the difficulties of inviting foreign participants. For example, one had to be especially careful in inviting Western scholars, lest they say something radically non-Marxist and thereby spoil the careers of their Soviet colleagues (Rotenberg n.d.).

The symposium was very successful: major scientists from the USSR, Western Europe, and the United States attended,[9] and the result of this meeting was a gradual change of attitude toward psychoanalysis. Being a major event for psychology in the Soviet Union, the symposium was also a meeting place for parapsychologists from different countries. Since psychology has long been legalized and parapsychology, on the contrary, finally discredited, there's no written record of it in the scientific literature. However, in 1979 both directions were in the same position: the problems of the unconscious were suspicious for the Soviet ideology because they did not fit into its primitive materialism. Nevertheless, Krippner's name was on the main program, and his paper was published in the four-volume collection *The Unconscious* (Krippner 1978).

Other guests and participants (but not authors of papers) at the symposium included Targ from the SCANATE project, the Murphys from the Esalen Institute, Krippner's junior colleague Jim Hickman, Naumov, and psychic and healer Djuna Davitashvili. Shortly after the symposium, Djuna moved to Moscow on Naumov's initiative to participate in research on her psychic abilities and to treat members of the Politburo.[10] From then until the late 1990s, Djuna remained an important player in Soviet alternative science.[11]

While scientific literature covered the symposium as a breakthrough in the study of the unconscious, popular science magazines preferred to cover its parapsychological part. For example, eight pages of the March 1980 issue of *Tekhnika Molodezhi* were devoted to psychics, telepaths, and philosophers who supported them (*K tajnam podsoznanija* 1980). The selection included parapsychologist and hypnosis specialist Viktor Raikov, philosopher Alexander Spirkin, as well as an interview with Djuna. From other sources, such as Targ's memoirs or a 2015 interview with Djuna, one can learn that the symposium participants not only discussed scientific problems, but also conducted telepathic experiments (Targ and Harary 1984; Djuna 2015).

When RAND Corporation employees P. T. Van Dyke and M. L. Juncosa wrote in their report for DARPA, "The fraternity of psychic researchers, in both the Soviet Union and the United States, is closely knit" (Van Dyke and Juncosa 1973), they hardly suspected that very soon these two communities would be tightly united with each other to begin an active struggle to end the Cold War.

"The Kingdom of Words Is Dead": A Screen Utopia by Joseph Goldin

In Tbilisi, the Murphys made the acquaintance of Iosif Goldin (Joseph Goldin in the American press). He often introduced himself as an "impresario" or "freelancer," which sounded rather exotic in the Soviet context. At the same time, Goldin's profession is difficult to define in any other words. He worked, as we would say today, on projects. He eked out a supplementary income as a sailor on cargo ships in the Arctic and as a scriptwriter for Gosteleradio, the state broadcasting service. He conducted "suggestopaedic" séances at the Taganka Theater in Moscow following a method developed by the Bulgarian psychologist Georgi Lozanov.[12] He penned articles on telepathy and the "hidden reserves of the human body." He organized conferences. An established figure in Moscow throughout the 1970s and 1980s, Goldin collaborated with various institutes of the USSR Academy of Sciences, contributed to popular science magazines and the *Literaturnaya Gazeta* (Literary Gazette), among other publications, and was also well known in theater and cinema circles. Yet he produced very few written texts, his endeavors being predominantly oral in nature. There're few references to Goldin in other publications, but writers, bloggers, and forum contributors who do mention him invariably emphasize his eccentric, singular personality.

He's variously described as "an idiosyncratic individual who earned himself the reputation of a wacko" (Sazikov 2014); as a "social hacker" (Fedotov 2012), "an enterprising dreamer" (Pozner 2012), and "a 'crazy person' (in a good way)" (Raushenbach 2003); and, finally, as a "sad genius," "a wacko of biblical proportions," and "an intellectual gangster who got beaten down by life" (Khiltunen 2008).

Since the late 1970s, the Murphys and other American parapsychologists often visited Goldin in Moscow and supplied him with literature. He was also friends with famous academicians. Therefore, many of Goldin's acquaintances wondered if he was a secret informant or perhaps a KGB agent. Here is how Leonid Kitaev-Smyk, a specialist in the psychology of stress and an associate at the Institute of Psychology, describes his acquaintance with Goldin and answers the question:

> In the late 1970s, a colleague came to me and said that I was called to a certain room. I knocked and entered. The room looked like a closet from the inside, and there was a man sitting in it, the KGB curator of the institute. He pulled out a newspaper with an interview of Iosif Goldin and asked: "Do you know him? A very interesting person, he also works on stress problems, but not as a scientist, rather as a publicist. If you are interested, meet him." I realized that the KGB was now interested in both him and me . . . Goldin was a very public person, so he was completely under control and never tried to get out from under it. He was the kind of dissident who didn't do anything secret. He was like a plant, sprouting through the smallest cracks in the concrete of Soviet power, destroying that concrete. (Interview, June 2, 2018, Moscow)

Goldin and Kitaev-Smyk became friends. They organized the first Soviet-American spacebridge together. Kitaev-Smyk knew the Murphys but he learned about the parapsychological interests of Michael Murphy and Goldin from me during our interview: Murphy introduced himself as a person interested in stress psychology. In the mid-1980s, Goldin and Murphy parted ways.

However, when they met in Tbilisi in 1979, Goldin and the Murphys were astonished at the extent to which their respective views aligned. They may have used different terminology—"human potential" versus "reserve capacities"—to describe their sphere of endeavor, but in fact they were interested in the same thing. Most likely, this meeting would have ended with another telepathic session, of which there would have been no trace, if it hadn't been for Dulce Murphy. Having discovered fellow thinkers in the USSR, she realized that American and Soviet researchers' shared interest in extrasensory perception represented a very different kind of potential. Upon returning to California, the Murphys decided to inaugurate a new project within the framework of the Esalen Institute: the Esalen Soviet–American Exchange Program.

In 1980, Esalen convened a conference—the first of its kind—on Soviet–American relations, prompting Joseph V. Montville, a diplomat friend of the Murphys, to coin the term "*Track II diplomacy*." The Soviet–American Exchange Program would subsequently come to dovetail with the increasingly popular idea of "citizen diplomacy."[13] Dulcy invited Krippner's student Jim Hickman, an enthusiast of extrasensory perception studies and a participant in the Tbilisi symposium, to lead the program.

Although the acquaintance of Hickman and the Murphy couple was made possible by their shared interest in parapsychology, it turned Hickman's biography in a very different direction. He summarizes the transition from parapsychology to political activity as follows:

> I am one of the thousands of people whom Stanley [Krippner] opened up to other parts of ourselves, giving us, in a sense of way, seeing opportunities about our lives. That has taken me to a vast range of what I would call "communication." So, I spent 25 years, for example, working on US-Soviet relationship. . . . The program itself grew far beyond the psychic world and eventually touched international politics in a way that, we believe, helped give rise to what was then called "citizen diplomacy." (*Jim Hickman's Reflections* 2019)

Meanwhile, Goldin plugged his new friends from Esalen into his turbulent activities in the USSR. At the very end of the 1970s—not long before his death—Academician Berg, cyberneticist and long-time chair of the Cybernetics Council of the Soviet Academy of Sciences, took charge of the Commission for Human Reserve Capacities. The journalist Valery Hiltunen, a friend of Goldin's and a fellow member of the Commission, remarked that the efforts of Konstantin Mazurov, then the First Deputy Chairman of the USSR Council of Ministers, were indispensable to its creation. Mazurov persuaded Berg to become the Commission's chair, thereby raising its status within the Academy of Sciences:

> Mazurov, fighting off Joe (Joseph Goldin), who was attacking him: "Well, you're a smart man and you realize that the country of dreamers and scientists should . . . ,"—he stuck his finger into the phone dial and asked tiredly: "Axel Ivanovich, dear, you have had experience of communicating with brilliant lunatics, you had Lev Termen working for you, right? We'll have to shake you again. . . . Well, I realize that the Cybernetics Council of the Presidium of the Academy is not the best place to collect paranormal. . . . But where else should I put them?" (Khiltunen 2008)

According to Khiltunen, the Commission's other members included academician Boris Rauschenbach, surgeon Amosov, chemical engineer Oleg Avdykovich, philosopher Spirkin, who chaired the Department of Philosophical Problems of Cybernetics of the Scientific Council on Cybernetics of the Academy of Sciences of the USSR, hypnotist Mikhail Shoyfet, psychic Djuna, parapsychologists Naumov, Veniamin Pushkin, and Zdeněk Rejdák, author of the waterbirth concept Igor Charkovsky, as well as the Murphy couple.

It is difficult to find out how many times the Commission has met and whether its archives exist, as there is practically no information about it. Several papers have been published under its auspices, including a collection of articles on problems of "human reserve capabilities," but they are mainly devoted to sports medicine and psychology.[14] In a brief comment on his website, Khiltunen mentioned that the meetings had been held "project-by-project" to avoid conflicts among the commissioners. The only mention of the commission from people who were not members of it, I found in the memoirs of Alexander Kutikov, a musician in the band *Mashina Vremeni*. He witnessed the meetings held at the premises of the State Institute of Theatre Arts (GITIS):

> At the GITIS studio, we had a very interesting time, a kind of "Athenian school." A commission of the USSR Academy of Sciences for the comprehensive study of human reserve capabilities operated on the basis of the studio. All the followers of alternative forms of study, yogis, ufologists, magicians came there. There were a lot of interesting people there, during two years of communication with whom I learned more than during all the previous years of my life. Although, of course, among these people there were a lot of charlatans, swindlers and crazy people. (Kutikov n.d.)

Apparently, the commission's activities did not satisfy Goldin. He was neither a theorist nor a researcher, but a producer and art curator, and he wanted to take practical actions. In 1982, Goldin learned that the U.S. Festival—organized by Steve Wozniak, cofounder of Apple—was to be held in San Bernardino. The festival stage had to be flanked by two fifteen-meter Eidaphor screens, with a Mitsubishi Diamond Vision screen suspended above it. Measuring nine meters by six, the latter was at the bleeding edge of the era's technology. Goldin suggested that the Murphys cooperate with Wozniak and use these screens, as well as satellite television technology and the resources of Gosteleradio, to conduct a Soviet-American telemost, or spacebridge. And indeed, they managed to mobilize all their contacts on both sides of the Iron Curtain and implement the first Soviet-American project: the "Moscow—Space—California" spacebridge.

In the United States, employees of the Internews organization, which had been created specifically for this purpose,[15] engaged in talks with Wozniak and the Soviet ambassador Anatoly Dobrynin. In Moscow, meanwhile, Goldin succeeded in securing the involvement of Gosteleradio as well as the Commission for the Study of Human Reserve Capacities of the Soviet Academy of Sciences, including the academicians Yevgeny Velikhov and Rauschenbach.[16] Goldin himself took on scriptwriting duties, with Yuli Gusman invited to direct. The format was shockingly novel. Goldin and Gusman decided that the initial contact necessitated nothing more than an exchange of music. And so performances from the U.S. festival stage were broadcast from San Bernardino to Russia, while the Soviets reciprocated with broadcasts of such forward-looking artists as Alla Pugacheva, the rock groups Voskreseniye and Arsenal, Nadezhda Babkina's Russkaya Pesnya (Russian Song) ensemble, and others.

According to the memories of psychologist Kitaev-Smyk, who also helped Goldin with the organization of the spacebridge, the hardest thing was to invite Pugacheva:

> She was quite modest then, and he could talk to her. But she said: "No, no, I don't want to." And he said, "Alla Borisovna, well, who but you can get into space and connect us with America?" And he talked her into it. (Interview, June 2, 2018, Moscow)

Since Soviet television neglected to broadcast the spacebridge, it was watched only by "immediate" viewers—predominantly students who'd been invited to the studio. Yet Americans, too, got to see only the very beginning. It would subsequently emerge that the broadcast had been cut short by Bill Graham, the Grateful Dead promoter and one of the festival's organizers. Born in Berlin in 1931 into a family of Jewish émigrés from Russia, Graham wasn't exactly enamored of the Soviet Union. "Convinced that the whole thing was a KGB trick, and that none of it was actually coming from Moscow," Graham "literally pulled the plug halfway through the concert" (Kripal 2007, 334). The Moscow studio continued to watch what was happening on the stage in San Bernardino, while the audience of the California festival did not see the Soviet participants. Nevertheless, the effect they exerted on those Soviet people who could see it was tremendous. Sol Shulman, a writer-director and a friend of Goldin's, recalls the reactions of people invited to watch in the studio: "'Now I'm a pan-planetary man . . .' someone shouted. They had glimpsed the world. They'd seen that there were cheerful young people there—people just like them" (Shulman 2017).

The first spacebridge was followed by the second. "Everything seemed to be going OK, but you felt kind of mute," Gusman recalled. "We couldn't talk [. . .]. It was all singing, all dancing, but what we really wanted was to talk. I could manage 'hi' and 'bye,' of course, but I didn't have enough words for a conversation, a discussion. Neither Iosif nor myself had had that level of language practice" (Telemost 2012, 36). In an effort to instigate a dialogue beyond an exchange of musical numbers, Goldin invited the bilingual Vladimir Pozner, then working in the Foreign Broadcasting Service, to host the link-up. Because households across the USSR tuned in to watch this time around, Pozner was propelled to television stardom.

After the third, Pozner-fronted broadcast, the Gosteleradio leadership relieved Goldin of his duties as spacebridge organizer. Nonetheless, the success of the first link-up, in combination with Goldin's strong informal ties with the Esalen Institute, enabled him to continue elaborating his notion of global telecommunications. It became his life's work.

One of the few researchers who has written several articles on Goldin's activities, media art historian Alexei Sazikov, reconstructed a possible train of thought of his hero. According to Sazikov, the idea of the spacebridge came to Goldin after a visit to the 1959 American National Exhibition in Moscow:

> The exhibition's centrepiece was a geodesic dome—the "geo-house" created by the famous American engineer, architect and designer Richard Buckminster Fuller. The interior of the "geo-house" boasted seven large screens, and it was on these screens that the film *Glimpses of the USA*, produced by the designers Charles and Ray Eames, had its premiere. (Sazikov 2014)

For America itself, this multiscreen installation represented a milestone in design, with the Eameses describing it as an "information machine" complete with an "electronic brain" (a "huge RAMAC 305 computer") (Colomina 2001). In the Soviet Union, screen production lagged behind the United States by about the same 20 years as the entire computer industry. The advanced projects developments were unique, did not go into industrial manufacturing, and remained in history as invariably one-off monuments to the ingenuity of Soviet engineers.

Here, for example, is what happened at the most advanced Soviet television factory, Elektron in Lviv, where Glushkov's team in 1967 installed the first automated control system. This system provided real-time information about the functioning of the various factory floors. Since it was supposed to improve the various indicators of "socialist competition," all members of staff were obliged to keep tabs on how things were progressing. The new set-up assumed the use of a common screen. According to the administration's idea, if all workers followed the progress of the socialist competition, it would improve the factory's performance. However, such broad access to information required a large screen in a public place, and there was no such screen at the TV factory. Teams maintaining the system came up with an ingenious solution: they'd get an electromechanical display of the kind normally seen at railway stations:

> Elektron bought an imported display for $100,000 and we installed it in the underground passage to the canteen, where thousands of factory workers would see the results of their efforts on a daily basis. (Bondarenko 2017)

In order for the system to work, it was necessary not only to buy a scoreboard, but also to connect it to the ACS through a chain of media and decoders: magnetic tape reels, punched tapes, teletype, original software. With this context in mind, it is easy to understand Goldin, who reacted so enthusiastically to the information about the screens in San Bernardino. Created with the latest technology, these screens were rare and expensive even for the United States and Japan, and certainly science fiction for the USSR. After the successful launch of the spacebridges, Goldin developed his project. In 1983, he had an idea to organize worldwide communication centers connected to each other. Such centers were supposed to help solve global conflicts like the Cold War (Sazikov 2014, 187). In 1985, when a group of chemists discovered a new form of the carbon molecular compound fullerene (also known as "buckyball"), Goldin decided that there should be sixty such communication centers, according to the number of compounds in fullerene, and each should look like Fuller's geodesic dome with large screens placed inside, exactly like the 1959 American exhibition in Moscow. In this way, the globe becomes a metaphor for fullerene, or a "thinking molecule."

While Goldin was working on his global project, he developed the idea that communication through a screen is direct and, consequently, allows such communication to convey human emotions. It differentiates telecommunication from text-based communication. In an interview in *Mother Jones* in 1986, Goldin said: "The kingdom of words is dead. Atomic weapons have created a new kind of silence. We must see each other [. . .]. We must reach a new level of consciousness" (Hochschild 1986). In another interview the following year, Goldin extended this line of argument: "Large groups of people," he asserted, must "interact spontaneously and directly via huge screens" (Gilman 1987).

In fact, Goldin developed his original theory of media: spacebridges and teleconferences free communication from all unnecessary things, providing an opportunity for a "direct" exchange of information. This localized media theory contradicted Marshall McLuhan's famous theory that there was no such thing as neutral media. Like any theory, Goldin's was adequate to the situation from which it grew: the Cold War, the Iron Curtain, and the propaganda-filled official press forced people to seek alternative, transparent channels of communication. In the same way, cyberneticians had been searching for direct transmission of information a decade earlier, researching telepathy. Of course, unlike Goldin's and the citizen diplomacy generation, they did not mean to pursue explicit political goals. However, for them, too, telepathic transmission implied the direct broadcasting of information. Kogan's information theory of telepathy can be considered a typical example of this general desire for direct communication. Counting the amount of raw information in bits, he assumed that a person during a telepathic session is analogous to a computer (see chapter 2).

Thus, Goldin's spacebridges were a kind of post-telepathy that could be achieved technically and which, as he said in an interview, would lead to "a new level of consciousness." Also importantly, Goldin's theory evolved along with his practical actions. With words discredited by politics, he countered with real-time video transmission. And it worked. The most fruitful time for Goldin was the mid-1980s. He continued to think about his project, which was now called *Mirror for Humanity*, realizing it in several directions at once. First, he was looking for screens, as well as inexpensive ways to broadcast, since only the government could pay for satellite communications. Second, he was providing PR for the project.

American entrepreneur Joel Schatz provided Goldin with the broadcast technology. Having worked as an energy advisor to the governor of Oregon and as a consultant to a psychiatric clinic in Colorado, he relocated to California and became involved in the citizen diplomacy movement. With the help of Esalen's Soviet–American exchange program[17] and the Murphys' contacts in Moscow, Schatz quickly established contact with Goldin.

Like Goldin himself, Schatz had been struck by the communicational possibilities that had suddenly opened up during those years, not least in the context of United States–Soviet relations. The Cold War, as it now seemed, would not last forever, and the Iron Curtain was not hermetic, with people on both sides of the divide eager to communicate with one another. But pacifism, the keystone of citizen diplomacy, wasn't Schatz's only motivation. Like Dulce Murphy, he was more of an entrepreneur than a researcher or activist and quickly realized that building communicational bridges with the USSR could augur well for business development. At this time, a phone call from the United States to the USSR could only be made by appointment, and there was only one AT&T phone company line for this purpose. Against the backdrop of a shortage of communication methods, by the mid-1980s the need for communication became very high. Teleconferences, Schatz believed, would serve as an effective stepping-stone toward the establishment of regular links, and in 1985 he founded the nonprofit organization San-Francisco Moscow Teleport (SFMT).

Before Schatz's next visit to Moscow, Goldin asked him to bring slow scan television (SSTV) equipment. This technology was used in American medicine whenever a photographic image had to be urgently dispatched to a specialist in another city. It involved transmitting images over a standard telephone line without the use of a costly satellite link: the system sent sequences of stills—one every 5–10 seconds—to a special receiver, thereby producing something akin to a slide show. Goldin came up with the idea of adapting SSTV to teleconference needs, and Schatz, at his request, brought equipment for this purpose.

Schatz and Goldin initially focused on professional teleconferences between scientists, astronauts, doctors, and teachers. Satellite linkups were prohibitively expensive, while Russia's telecommunication wires were tsarist-era copper affairs. At the pair's request, engineers attempted to boost the signal by means of terminals, but this was insufficient even for SSTV. For the first session, Goldin—his thinking characteristically global in scope—decided to enlist the involvement of Rauschenbach, a Soviet physicist responsible for the first photographs of the far side of the Moon. Rauschenbach and two American Nobel Prize–winning physicist colleagues were to show one another the workspaces where they'd made their respective groundbreaking discoveries.

In 1972, the unique 235m2 ELIN screen was manufactured in the city of Vinnitsa using light element pulse control technology. "The ELIN was effectively a full-color 'television' that boasted 102,900 automotive incandescent lamps covered with red, blue and green filters," Sazikov writes (Sazikov 2016). The screen was installed on Kalinin Prospekt, but for a long time no institution wanted to put it on its books: because of the unique design, technical support was too expensive. Plus, no one but Goldin understood how ELIN could be used other than to broadcast television programs. For him, however, the giant screen was a dream come true: it was installed on the street and was ideal for his *Mirror for Humanity*. Given that the SSTV technology was already implemented by Goldin and Schatz, all that was still needed was for all parties to agree.

Goldin got acquainted with the group of engineers who had created ELIN, involved Shatz and state television, and together they conducted several teleconferences. These were local (teleconference with the Grauerman birthing center, "New Year's Holiday on Arbat"), long-distance ("Moscow—Novosibirsk") and international ("Moscow—Vladivostok—Tokyo"). In the same year, 1986, the Ministry of Communications organized the teleconference "ELIN" using orbital station "Mir," involving expensive satellite communications (Sazikov 2014, 190). So Goldin's idea was taken up by the state.

Goldin also promoted his project on a large scale. In 1986, together with Schatz and the Esalen Institute, he organized the publication of *Citizen Summitry: Keeping the Peace When It Matters Too Much to Be Left to Politicians* (Carlson and Comstock, 1986). Several sections contained essays by American and Soviet authors, including Goldin and Schatz, on the threats of nuclear war and nuclear winter, on citizen diplomacy and Soviet-American spacebridges, and on the transformation of consciousness in the coming era when humanity will find ways to be united.

In 1987, the journal *Znaniie—Sila* (*Knowledge Is Power*) published a series of papers under the title *Mirror for Humanity* (*Zerkalo . . .* 1987). The big photo of ELIN on Kalininsky Prospekt was followed by a fragment of Khlebnikov's poem *Swanland in the Future* as an epigraph:

> In cloudy weather the clouds themselves were used as screens, the latest news were projected directly onto them. (Khlebnikov, *Collected Works . . .* 1987, 344)

Khlebnikov's poetry was closely related to different technologies, particularly radio (see chapter 1), and his vision of the future is often cited when it comes to prophecies of the global network. Although Goldin did catch the time of the internet, he developed his own vision of ideal communication and an alternative network built on screens and video. For him, Khlebnikov's screens were rather a prophecy of a *Mirror for Humanity*.

The epigraph was followed by quotes from the speeches of Mikhail Gorbachev and Velikhov, Vice-President of the USSR Academy of Sciences, and then by a short commentary by Goldin, in which he described the *Mirror for Humanity* concept:

> If, with the help of "space bridge" technology, one realizes the observation of the sunrise simultaneously on all continents of the Earth and does it regularly, turning it into a form of bringing people together, there may be no nuclear catastrophe. *Mirror for Humanity* will allow people to see how the Sun will rise over the Earth, with the main glissando transmitting it from one giant video screen to another, changing landscapes and the appearance of the population. In some countries, it is still "yesterday's" twilight, in others, it is deep night, but everywhere people, young and old, stand with eyes squinting, or hands folded in prayer, or hugging each other, watching the Sun now rising at the edge of the Earth, their eyes catching more and more streams of light. (*Zerkalo* . . . 1987, 22)

According to Goldin, this process was intended to prevent nuclear war and push humanity to a new stage of evolution and a new consciousness. The *Mirror for Humanity* project would occupy his attention for literally the rest of his life. He sought technical possibilities for its realization, involving people of all kinds of professions and status and constantly adjusting the idea. Watching the sunrise was replaced by the idea of broadcasting the main sights of different countries, which he called "the wonders of the world":

> Sakura (flowering cherry) in Japan at the foot of Mount Fuji, the Bronze Age observatory at Stonehenge in England, the Sistine Chapel in Italy, a view of the Moscow Kremlin from the Moskva River, the Zwinger in Dresden and the dolphinarium in Hawaii. (Hochschild 1986)

Among his visionary ideas was a tour of Europe, complete with performance art and other events, in an SS-20 missile carrier truck; the construction of a communications center in Gorky Park, and a joint sunrise observation session during a meeting between Gorbachev and Japanese prime minister Toshiki Kaifu. Having failed with the presidents, Goldin contacted the Japanese construction company Takanaku, which by then had designed Sky City 1000, one of the tallest skyscrapers in the world, and agreed to merge Sky City 1000 and *Mirror for Humanity*. In 1988, he penned a screenplay for a documentary of the same name, which the actor and filmmaker Rolan Bykov was slated to direct (Bykov 2011, 318).

None of these ideas did Goldin manage to realize to the end. The film was not made, the skyscraper was not built, the sunrise broadcasts were not organized. The era of crazy enthusiasts was replaced by a new era of businesspeople. Telepathy found its way onto television shows and a dream of universal contact became, as Lemon wrote, a consumer item (Lemon 2017, 101; Golubev 2020). Finally, internet technology has proven to be more convenient for fast communication. And Schatz understood this much better than Goldin.

Prior to his arrival in Moscow, Schatz's IT expertise was minimal: he had, in fact, bought his first computer specifically with a view to improving links between the United States and the Soviet Union. He already understood then that manually organized spacebridges and teleconferences were not as promising as systemic communication between the countries, the need for which was growing every year. And it was clear that this connection would be the internet. In 1986, the same year that Goldin began work on his *Mirror for Humanity* project in the hope of achieving universal peace through screens, Schatz proclaimed:

> This technology is going to revolutionize human communications! Think what it will mean when you can get thousands of Americans and Soviets on the same computer network. Once scientists in both countries begin talking to each other on these machines they won't be able to stop. And we'll be taking a running leap over the governments on both sides. (Hochschild 1986)

Several ingredients were needed for the business to succeed, and Schatz, a talented entrepreneur, was able to put them all together. First, technical access to the global network: as it turned out, this had existed in the USSR since the early 1980s at the All-Union Institute of Applied Automated Systems (VNIIPAS). Second, contacts with influential people to get this access: these Goldin provided to Shatz. However, Schatz recognized the historical moment from the very beginning: the need for the internet and even proto–social networks had long existed; all that remained was to provide an electronic connection. Below I will look at all of these components separately.

VNIIPAS: Hooking Up to the Internet in 1982

The International Institute for Applied Systems Analysis was founded in 1972 as a joint US–Soviet project. The idea for such an institution had emerged years earlier and was championed by U.S. president Lyndon Johnson. In an October 1966 keynote policy address, Johnson stressed the need for the United States and the USSR to undertake joint peace efforts, with the scientific ties between the two superpowers integral to any such initiative. The Cuban Missile Crisis was a recent memory, and the Vietnam War, escalated by the Johnson administration, was at its height. The proposal to inaugurate a Soviet-American institute may have been unexpected, but it was hardly a throwaway suggestion: over the course of 1966, Johnson had repeatedly spoken of "building bridges" with the Eastern Bloc. So began efforts to initiate negotiations with the USSR—efforts which involved former presidential security advisor McGeorge Bundy, USSR Council of Ministers chairman Kosygin, and (in due course) Dzhermen Gvishiani, who not only played a part in the inauguration of the International Institute for Applied Systems Analysis (IIASA) in 1972 but also became the first director of its Soviet branch in 1976.

Gvishiani's involvement was far from accidental. The son of an old Bolshevik and an ally of chief of the NKVD Lavrentiy Beria, he graduated from the Moscow State Institute of International Relations (MGIMO)—a breeding ground for Soviet diplomatic personnel—where he met Kosygin's daughter and became his son-in-law. His familial affiliation with several clans of the Soviet political elite, his progressive scientific interests (control theory, systems theory), his proficiency in foreign languages—all this made Gvishiani an ideal candidate for facilitating scientific cooperation with America in an era of proxy wars when only cybernetics and systems analysis seemed capable of saving humanity from its own unreason. The institute inaugurated with his involvement became a genuine "window into Europe," linking liberal forces in the West and the USSR for two generations.

The history of the Institute of System Analysis is recounted in detail in Eglė Rindzevičiūtė's *The Power of Systems*, a work that explores the roles played by cybernetics and system analysis in state-building on both sides of the Iron Curtain. Rindzevičiūtė described the relationships Gvishiani developed with the USSR's political and scientific elite, dwelling on his ability to network, which, in combination with his family connections, yielded tangible results:

> Higher education was indeed crucial for the formation of Soviet governmental elites that eventually came to occupy leading positions after World War II. For example, it was at the Industrial Academy in Moscow in 1929 that Nikita Khrushchev met Stalin's wife, then also a student, who brought him to the

> attention of the leader. Later Dzhermen Gvishiani would help Khrushchev's grandson gain a position at the Institute of Systems Research [sic]. Furthermore, Dzhermen Gvishiani's sister married Evgenii Primakov, who would later become the director of the Institute of World Economics and International Relations (IMEMO) and, after the collapse of the Soviet Union, the head of the state security agency and prime minister under Boris El'tsin. (Rindzevičiūtė 2016, 39)

In 1982, the Institute for System Analysis of the Soviet Academy of Sciences and the Austria-based International Institute for Applied System Analysis (IIASA) established a dedicated communications channel between Moscow and Laxenburg, a town near Vienna. The link between the two institutes was a unidirectional one, with the Soviet institute's staff predominantly availing themselves of information retrieval systems (Dialog, DataStar, and so forth) and bibliographical tools. The Austrian network was directly connected to the American military one, the ARPANET, and in the early 1980s there were still stringent restrictions on access to information for Eastern Bloc users. Nikolai Saukh, an engineer at the Institute for System Analysis, offered the following overview of the situation in a 2003 interview:

> The Americans took a dim view of our endeavours from the word go. They kicked up a real fuss: it was like, "Those Soviets are pumping out information behind the smokescreen of an international institute." Then they went into total hysterics, and we agreed with Radio Austria (a semi-governmental communications organization) that our channel would end there. But from there, one could get access to all the information sources we needed. (Ivanov 2004)

Access to the Moscow–Laxenburg channel did not yet constitute access to the internet as such—or at least not to the internet as a social phenomenon. Entry to digital databases did not entail the possibility of communication, which materialized only in the late 1980s, and even then, only for a narrow circle of Soviet users. Be that as it may, further developments linked to the emergence of grassroots bilateral communication between the West and the USSR were all directly related to the channel's existence—and, ultimately, depended on the political will of Johnson and Kosygin, on the one hand, and on the diplomatic talents of Gvishiani, on the other. Although Soviet cyberneticists failed to build their own computer network, cybernetics proved a useful diplomatic tool. It was Gvishiani's interest in cybernetics that prompted him to secure access to the American computer network.

In 1983, Gvishiani, the institute's director, summoned the biochemist Anatoly Klyosov to a meeting and showed him a letter from the UN Industrial Development Department. The letter contained an invitation for Soviet scientists to attend a major international online biotechnology conference, with Klyosov's name floated as that of a potential moderator. Klyosov had spent a year working in a biophysics lab at Harvard University in the mid-1970s and gone on to become a UN biotech consultant, earning himself a degree of renown in America (Klyosov 1985; Klyosov 2010; Pototsky 2014).

Internet access was provided by the Institute for System Analysis via the Austrian link. The link enabled Klyosov to access the website of Stockholm University, which provided a connection between Western countries and Warsaw Pact members throughout the conference. The event, which proved a success, is documented not only in Klyosov's recollections and articles, but also in a report in which the Canadian moderator remarks on the USSR's participation alongside various other countries (Balson 1985, 26).

Access to the internet didn't disappear after the conference: Klyosov continued to take advantage of it into the late 1980s. For several years, he remained one of the few Soviet scientists in cyberspace. Technically, this was the same internet of which the American military network ARPANET constituted a component part. In his memoirs, Klyosov singles out Oleg Smirnov, director of the All-Union Scientific Research Institute of Applied Automated Systems (VNIIPAS), for mention, noting that Smirnov covered up for him, as using computer networks for purposes other than work was completely illegal (Klyosov 2010, Ivanov 2004).

From Contacts to Connection

In order to become an internet provider, in addition to having technical access to the network, it was necessary to negotiate with VNIIPAS for a permission to access the network. Goldin, who was friends with academicians and influential people, provided Schatz with contacts. Most important for further networking was Velikhov, director of the Kurchatov Institute and vice-president of the USSR Academy of Sciences.

Since the early 1980s, Velikhov has been an active advocate of peace and nuclear disarmament. In 1983, he founded the Committee of Soviet Scientists for Peace and Against the Nuclear Threat and became its first president.

That same year, during the second teleconference between the United States and the USSR, Velikhov compared nuclear weapons to a cancerous tumor. This speech astonished the American side and made the academician a television celebrity in the United States (Gilman 1987; Malcomson 2017).

In 1986, Velikhov took advantage of his high position in the USSR Academy of Sciences, his connections with American and European scientists, and his friendship with the Murphys and other Californians to organize the VelHam Project with Carnegie Corporation President David Hamburg in order to establish a direct line of communication between American and Soviet schoolchildren. To enable Soviet schoolchildren to communicate with American ones, Velikhov helped to establish the Children's Computer Club in Moscow. Computers for the club were purchased by chess player Garry Kasparov, and the club was headed by Stepan Pachikov, the future developer of the Evernote application. The first successful session took place in 1987 (Malcomson 2017).

It is difficult to say to what extent his peace activities were related to parapsychology, as was the case with Goldin and the Murphys. Velikhov was interested in consciousness issues, he participated in round tables on the subject, his articles were published in editions of collected papers, he even tried to organize the Commission on Problems of Consciousness at the USSR Academy of Sciences. According to the American journalist Scott Malcomson, Velikhov's primary interest lay in the notion of extrasensory abilities and human reserve capacities, as he has "mystical faith in spiritual communities and new forms of consciousness, in pedagogical and social optimism and new ways of thinking" (2017). In spite of Velikhov's friendship with psi-sensitives and telepaths, not a single source—his own book of memoirs included—references any publications of his that deal directly with the topic of extrasensory perception.

What is certain about Velikhov is that as a well-known Soviet scientist and functionary close to the government, he was also a liaison between different groups of people interested in contacts between the United States and the USSR: citizen diplomats, environmental activists, physicists, sociologists, parapsychologists, teachers, businessmen, philanthropists, scientists, and so on.

In addition to connections, Schatz needed money. Through the contacts of the Esalen Institute, he met Soros, who became the first serious investor in a company called San-Francisco Moscow Teleport. Soros first came to

Moscow in 1987 and found himself in the company of scientists, activists, and entrepreneurs that brought together people of different professions and social status, from the vice-president of the Academy of Sciences, Velikhov, to the unemployed "impresario" Goldin. Soros founded the Cultural Initiative Foundation (formally it was a joint project with the Soviet Culture Foundation and the Soviet Peace Foundation). Later, he recalled how his foundation included a wide variety of people, including those who would subsequently find themselves on the other side of the political spectrum:

> I first went to Moscow as a tourist, hoping to convince Andrei Sakharov to head it. He strongly advised me against going ahead, because he was convinced that the money would end up in the coffers of the KGB. But I persisted, and I managed to assemble a governing board. It was truly an odd collection, for it included people who normally wouldn't even speak to each other: on the one hand, the historian Yuri Afanasiev and the sociologist Tatyana Zaslavskaya, and on the other hand, the writer Valentin Rasputin, who has since become an extreme nationalist. Such a combination would be unthinkable today. (Soros 1995, 128)

Soros made major investments in network infrastructure a little later.[18] Nevertheless, thanks to the Cultural Initiative Foundation, conditions were created for the further development of real-life networking or bringing together various active groups of people and creating social networks in the original, pre-digital sense of the word. In an account of his experiences at the Cultural Initiative Foundation, Gleb Pavlovsky explicitly refers to the "informals" as a civil society movement, describing cooperatives as civil society's "resource hubs" and the web of social connections between its constituent elements as a proto-internet:

> It's interesting to note that, though there was no Internet back then (in the current sense of the word), the network was known as an "information environment." We might say that the Internet was concocted for us by Soros. (Shubin 2006)

SFMT first became a nonprofit internet service provider that provided e-mail access for Soviet and American activists and scientists. Here is how Igor Ovchinnikov, a former participant in Soviet-American antiwar and environmental projects, describes his user experience:

> With the Cold War starting to recede into the background, the perestroika wave spawned public initiatives in America and the Soviet Union, these initiatives, it would appear, emerging spontaneously yet simultaneously. Through an organization called Doctors for the Prevention of Nuclear War, we—still youngsters then—made the acquaintance of a group of Americans who were also involved in various anti-war projects. This acquaintance gave rise to an entire range of piecemeal endeavours and (eventually) full-fledged projects. We organized multi-city events across the US and the Soviet Union, giving speeches, gathering people together, staging demonstrations against the nuclear threat and weapons stockpiles, and so on. . . . While all these efforts were still in their infancy, we had Macs equipped with what were still external modems sitting in our homes, and these modems would connect to the telephone network with crazy bursts of crackling and flurries of odd electronic sounds and blinking lights. . . . Back then, I remember, there was this system GlasNet. We immediately started using it, which first and foremost meant electronic mail access. This was an unprecedented communication channel at the time: you'd send a message whenever and two hours later it'd reach its addressee. (Interview, 01.11.2016, Moscow)

By the late 1980s, all of these perestroika figures had become part of a single social network that extended to both countries, the United States and the USSR. Each group contributed in its own way to the process. Murphy, Goldin, and Velikhov connected Soviet activists with American foundations and individual philanthropists, citizen diplomats—with the Academy of Sciences and state authorities. Soros gave money and mobilized people inside the USSR, and Schatz provided them all with the internet. Here's how SFMT employee Andrei Kolesnikov described it in an interview with *Itogi* magazine:

> [Soros] often sponsored San Francisco-Moscow-Teleport nonprofit initiatives through his foundations. I remember my first meeting with him: around 1989, he flew in from America and was sleeping on the floor on a mattress in Joel [Schatz]'s office in Maly Afanasievsky Lane. He was very tired after the flight, and we had a mattress on which the guards slept. So, he lay down to rest. In those days he often visited us in Moscow.
>
> On our side, social internet projects were driven not by millionaires, but by very remarkable individuals. For example, Iosif Goldin, a man about whom, unfortunately, very little is known, but who, in my opinion, played one of the most important roles in breaking the Soviet consciousness. (Pokataeva 2012)

Participants in pre-digital social networks during perestroika, although they talked about the entire Soviet Union, primarily meant just Moscow. The city with the maximum concentration of resources, Moscow remained in memoirs and in the press the most prominent place where new communities were formed. Still, the perestroika turbulence touched other cities as well. The second important place was, logically, Leningrad, which, as early as the 1970s, was considered much freer than Moscow and therefore more difficult to control (see chapter 4). Another important point on the map of perestroika in Russia was Novosibirsk.

In 1985, Novosibirsk scientist Gennady Alferenko published an article in the newspaper *Komsomolskaya Pravda* inviting readers to share ideas for possible "social inventions" that would help implement perestroika. Alferenko, a geophysicist who worked for many years at the Akademgorodok Institute, founded the Terpsichore Society of Dance Lovers in Novosibirsk back in 1973. It was a unique phenomenon for the Soviet era: a truly public organization, which was not subordinate to any government agencies, had its own budget and its own bank account. By initiating an article in *Komsomolskaya Pravda*, Alferenko extrapolated his experience of local grassroots initiative to the whole country.

After the publication of the article, the newspaper received so many letters that journalist Khiltunen called in the help of "informal [*neformaly*] sociologists" Pavlovsky, Grigory Pelman, and Boris Kagarlitsky to analyze the letters. The Children's Computer Club, founded by Velikhov, offered computerized text processing. Soon the help of the authorities arrived. As Alferenko said in an interview in 2014, an article in *Komsomolskaya Pravda* was seen by Raisa Gorbachev, after which he "received a call from Mikhail Gorbachev who promised his support" (Samouvazhenie 2014). This is how a network of civic initiative foundations emerged, where ideas for further changes in Soviet society were collected and discussed.

In 1987, taking advantage of Moscow colleagues' contacts with the Esalen Institute, Alferenko was able to find financial support from Henry Dakin (who already supported Esalen's Soviet-American Exchange Program as well as parapsychological researches) and created the American twin brother of his Social Invention Foundation with offices in San Francisco, New York, and Juneau (Alaska). Two years later, in 1989, the Esalen Institute and the American Social Invention Foundation organized the first trip to the United States for Yeltsin, then a deputy of the Supreme Soviet of the USSR and a promising politician (Virginia Thomson et al. 2020; The History . . . 2023; Sukhanov 1992).

It was the famous trip on which Yeltsin met with President George W. Bush and other American politicians, and on his way to NASA asked to stop at a supermarket. His curiosity and the willingness of the Americans accompanying him to change the travel plan turned his own life upside down and, in a sense, hastened the collapse of the USSR. After counting the number of sausages and asking the supermarket staff about the assortment, Yeltsin and his assistant Lev Sukhanov came out deeply shocked. Sukhanov recalled: "The American reality, on the example of this supermarket, looked 100 times more convincing than any Soviet theories" (1992). According to Sukhanov, it was then that "Yeltsin's last faith in his Bolshevik way of thinking finally collapsed" and he decided to leave the CPSU. Here is how Sukhanov recalls Yeltsin's reaction on the way back: "Well, how the people were fooled . . . And now, it is clear why Soviet people are prevented from traveling abroad. They are afraid that people's eyes will be opened" (1992). A few months later, during the CPSU Congress, Yeltsin announced his resignation from the party. This greatly changed the political balance of power, and a year later Yeltsin became the first president of Russia.

In the 1980s, things happened very quickly. Only five years passed between the first spacebridge organized by the Esalen Institute and Goldin and Yeltsin's first trip to the United States. During this time, the USSR received access to the internet and Goldin's techno-utopia was no longer relevant, it just no longer fit reality. The people he had recently been inventing new media with were now founding their own companies and wiring the internet. In 1986, Schatz created a commercial organization, SovAm Teleport, on the basis of SFMT and started selling internet access to entrepreneurs, banks, and news agencies. He turned his attention to this business—expanding and multiplying companies, merging them again, acquiring and selling them, and eventually making good money.[19]

4

User Revolution

"In 1923–1924 it was generally accepted that stable long-distance radio communication was only possible on long waves," said the radiophysicist Alexander Mints to the authors of the book *Reporting from the XXI Century*. "But radio amateurs challenged that conventional belief and, with radio stations of limited power, operating on short wavelengths, set fantastic records for long-distance radio communication. Muscovites were talking to Australians, Parisians to Canadians, Argentinians to Japanese. And the theorists had to reconsider their positions. The reflection of short waves from the ionosphere was discovered. These waves became the basis for long-distance radio" (Reportazh 1963, 335). Mints believed that "huge masses of radio amateurs" should be involved in scientific discoveries, not only because there were more of them than scientists, but also because they were much more courageous. Amateurs generally are not threatened by criticism from colleagues, they spend their free time rather than government salaries, they are not burdened by theories that may contradict their discoveries, and finally, they are young and do not trust authority figures.

The conversation took place in the late 1950s, against the backdrop of the boom in the ham radio movement not only in the USSR, but all over the world. Academician Mints hoped that a new generation of enthusiastic engineers would help make radio engineering more miniaturized. And beyond that, he counted on their more general contributions to radio communications research. Since these young people were not subject to the tasks set by the Academy of Sciences, Mints did not know in which particular area they would make a breakthrough. What was clear for him was that there was a great force behind the ham radio movement. Today crowdsourced research is a normal practice, for example in astronomy, where it takes many people to observe celestial bodies, and this is made possible by the internet, which allows the rapid exchange of data. But in the late 1950s, the idea of involving amateurs was quite extravagant, especially given the secrecy of much research: during the Cold War, communication was a strategically important field.

Here lies a series of paradoxes: a state needs its citizens to develop technology but wants to retain a monopoly on the product and control over its usage; hired professionals perform the given task, while amateurs are free in their imagination and in some cases can be more efficient; finally, the tasks of developers often contradict the expectations of both commissioners and users. Such tension between different social forces and their diverging goals is a key mechanism of the transformation of communication technologies into social networks and virtual communities. And radio enthusiasts have played a major role in this process.

Hackers and Phreakers: Virtual Communities Before the Internet Era

Various kinds of virtual communities existed even before the internet became widespread. They were very similar in the United States and in the USSR: though their members were not political dissidents, they took care to operate under the authorities' radar. Their interest in communication technologies led them to discover new domains of remote communication and to develop their own security protocols and ethical codes. They called themselves radio pirates, hackers, and phone phreakers (*phreaker* being a portmanteau of *phone* and *freak*), and they were part of a new semi-underground subculture that emerged in the late 1950s with the mass popularity of radio and other communications technologies. As they came of age, they enrolled in university computer science programs and eventually became the first generation of USENETters in the 1980s.

The key figure in this story was John Draper, who called himself a *hacker* in the old sense of the word—a person who explores technologies. At least until the mid-1980s, the term did not have a negative connotation:[1] it became synonymous with "criminal" later, when intelligence agencies considered all radio amateurs and hackers to be potential information security violators. It was in this situation that Draper became a celebrity: he was one of those tech enthusiasts who came to be regarded as cyber criminals in the Cold War–defined political environment.

Not a historical figure in the classical sense, Draper would often wind up where the important action was, literally stumbling into history. A tech lover since childhood, Draper built several pirate radio transmitters in his time; while serving in Alaska as a U.S. Air Force electronics engineer, he also hacked into a telephone switchboard so his fellow service members could call home for free. One day, while testing out yet another pirate radio station, Draper encountered a coterie of *phreakers*—hackers who exploited the technical idiosyncrasies of telephone networks to make free calls all across America (Lapsley 2013).

The phreakers turned out to be visually impaired teens, kids for whom virtually no other leisure activities existed at the time, and who possessed sufficiently developed pitch to deceive AT&T's automated operator. The telephone connection was based on tone dialing: in order to access the long-distance service, it was necessary to produce a series of tones of a certain frequency that were interpreted by the automatic operator as a signal to switch. The teenagers used musical instruments to imitate the tones. In some cases, toy whistles found in Cap'n Crunch cereal boxes emitted a 2,600 Hz tone—ideal for manipulating AT&T's automated operator.[2] When Draper joined the community, the phreakers told him about their methods of dialing, and he adopted the nickname Captain Crunch, by which he later became famous across America.

To make life easier for themselves, the phreakers asked Draper to construct a "blue box"—an electronic portable tone generator capable of producing sounds of the desired frequency. The blue box was ready a few days later: phreaking had now been automated, greatly expanding its potential. The subsequent evolution of phreaking was a natural consequence of the internal contradictions in the development of communication technologies. The telecommunications industry receives funding and key development stimuli from the state because major inventions and their implementation require large resources, which smaller players do not have. However, when technologies have already been invented and have spread, the state seeks to control their use, as it considers communication potentially a danger to information security. In a situation where devices based on such communication technologies come into the possession of users, it is already quite difficult to control them: people want to communicate with each other without the involvement of any institutions. That's what happened in the 1920s with radio; it was exactly the same situation in the 1960s and early 1970s with telephone networks. Although phreakers' activities were detrimental to telephone companies, their probing of the networks' capabilities was generally more akin to "telephone hooliganism" than to economic criminality. And perhaps in another historical situation, the case would have ended with a couple of fines, but in the climate of the Cold War, the very fact of uncontrolled communication got the intelligence services interested.

With the emergence of Captain Crunch, phreaking experienced a surge in growth: young people began to embark upon long-distance telephonic journeys while enlisting ever more followers, and not only among their friends—other visually impaired teens—but also among students from various technical colleges . . . and simply random youngsters. They learned how to organize conference calls and hold communal broadcasts from different corners of America. ARPANET was in the design stage at the time; the internet proper wouldn't materialize for another decade, with the Web protocol still twenty years away and social networks more than thirty. "It was the 'the coolest thing in the whole wide world!'" telephone conference participant Bill Acker would later recall. "I was willing to work in isolation but to think that there were people out there that I could *talk* to" (Lapsley 2013, 157).

The community became so extensive that even the uninitiated began to take notice. In 1971, *Esquire* published its now-infamous "Secrets of the Little Blue Box" article—a piece in which phreakers were described as harmless geeks, but which also quoted Draper as saying, among other things, that it would be "possible for three phone phreaks to saturate the phone system of the nation. Saturate it. Busy it out. All of it" (Rosenbaum 1971). It wasn't just the hundreds of thousands of the magazine's readers who began paying attention to the phreakers following the article's release—the telephone companies' security teams and, more importantly, the FBI itself, did so too.

State-level paranoia surrounding hacker-espionage for the USSR claimed many victims. The phreakers and hackers were formally accused of "fraud by wire, radio or television,"[3] but if the corporations were genuinely concerned, first and foremost, about the losses they were incurring, the intelligence agencies were guided by the need to defend against state-level threats—and their response was out of proportion to the real facts. "Ten or twelve FBI agents jumped out of the cars and said, 'You're under arrest!'" Draper would recall some five years later (Long 1977, quoted in Williams 2015). He was arrested and sentenced to five years' probation.[4]

Stories about omnipotent hackers capable of remotely destroying computers and "starting a nuclear war by whistling into a payphone" consistently provoked panic throughout American society (Mitnick 2012, 42). There was an almost mystical sense, fueled by the Cold War, of the omnipotence of information technologies and those expert in using them—hackers—on the one hand, and, on the other, of the public's technical illiteracy. Being well funded, the development of these technologies took place very rapidly, often under conditions of complete secrecy. It stands to logic that the ability to control computers and infiltrate networks came to be regarded as dangerous magic by the man in the street. Newspapers and films, with their chilling stories of superheroes and "Robber Nightingales," massively facilitated these beliefs.

Eleven years ago, when hackers were generally considered criminals, Draper changed his mind. In a 2014 interview, he commented on his attitude toward modern hackers: "I have mixed feelings . . . due to media exposure and new hacker law enforcement tools, hacking is very dangerous, and I discourage it, and No, the law enforcement people did not tell me to say that" (Draper 2014). So, first-generation hackers had to give up their identities: a boyhood fascination with technology was no longer a socially acceptable hobby.

Soviet Phreakers: Underground Telephone and Radio Broadcasts

The history of the battles waged by the telephone companies and intelligence agencies against some of society's mavericks—blind teenagers, tech-head students, and solo hackers—wasn't uniquely American. Certainly, an important role was played by the technological specifics of American telephone networks and the community of users, which materialized against the backdrop of their technological peculiarities and entered into a typically American relationship with the media, law enforcement, and the courts (to say nothing of the typically American object that came to symbolize the movement—a cereal-box toy whistle). However, the pattern of the relationship between technology enthusiasts and the system was the same. Hackers, phreakers, and underground networks had existed in the USSR since at least the late 1970s. Less extensive than their American analogues but functionally very similar, these nascent virtual communities, each with their own rules of etiquette and security, were persecuted by the authorities and intelligence services even though they intended no damage to the state or its ideology.

Due to the idiosyncrasies of their design, Soviet period telephone exchanges generated "unclaimed" telephone numbers. If you dialed such a number, you could enter into the space of a communal conversation—something akin to a telephone conference or a voice chat. Having discovered this technical flaw in the system in the 1970s, Leningrad residents began to exploit it for communication purposes, giving rise to the so-called *telefonnyi efir* ("telephone broadcasts"). The economic damage caused by the use of redundant phone numbers under planned-economy conditions was impossible to calculate; far more significant in the eyes of the state, moreover, was the actual fact of noncontrollable communication, since communication technologies had been tightly controlled by the intelligence services since the very beginning of the Soviet era. Though telephone exchange managers regularly deactivated the unclaimed numbers, the networks were so configured that new ones could always be found. Furthermore, many exchange personnel were themselves participants in—and even organizers of—such broadcasts. A far greater threat was posed by the intelligence services.

In the late 1970s, Leningrad was a city with a flourishing unofficial culture—artists and musicians occupied squats, organized themselves into communes, arranged underground exhibitions and concerts (Kompost n.d., Gromov and Kuzin 1990). Independent artists and unofficial youth collectives were closely monitored by the KGB: among intelligence personnel, Leningradians were regarded as those least likely to toe the line. The former KGB major general Oleg Kalugin told the *Argumenty i Fakty* newspaper in 1992:

> [Leningrad] was always notable for its inclination to dissidence—an inclination consistent with the very spirit of St. Petersburg, whose residents have traditionally been independent in their judgments and difficult to re-educate. When I was about to go to my new post in Leningrad, I remember that Andropov gave me some parting advice: bear in mind that this is a special city, a city where the remnants of the old empire continue to prosper. People say—and not without reason, either—that if a rebellion comes to Russia, it'll originate in St. Petersburg. (Kalugin 2003)[5]

By no means all the users of the Leningrad *efir* were dissidents, but, in the eyes of the authorities, they were all fringe elements doing their utmost to dodge state control. *Fartsovshchiki* (black marketeers), currency traders, *spekulyanty* (speculators) and other players in the shadow economy used the *efir* to find clients and arrange meetings; so too did "unofficial" youth collectives—hippies, rockers, punks, breakers, metalheads, mystics, and yogis—and in-the-know seniors from ordinary Leningrad schools (Gaddy 1991, Yurchak 2002, Kozyrev 2013). Members of even the most ideologically innocuous, but still underground, network, ran the risk of being expelled from school or university or fired from their jobs and were risking their professional futures. Which is why the use of real names was a no-no: all regular participants had chat names.

The next generation of phreakers, who began using the Leningrad *efir* during the perestroika days of the late 1980s, no longer feared the Komsomol (The League of Young Communists) and the KGB. In 1988, a group of activists even organized a meeting with the Komsomol City Committee in an attempt to transform the *efir* into a legal phenomenon: "We wanted official status so we wouldn't have to make clandestine calls," the Leningrad *efir* participants recalled some fifteen years later. "This was 1988–89" (Balaganov 2008).[6]

Though these were novel times, the *efirshchiks* ("broadcasters") retained some of the traditions practiced by the previous generation. In particular, they preserved the use of nicknames: Oborona (Defence), Dyuimovochka (Thumbelina), Begemot (Behemoth), Lomonosov, and so forth. But the set-up was now more akin to that of a club with regular members, well-defined social roles, and a high degree of self-organization. The elected "kings of the *efir*" were responsible for organizing meetings in the city—they'd phone people up and arrange the time and place. Music would be broadcast from participants' home telephones (these hooked up to tape recorders), and unrestrained conversations flowed. The bulk of the *efirshchiks* would quickly get to know one other before exchanging phone numbers and meeting up somewhere in town. But by night, as participants recall, long and interesting conversations were conducted over the *efir* itself (Synerj 2008). The *efir* of the time was most closely reminiscent of the earliest chat rooms, with the geographical caveat that only Leningradians had access to it. That said, the *efirshchiks* themselves, endeavoring to safeguard the memory of a phenomenon close to their hearts, have pointed out serious differences between the former and the latter. "These were lively conversations, not twaddlings!!!"

someone with the handle *Oborona* remarked on an *efir*-themed forum. "Online, everything's organized by interest. You just try chatting to animal lovers about enemas—no one'll listen to you and you'll quickly earn yourself a ban! The *efir* wasn't like that" (Oborona 2008).

The Leningrad *efir* remained in existence until the early 2000s, when the telephone exchanges updated their equipment. But unlike American phreaking, vanquished by the telephone corporations and the intelligence agencies, the *efir* died a natural death: it was gradually superseded, from the mid-1990s onward, by the first online chat rooms. It had formed its own pantheon of heroes and acquired its own mythos over the course of its existence, although mainstream media pieces about the *efir* began to appear only in the 2010s (Lurje 2009).

A similar social network, albeit on a much smaller scale, was set up by the residents of Moscow's Solntsevo District in the mid-1980s. They used the nighttime cessation of cable radio transmissions to chat and broadcast music. By the middle of that decade, all Soviet apartments, production facilities, and institutions had been equipped with so-called *radiotochkas* (small, wired radio sets). Public broadcasting began at 6 a.m. and drew to a close at 1 a.m., with radio silence reigning for the rest of the time; as Solntsevo residents came to discover, the *radiotochka* could be used for communication purposes in combination with an amplifier and headphones. As Solntsevo radio net member Boris Gordon recalls, it was high school seniors—people willing to devote sleepless nights to conversation—who comprised the bulk of the underground network's users:

> I had this classmate. He told me at some house party that after broadcasts ceased for the night, something else would start to happen—voices and things. People, he said, were communicating with one another via the broadcast system. (Interview, 30.03.2016, Moscow)

Radiotochka broadcasting was limited to a single district—limited, that is, by communal cables: the signal passed through no transformer, and audience reach was therefore minimal. There would be five or six people—mainly seniors from district schools—on air simultaneously:

> We had several people from my area, five people from a neighboring area, and even one war dog from the local military base. He just had some headphones, nothing else, so he listened through them—and yelled through them, too. You

could actually hear him: the headphones functioned like a dynamic microphone. (Interview, 30.03.2016, Moscow)

The topics discussed by members of the Solntsevo network included neither politics, nor philosophy, nor local news—they generally just put music on and discussed the quality of the connection. Much like contemporary social media users, the Solntsevo radio community set great store by its rules of communication. Violating certain etiquette norms was a no-no: you couldn't air two songs in a row, for example, because that'd prevent people from chatting.[7] And there were security rules as well: no real names, digital handles only. "Times were tough—the KGB was still around, and folks were afraid," says Gordon. "So real names were never used. We had digital code names instead."

The takeover of radio frequencies has been a familiar practice since the 1960s in the USSR, America, and Europe, where radio pirates normally dropped tunes and earned money from illegal advertising. In the language of Soviet law, this practice came to be known as "radio hooliganism" in 1963, when a decree of the Plenum of the Supreme Court of the RSFSR equated unauthorized broadcasting with "disturbing the public peace" (Chalidze 1977). Soviet radio hooligans pursued no commercial ends: like their Leningrad cohorts, they were simply engaging in unfettered mediated communication. Until the late 1980s, they had to contend with the very real threat of being caught by the police for their nightly takeovers of radio broadcasts. We know of such cases predominantly from pieces published in *Radio*, the departmental publication of the Ministry of Communications and DOSAAF (the Volunteer Society for Cooperation with the Army, Aviation, and Navy), but the actual number of individuals caught breaking the law was far greater.[8]

The Soviet secret services' archives are still closed to researchers, so Soviet amateur radio and radio hooliganism haven't yet received detailed critical attention, and we still don't know precisely how many pirate stations and communities there were, nor how many radio hooligans were convicted. The phenomenon was certainly extensive, however: in the 1970s and 1980s, there were pirate broadcasts in all of the country's major cities, and in villages, too, where they served as the sole form of entertainment for local youths.

The story of the relations between radio amateurs and the authorities in the USSR was a convoluted one. On the one hand, the Soviet state encouraged amateur radio fans—it published magazines and textbooks featuring technical drawings of radio receivers and transmitters, and inaugurated DOSAAF hobby groups. Mass-scale militaristic education included the training of skilled radio engineers and communications workers. On the other hand, unregulated amateur radio posed a threat to the regime—both in and of itself, as it created the opportunity to broadcast freely, and gave listeners potential access to foreign voices: Voice of America, the BBC, RFE/RL. Beyond the traditional risk group, the urban intelligentsia, these "voices" were listened to in the villages. Gennady Vdovin recalls his radio amateur days of the late 1960s:

> Me and my granddad, who'd served his time in all the camps and fought in all the wars, took great pleasure in building the tallest antenna in the village of Oster, in the Roslavlsky District of Smolensk Oblast. Back then, BBC and Voice of America broadcasts were weak there and tended to disappear, and they were rebroadcast from Minsk on the "Detinets" radio station. (Interview, January 25, 2017, Facebook)

This flip side to Soviet militarization, and to the popularization of engineering/technical education, manifested itself very quickly: the 1960s witnessed the emergence of an entire generation of technically literate young people. Not only were these youngsters capable of assembling receivers, but they were also just as adept at putting together transmitters. Some failed—on principle—to obtain a radio amateur license, preferring the romance and freedom of radio piracy. Others would have liked to be able to broadcast legally, but the DOSAAF enrollment system was too unwieldy, and it was therefore often impossible to obtain legal status. The contingent primarily consisted of high school seniors, technical college students, and sometimes university freshmen—young people with the time and opportunities to establish underground radio stations.

If pirate radio stations primarily broadcast music and innocuous discussions, with political topics given a wide berth, Western radio stations represented a far more serious issue for the Soviet authorities—their reach, by some estimates, encompassed almost half of the USSR's urban population (Lisann 1975, 127; Trinkner 2014, 64). The CPSU Central Committee never did manage to deal with the problem of "foreign voices," although it had discussed it in the Presidium since as early as the late 1950s. The "Report of the CPSU Central Committee on the Jamming of Foreign Radio Stations" (August 6, 1958) lamented:

> Despite all our efforts, despite billions of roubles in expenditure, radio jamming has not fulfilled its objectives. . . . Hostile broadcasts are being listened to throughout the country. . . . It would be advisable to give thought to the question of developing more effective means of protecting the population from hostile radio propaganda. First and foremost, our broadcasting to the USSR population must see drastic improvements: we must make it multi-programmed and diverse and ensure that it meets listeners' demands. (Pressa 2000)

Realizing that jamming was costly and failed to yield the desired results, Khrushchev proposed the development and release of a radio set incapable of receiving VHF broadcasts. But people didn't want to buy limited-frequency radios, which triggered proposals to recall VHF-capable sets or to stop producing them, leaving Soviet citizens with no choice in the matter. Sometime later, Alexander Yakovlev, head of the Radio Division in the Propaganda and Agitation Department of the CPSU's Central Committee, suggested an alternative course of action: a new music-heavy infotainment program could be used to drown out the "foreign voices," thereby "killing two birds with one stone, as it were" (Yakovlev 2005). Radio Mayak (*Beacon*) would be broadcast on the same frequencies as Western radio stations and, furthermore, via any *radiotochka*—that is, in literally every apartment.[9]

There was no difference, legally speaking, between the "radio hooligans" who used cable radio and those active in clandestine shortwave broadcasts. The nature of the social ties formed as a result of unlicensed broadcasting *was* somewhat different, however. The configuration of the wired networks facilitated simultaneous communication between all *radiotochka* owners based within a single district. Ordinary VHF pirates, in contrast, were solo operators who received feedback by way of special cards sent to them by other radio amateurs. Even if they eventually managed to find their way into a circle of fellow-thinkers, they did so only much later, in the 1990s, with the advent of online forums, guest books and other social network prototypes. But, unlike neighborhood cable radio communities, which were constrained by the wishes of fellow broadcasters, shortwave radio pirates could organize entire alternative radio programs and broadcast whatever they wanted—the feedback was episodic.

Although the Soviet authorities were afraid of the influence exerted by Western radio stations on the loyalty of the USSR citizens, studies demonstrate that, in reality, Soviet listeners were far removed from any political agenda: they'd switch over the moment they heard a news report or an analysis program and were far more interested in music and entertainment programming, conspicuously lacking across Soviet radio (Trinkner 2014). These preferences were largely shared by Soviet radio pirates of both the shortwave and cable variety. The radio amateurs themselves recall, as do their listeners, that underground broadcasts never featured political discussions. Nobody wanted to talk about the Soviet regime; nobody had any intention of becoming a dissident. Neither the amateur broadcasters nor their listeners needed an alternative news landscape—what they really craved was pop music and entertainment content. Which is why this kind of radio piracy practically vanished in the 1990s, as its functions were quickly replaced by licensed shortwave broadcasters of Western pop, rock, and other music previously banned in the USSR. And the radio pirates themselves happily migrated online.

From Military Solution to Smart Community

The telegraph and the telephone are typical inventions of the nineteenth century, where the work of enthusiastic inventors depended on funding and recognition directly from the state or other large systems: academies of sciences or investors. The most famous case is the invention of the "sonic telegraph" by Alexander Graham Bell. In order for Bell to perfect the system and obtain the patents that formed the basis of the future AT&T Corporation, his father-in-law, Gardiner Greene Hubbard, first funded his son-in-law's research and then commercialized his invention. As a lawyer and financier, a well-known man in New York City, heir to old money, and grandson of the founder of the state of New York, Hubbard was a major player in both business and politics. At the same time, other people were making similar inventions: the German engineer Johann Philipp Reis, Thomas Edison, and others. But Bell's contribution proved to be the most famous and gave its name to the U.S. telephone monopoly.

A similar story happened to Samuel Morse, the inventor of the telegraph, who secured political support for his invention in time to make it a successful business model. At the same time, dozens of people were inventing roughly the same electric telegraph. But while the British government refused to fund the technology as "wholly unnecessary" during a demonstration of Francis Ronalds's telegraph in 1816, Morse received support directly from the White House. It happened just thirty years later.

If until the middle of the twentieth century there was a huge distance between the invention itself and its user, the invention of the internet belonged to a different era. Accordingly, the model of relations between the state and the customer, developer and user communities was different. Until recently, however, the story of the creation of the internet on the basis of military network technologies of the ARPANET repeated the pattern of earlier inventions. In its most complete form, this story has been told by Kathi Hafner and Matthew Lyon in *Where the Wizards Stay Late* (1996). I'm summarizing this story below to focus on the model of the new relationship between customers, developers, and users.

The launch of a Soviet satellite in 1957 impressed President Eisenhower, who initiated the creation of an agency under the U.S. Department of Defense (ARPA, which later became DARPA, with the word "Defense" added to its name). Commissioned by the Pentagon, the agency hired engineers and developers, including entire companies, to build the computer network. Hafner and Lyon provide anecdotal evidence of the networks' transformation from a system for sharing computer capacity to a means of human communication in the ARPANET era. One ARPANET developer, who had forgotten his razor in a hotel room during a conference in the U.K., used a work chat to ask a colleague to pick it up and bring it back to the States (Hafner and Lyon 1996, 122). In this story, the computer network showed the potential of social networking even at the stage of invention, despite the very different goals of developers and customers. The subsequent development of the internet as a global communications network was determined by the fact that ARPANET's tasks became obsolete before it was fully operational, while the microchip revolution made the internet possible in the home.

An important part of this narrative is the question of who was responsible for creating the internet, the government or the developers, whose agendas were very different. The military gave Joseph Licklider a million dollars, and the project was realized. Scientists, on the other hand, came up with the idea of creating a computer network and found ways to do it using state financial support. Stephen J. Lukasik, director of DARPA from 1967 to 1971, during the development of the ARPANET, believed and still believes that the agency's activities were completely subordinate to the Pentagon's goals:

> The goal was to exploit new computer technologies to meet the needs of military command and control against nuclear threats, achieve survivable control of U.S. nuclear forces, and improve military tactical and management decision making. (Lukasik 2011)

Other involved parties disagree with this view, however. Hafner and Lyon relay the stance of Robert Taylor, Licklider's student and co-author and the project's immediate supervisor:

> The project had embodied the most peaceful intentions—to link computers at scientific laboratories across the country so that researchers might share computer resources. Taylor knew the ARPANET and its progeny, the Internet, had nothing to do with supporting or surviving war—never did. (Hafner and Lyon 1996)

Charles Herzfeld, ARPA director between 1965 and 1967, expresses himself even more categorically:

> Why was the ARPANET started? Most of the early "history" on the subject is wrong. As Director of ARPA at the time, I can tell you about our intent. The ARPANET was not started to create a Command-and-Control System that would survive a nuclear attack, as many now claim. . . . Rather, the ARPANET came out of our frustration that there were only a limited number of large, powerful research computers in the country, and that many research investigators who should have access to them were geographically separated from them. (Bellis 2016)

Taylor and Herzfeld hold to the view that, although ARPANET was completely dependent on the Pentagon for its budget, the endeavors of the project's researchers and engineers were fundamentally different in nature, their goal being to provide scientists with access to computers. It only remained to convince the authorities of the need for funding, and so, with the military's consent, Herzfeld transferred a million dollars from a ballistic missile defense program to Taylor's budget.

The late 1990s saw the publication of *Media, Technology and Society. A History: From the Telegraph to the Internet* by media historian Brian Winston. Examining the history of computers and computer networks in the context of the Cold War, Winston argued that there would be no computer science if it were not for military objectives. He called the internet a "spin-off" of the national security project, and sympathized with the "cognitive dissonance" that the developers who insist on the purely scientific objectives of the project must be experiencing:

> Although the scheme that became ARPANET was clearly focused on academic sites, this does not mean that the computer science agenda was entirely dominant. It should not be forgotten that all these machines were still closely bound into defense work of one sort or another wherever they were sited . . . Those who seriously believed they were in a brave new world of free and democratic communications were simply ignoring the reality of their situation. (Winston 1998, 325)

This stark choice in determining the most important force behind the emergence of the internet—between the state and citizens, military tasks and scientific ones, budget and intellectual resources—characterized the debate of the mid-1990s when the internet in the United States became both a legitimate medium and a business commodity. The subsequent years of research introduced new explanatory models that eliminated this rigid contradiction.

BITNET, USENET, and BBS: Users Are Taking Over

In the approach described above, there are only two parties: the customer and the developer. The user appears in this model only when the declassified technology is released, and personal computers become available. This was indeed the case with the telegraph and the telephone, but, as discussed above, the invention of the internet took place in a new era: its user was directly involved in and influenced the invention process. Moreover, by the time big government funding began pouring into network technology, radio amateurs and members of underground telephone communities had already built their social networks and their subculture of grassroots communication. That is, the demand for computer networks overtook their invention.

Another internet historian, John Naughton, wrote about how users participated in the creation of the internet. According to Naughton, the communities of the 1980s and 1990s owed their atmosphere of volunteering and cooperation to the ARPANET network, broadly reliant as it was on student labor. And it was the ARPANET age that witnessed the emergence of network ethics as well as other features common to later networks—features attributed by their initial users to the very format of electronic communication. Naughton notes that although the ARPANET project was a conventional success in terms of project management, it stood out for its unusually collegial approach:

> This was sensible for several reasons: the network was intended to link high-profile researchers working in elite institutions, and such individuals are not easily herded, plus it made sense to harness the collective IQ of that community at every level, including that of graduate students. For that reason, for example, design of the central protocols of the network was entrusted to a Network Working Group that largely consisted of students. In this way was established the collaborative ethos that has been an important feature of Internet technical development up to the present day. (Naughton 2016, 8)

Thus, the model of previous discoveries in the field of communications did not fit the internet era, when not one inventor or a small group of people, but many managers, engineers, scientists, and their graduate students were engaged in building a computer network. They were its first users, and a little later they became the basis of the first virtual communities of BITNET, USENET, and local BBSs.

From the beginning, ARPANET existed through university computer centers and was closely tied to the academic community. Using the same infrastructure, BITNET and USENET were no longer dependent on a military project. Launched in 1981, BITNET began as a cooperative network that facilitated communication between university computer centers. However, access to BITNET was limited to university employees, and the governance structure was centralized. University computer center directors elected an executive committee, hammered out a set of interconnection rules, standards, and principles, and established a taxonomy and hierarchy of users (Grier and Campbell 2000).

Unlike BITNET, USENET was a system of newsgroups that offered unlimited subscriptions, existed beyond institutional confines, and was proudly dubbed "collective anarchy" by its users. Technically USENET arrived a year earlier than BITNET: programmers Tom Truscott and Jim Ellis launched it in 1980. As a high school senior, Truscott competed alongside his friend Bruce

Wright in a computer chess tournament conducted by Bell Labs staff (Hauben and Hauben 1997). They found themselves in the company of the developers of Unix, an operating system that could be run on almost any kind of computer and one that had become a popular network creation tool. Missing his colleagues at Bell Labs, Truscott started working on a connection between Duke University and the Lab together with other student aficionados of Unix. And so, USENET was born out of a necessity to connect with friends and colleagues. It was initially expected that traffic would amount to something like two messages a day and that the network would support a hundred sites.[10]

Duke University had access to the ARPANET mailing lists. Truscott and Ellis came up with the idea of building their own network based on their familiarity with this network and their desire to build a network without access restrictions. Unlike ARPANET, which was built around a list of electronic addresses, BITNET and USENET were built around "news," that is, users' messages. This constituted a completely different philosophy: central control over message recipients was given up in favor of a system in which the recipients themselves exercised control over what they received. This user-oriented approach meant a far greater degree of network openness and, by extension, a different quality of community.[11]

Nevertheless, both networks consisted primarily of university professors and graduate students, as well as employees of large corporations associated with the IT industry, such as Bell Labs and IBM. Truscott would not have built USENET without his desire to create an "ARPANET for everyone" and his contacts with university computer centers. Among other things, these networks inherited ARPANET's packet-switching technology.

The most accessible—and yet the least massive—were the networks based on BBS technology (Bulletin Board System). The first BBS appeared before USENET, in 1978, when two young men, Ward Christensen and Randy Suess, who had known each other from the Chicago Computer Club, connected two computers via modems and a phone line during the Great Blizzard. The system became extremely popular because it required minimal resources. In fact, all you needed was a computer, a modem, a phone line, and a piece of software written by Christensen and Suess.

Grassroots BBSs and the Legacy of Ham Radio

Kevin Driscoll begins his detailed study of BBS networks by analyzing the 1990s mythology of the internet's origins in the ARPANET network and contrasting it with the history of the "modem world"—the many local communities that sprang up around the world in the 1980s. While BITNET and USENET, which grew out of the ARPANET project, "were used mostly by graduate students and university staff, BBS communities were the place where different sorts of people were connected." They were not set up by universities or government agencies, but by individuals, people who "paid their own phone bills." This meant that the connection had to be as inexpensive as possible. Computers were built from parts, software was distributed for free and improved by enthusiasts in their spare time, and to save on telephone costs, all messages were accumulated and sent and received once a day—usually at night—in a single packet.

Sometimes these networks, while remaining predominantly local, brought people together not geographically but by interests: there were BBS communities of Doom or Batman fans, baseball players, an information network on HIV research, as well as FidoNet, which represented an exceptional case of a worldwide BBS network (Driscoll 2016). Jason Scott, the author of *BBS: The Documentary*, believes that there were at least 106,418 BBSs in operation between 1978 and 2004 (Scott 2005).

According to Driscoll, the fundamental difference between BBSs and the "ARPANET family of networks" was not only technology but also organizational structure and community ethics. First, BBS networks were created "by community-oriented amateurs and entrepreneurs—hobby radio groups, computer clubs, software pirates, and activist organizations." Second, they provided "a low-cost alternative to commercial packet-switching systems and closed research networks" through "the creative appropriation of the North American telephone network." Because all users still had to pay for telephone service, however minimal, these networks could only be local.

Hence the lack of centralized management and the spirit of mutual support that Driscoll sees as a legacy of the ham radio subculture. It must be said that before the proliferation of microchips and personal computers, ham radio was one of the few possible hobbies for those interested in technology. It makes sense that both Christensen and Suess were hams, and that the BBS they invented was in fact a marriage of computer science and ham radio.

Of the communications inventions of the nineteenth century, I have mentioned in this chapter only the telegraph and the telephone, not radio. Although radio was originally seen as a replacement for the wire telegraph, there was a fundamental difference in the technology: radio did not require the construction of a huge infrastructure, which is usually beyond the capacity of private capital without public funds. Yes, Guglielmo Marconi worked hard to make radio a widely accepted form of communication, and his company prospered. But the support he received was incomparable to previous investments in wire communications. Radio, requiring only a transmitter and receiver, was and is the most democratic means of communication. Directly related to this fact is the imaginary behind the history of virtual communities on the internet.

Driscoll describes the rise of the amateur radio movement in the 1960s, when radio technology shifted to electronics and amateurs switched to local repeaters (Driscoll 2016, 41–42). In the USSR, as mentioned earlier, radio was no less important than in the United States because there were virtually no alternatives for free information. The MIT report commissioned by the CIA, *Amateur Radio Operation in the USSR* (1965), gives statistics on the growth in circulation of the Soviet magazine *Radio*: from 20,000 in 1946 to 800,000 in 1965. These figures are much more revealing than the number of registered radio amateurs, since a significant proportion of *Radio* readers did not register their stations.

Even if not all users of local BBSs had a passion for radio in their background, we can assume, following Driscoll, that early online communities did indeed inherit the radio amateurs' subculture . . . which included in its coordinate system, first, a fundamentally horizontal model of communication and, second, the value of free access to information.

FidoNet in the United States and USSR/Russia

FidoNet became the only truly global BBS network. Remaining independent of government and academia, FidoNet grew from 12 nodes in 1984 to 40,000 nodes in 1996, connecting literally every region of the world. One of the reasons for FidoNet's popularity was the constant work of the programmers (as in most other BBS networks, they were the users) to optimize telephone bills, including those between continents.

In the USSR, the first FidoNet node appeared in 1990,[12] and in the soon-to-be post-Soviet Russia and some other post-Soviet countries (most notably Ukraine), it became a more mass phenomenon than the "proper Internet." FidoNet also lasted much longer among popular forms of communication than in the rest of the world: while world statistics show a decline since

1996, in post-Soviet countries it was more popular than the internet at least until the early 2000s due to high prices for ISP services.

As in the case of radio, the possibility of free software exchange and uncontrolled communication with each other was extremely popular in the late USSR and post-Soviet Russia. Freedom of communication was an absolute value—in this sense, the first virtual communities in the USSR and Russia were very similar to the first American ones that appeared a decade earlier. The organizational structure of the network, consisting of points and nodes of different levels, was also ideal for Russian users, as it did not require official permission or affiliation with universities or the Academy of Sciences.

All of the above should suggest that the Soviet (and post-Soviet) segment of FidoNet was no different from the American one. In both cases, users came to the network primarily for free software and only then for free communication; nodes were local, so their points were often collected offline, and "everyone knew each other" (this is particularly how Fido-veterans describe the early years of the network in the former USSR [*Asia Patrysheva* 2019]). However, there was a crucial difference: post-Soviet nodes almost never paid for long-distance calls themselves, but instead used a working phone line.[13]

Sometimes, these were commercial companies, but more often, they were government organizations. In interviews with me and in online archives of FidoNet history, users in the early 1990s mentioned the First Medical Institute and a children's psychiatric hospital in St. Petersburg, the Presidium of the Academy of Sciences and the Ministry of Defense in Moscow, as well as some university departments, research institutes, commercial IT companies, and other institutions, often random ones. These were places that had computers, paid for long-distance and international phone lines, technical staff motivated to start their own FidoNet node, and cooperative superiors who allowed the use of resources. "Fido nodes formed wherever there were experts who wanted to organize them," as user Vlad (nickname Vatson) told me in an interview. In an archived recollection of the early FidoNet, one veteran first "worked out the long-distance charges with his bosses" and then started his own node, connecting to a network of BBSs in Tallinn. Another worked for a commercial company "just for the free international calls."

Access to office phone lines offered post-Soviet users much greater opportunities than the private phones of American ones. American home users typically had a phone line at home that they paid for and had to keep free for actual phone calls. This severely limited the amount of downloading of files and correspondence. Journalist Benj Edwards tells a typical story. In 1992, as an 11-year-old BBS enthusiast, he begged his parents for his own phone line so he wouldn't have to borrow the house phone. And after befriending an operator from a neighboring state, he received a $200 long-distance bill that made his father "very angry":

> After (him) locking my computer, which disabled the keyboard, I found a spare key. Then he just took away my keyboard. After he restored my privileges, I proceeded to do it again—and another $200 phone bill showed up. I called that BBS hundreds of times. Its sysop was my best friend—or so I thought. (Edwards 2022)

In post-Soviet Russia, the late 1980s and early 1990s was a time when Western concepts like private property or copyright had not yet become the norm, and commercial opportunities had already been added to the socialist habits of using state resources for private purposes. Therefore, on the one hand, distributing pirated software was not considered a crime. On the other hand, private programmers used their employers' equipment and telephone lines to distribute their own programs on the net for free. According to research and memoirs of American BBS users, this could not have happened in the United States. This was a situation specific to the late Soviet and early post-Soviet period, when people made no distinction between governmental, non-governmental, and private. It ended around the end of the 1990s, when a significant number of users had access to the internet, the Web protocol became widespread, and the internet was commercialized in Russia.

> "In the First Medical Institute there was a man who got a separate room and lived in it," says Vlad (Vatson). "In fact, he set up the production of alternative modems with original software adapted to Russian telephone networks." (Interview, Facebook messenger, 06.06.2024)

Another interviewed personality, the owner of the famous Moscow Night Director BBS, Ivan Sinelobov, worked in the Presidium of the Academy of Sciences of the USSR (after 1991 RF) in the Computer Center for Collective Use. The director of the Center was a former developer of the Soviet Elbrus computer, so almost every office had a computer that was often idle:

> That's what I taught my academicians, so that when they left, they dialed the BBS on their computer. And their phone line becomes available to the whole world. And since the academic day is Thursday,[14] and on the other days academics think, my Night Director BBS was the second largest in Moscow.

It should be noted that the failure to distinguish between public and private property was ubiquitous and affected, among others, state organizations and even authorities (Smolyak 2014). For example, according to user Vatson, when the St. Petersburg mayor's office decided to build an internal computer network, they invited FidoNet users for this purpose. Commercial services were scarce and expensive. Technically, FidoNet was simpler and cheaper than IP, so in the early 1990s it often replaced the expensive "normal internet." In organizations and scientific institutes, there were no special positions for IT specialists, and they were hired as junior researchers to be allowed to use the workplace for private purposes, as long as they provided the others with access to e-mail. If an organization had enough computers and phone lines free at night, it had a good chance of becoming the base for a large FidoNet node. In some situations, this factor not only worked for the private interests of the FidoNet users but also influenced the political situation. Here's one such story from Sinelobov.

He got the job of night director at the computing center of the Presidium of the Academy of Sciences, and with it access to all its computers, almost by chance: as a young graduate student, he was offered a job staying overnight to guard the property, and he took advantage of the situation. Taking this job at the Presidium of the Academy of Sciences in 1989, he created the Night Director node one year later, and it quickly became popular. The computers ran without interruption, which often limited other nodes, and also went online every night. In 1991, Night Director proved to be the only channel for emergency communication with another user from the Ministry of Defense, who was watching the destruction of the Moscow coup archives. This is how Sinelobov tells it:

> Warrant Officer Stepanov worked as a telephone operator in the Ministry of Defense. He sat under the stairs where the telephone exchange was, and he had about 20 telephone lines at his disposal. FidoNet was organized in such a way that if you downloaded some software, you could chat in parallel with the owner of the node from which you downloaded it. So, shortly after the coup,

> I went to the node of a warrant officer to download something, and he hit me in the chat and said that there were generals in the Ministry of Defense who were going to destroy the archive with their orders from the time of the coup, and a young lieutenant took a dagger and went to defend the archives. "He will be killed; we need Gorbachev now!"

Since the incident took place in the middle of that day, Sinelobov said he ran out into the hallway and started shouting "Help!" The head of the computer center called Yegor Yakovlev, editor-in-chief of the newspaper *Moscow News*, an important perestroika figure and Gorbachev's confidant. Through Yakovlev, Sinelobov managed to pass information to Gorbachev, and the archive was saved. But only for a short time: "It all ended sadly: the papers were officially handed over for destruction a few days later, and the young lieutenant who had guarded them was sent to a godforsaken place. But nothing could be done about the warrant officer, who remained at his telephone switchboard under the stairs."

This specific situation of blurred hierarchies and rules persisted for several more years. In the late 1980s and early 1990s, an employee of the Ministry of Defense could still ask for help via FidoNet chat, a graduate student could deliver information to Gorbachev, amateur computer specialists could be called in to build networks in a mayor's office, and a children's psychiatric hospital could turn out to be a major FidoNet node. And all the while, despite its physical connection to office phones and computers, FidoNet remained a truly grassroots network where home users shared software and talked about various topics.

"At first, FidoNet was warm, everyone knew each other, everyone was friends. Then thousands and thousands came running," Asya Patrysheva, one of the pioneers of the post-Soviet FidoNet, describes the situation in an interview with DataArt Blog (*Asia Patrysheva* 2019). Dmitry Zavalishin, another well-known early FidoNet user, describes the growth of the network in other words: "At that time, 90% of all FidoNet users knew each other personally, met, drank beer. . . . And, of course, it was partly a kind of Masonic structure, but now it's completely different."

By the end of the 1990s, "a kind of Masonic" FidoNet had attracted mass users, and the Russian-language segment of the network experienced the same crisis as all early virtual communities in all countries. Here, for example, is how BITNET and USENET participants described the mass-user crisis:

> We found a way to reach beyond the physical limitations that constrained others (though they didn't know it) and share information, viewpoints, and form friendships. We were bound together not just by common interests in computers or certain fields of study, but by the knowledge that we had stumbled upon a new world—a virtual world [. . .]. Now that everybody and their mother can get access to the Internet, some of that is lost to us. Because anybody can do it now, the experience is somehow less magical [. . .]. Some of that feeling of community is lost, because the thing that made us a community was the fact that we shared the secret of BITNET (Condon 2001).

The feeling of belonging to a secret community and the magic of communicating with remote users was replaced by irritation toward humanity in general. "People have disappointed me," this is how Sinelobov commented on this.

From Psychedelics to the Internet . . . and Back

Memories of Russian-speaking users of early FidoNet—and the internet in general—are decidedly about pragmatic things. Most remember getting access to free software and communicating with each other. Sometimes this is supplemented by joyful surprise at the first online encounters with "real foreigners," which post-Soviet users were much less interested in than communicating with each other. The mystical feelings of the Soviet 1960s about computer technology were replaced in the late 1980s by a search for engineering and software solutions to adapt American technology.

A very different kind of recollection can be found in nostalgic posts and articles about the old good BBS times in the United States. They more often evoke a certain spiritual quality to this experience of connection with other people. In the words of Edwards, it was a "whole-body teleportation" elicited by the "intimacy of direct, computer-to-computer connection" (2016). A direct analogy between psychedelics and the internet was made by Schatz in an interview with Andrei Loshak for *Holivar*, a documentary about the history of the Russian internet:

> Psychedelic experiments not only produced a dramatic increase in my perception of the interconnectedness of all elements of life. Why is it that, when we're not using these drugs, everything seems disconnected? My answer was, "Well, it's because we need to develop information tools for helping the

brain put those separate pieces of reality back together into whole patterns." (Loshak 2019)

The same line, though more ironic, is taken by Christensen, the author of the first BBS. In a 1985 interview he gave directly on his BBS, he called the Net a drug that allowed you to escape reality:

> I'm a negativist, hater of life, and have a short fuse—it doesn't take much to set me off. That's why I'm into computers—it's almost like a drug, letting you get so completely wrapped up in it, the "world passes you by," i.e. I've been known to have a bad headache or stomachache, but an hour of computing, and I'm oblivious to it, until I stop for something. It's a totally engrossing way to "pass the time." (Petersen 1985)

In its most mature form, the psychedelic projection of online communication affected early California virtual communities, to which a large body of memoir and research literature has been devoted (Rheingold 1993; Turner 2000; Gere 2002; Snider 2003; Alan 2016). For example, in *The Virtual Community*, a book about the BBS network The WELL, Howard Rheingold remarks that this "inexpensive public online service was launched because two comrades from a previous cultural revolution noticed that the technology of computer conferencing had potential far beyond its origins in military, scientific, and government communications" (Rheingold 1993). He notes that the generation of early online activists who became Silicon Valley businesspeople "were five to ten years younger than the hippies, but they came out of the zeitgeist of the 1960s and embraced many of the ideas of personal liberation and iconoclasm championed by their slightly older brothers and sisters." These include one of the founders of The WELL, Stewart Brand, counterculture icon and editor of *The Whole Earth Catalog*, a "hippie bible" which featured articles on ecology and philosophy as well as product reviews.

The Californian countercultural activists' path "from satori to Silicon Valley," as Theodore Roszak called it (2000), has been well documented: after the failure of psychedelics, the task of laying bare "the interconnectedness of all elements of life" fell to cybernetics. Several notable figures among those who recognized the possibilities of computer networks were Timothy Leary and

Terence McKenna. They saw computer-mediated communication as a "global consciousness" and prophesied a "cyberspiritual future" for humanity.

Within the spectrum of psychedelic and mystical expectations of online communication was a radical wing, the "extropians" movement founded by philosopher Max More (real name Max O'Connor). Extropian theories fuse the idea of cryonics with that of virtual communities, specifically BBSs, whose members Extropians were in the 1980s. Developments in technology, the theories suggest, will give rise to a system wherein whole-body preservation is no longer necessary, with essential brain data all now uploadable to a computer (More 1990). "It would be a historically brief phase transition from the human condition to a posthuman condition of agelessness, super-intelligence, and physical, intellectual, and emotional self-sculpting" (More and Kurzweil 2002).

The Extropian movement was not a mass one, and today, in the Age of Singularity, its theories look like naive retro-futurism. Interestingly, however, despite the California-specific density of such techno-utopias, their content was not tied to a specific place and time. When Wiener discussed the prospects of human travel via telegraph in the 1950s, it was also an attempt to imagine the transformation of the body into an electronic signal (Wiener 1954, Hayles 1999). Later, in 1969, the idea of downloading information from the brain into a computer and thus ensuring the immortality of the human personality was expressed by the writer Philip K. Dick in his novel *Ubik*, which described communication with the dead through a synthesis of electronic communication and telepathy.[15] That same year, in an interview with *Playboy* magazine, Marshall McLuhan, the prophet of the internet, described electronic media as a way to "amplify human consciousness," comparing it to clairvoyance and other occult practices and arriving at the concept of "global telepathy" (McLuhan 1969).

A few years later, a similar idea was expressed by the Soviet cyberneticist Glushkov in the pages of the magazine *Fantastika* (see chapter 1). In 1984, it was taken up simultaneously by William Gibson, one of the founders of cyberpunk, in his novel *Neuromancer*, and by the Californian philosopher More, the spiritual father of the Extropians. And if the Californian authors can still be suspected of direct borrowing, it is quite obvious that Academician Glushkov had nothing to do with them. Simply the transformation of personality into a digital signal and, as a consequence, digital immortality was the most radical version of the techno-utopia born at the intersection of scientific and technological progress and boundless fantasy about its possibilities. Both the USSR of the 1960s and the California of the 1980s provided ideal conditions for this kind of radicalism.[16]

I started this chapter with a comment by the Soviet radio physicist Mints about the radio amateurs who challenged "conventional beliefs" and made long-distance radio communication possible. The phenomenon of radio, from its invention in the late nineteenth century to the amateur radio movement a couple of decades later, to the BBSs of the 1980s, defined the characteristics of other twentieth-century techno-utopias.

Marconi himself, as well as other nineteenth-century inventors, imagined that his discovery would have existential consequences: for example, humanity would be able to hear the voices of the dead, up to and including Christ's "Sermon on the Mount" (Milner 2009). It is logical that the Italian professor Cazzamalli conducted his telepathic experiments in the 1920s in consultation with Marconi and the staff of his company. A great history of brainwave research followed (Shure 2018). But if the scientific direction had lost its power by the 1980s, the completely new type of community that emerged from dealing with radio technology was, on the contrary, in great demand in the postmodern era.[17] It was imagined as a truly grassroots community, self-regulating and ready to fight for the right to free communication.

5

The USSR Is Connected to the USENET

The younger generation of Soviet programmers that emerged in the late 1980s and early 1990s exhibited a markedly more pragmatic and down-to-earth outlook than their predecessors in the field of cybernetics. They did not entertain the notion of a promising future for humanity or anticipate groundbreaking scientific advancements. They were the children of the late USSR, and as a result, they espoused right-wing liberal political views. The ideological and economic crises of the 1970s, and even more so the collapse of the Soviet Union, completely discredited the leftist ideas. Furthermore, the absence of competitive IT developments and the underperformance of the Soviet computer industry contributed to the perception that American technology represented the pinnacle of achievement. When considering not only the cohort of programmers but the entire 1980s generation, it is obvious that the appeal of American technology was not the sole factor at play. The value system and lifestyle espoused by this generation were also of significant consequence. The 1990s in Russia were a challenging period for scientists, who faced significant declines in status and income or opted to pursue their careers in the West (the most desired destination of emigration was the United States) or become entrepreneurs.

Against this background, the gradual corrosion and fall of the Iron Curtain, the first professional contacts, and the first trips abroad without Communist Party "interviews" undoubtedly evoked a sense of joy among the Soviet people. However, this was not a sense of a miracle. A review of the archives of the initial online interactions between American and Soviet users reveals that this sense of wonder was, in fact, more typical for American network users. First and foremost, they perceived it as the cessation of the threat of nuclear war. Additionally, they regarded it as a triumph of democratic media—as McLuhan termed it, a "global village"—over the deceiving state-driven press. In this chapter, I will analyze the archives of the early online encounters between American and Soviet users, from the initial stirrings of an encounter with "others like us" to the political discussions that illuminated the starkly divergent positions of the two sides.

≈

On 1 April 1984, USENET subscribers received a message from a user calling himself Konstantin Chernenko. The USSR, so the message insisted, was going online:

> Well, today, 840401, this is the Union of Soviet Socialist Republics joining the USENET network at last and saying hallo to everyone. The reason we have joined this network is to have a forum for open discussion with the American and European people and make clear to them our resolute efforts towards maintaining peaceful coexistence between the peoples of the Soviet Union and those of the United States and Europe. (Beertema n.d.)

The message had been sent from *kremvax*—a typically structured USENET user address, where "vax" denoted a type of computer, and the initial part generally referenced the name of an organization. This April Fools' Day hoax, posted by the Dutch internet pioneer Piet Beertema in the year of Orwell's dystopia, became a colossal success among the USENET community. According to Beertema himself, the "Chernenko letter" was even appreciated at the Pentagon, the internet's birthplace, and provoked energetic discussions around information security there (Beertema n.d.). What made the joke all the funnier was the sheer impossibility of imagining an internet-connected USSR in 1984: no one expected real-life people to emerge from behind the Iron Curtain.

In 1985, Gorbachev became General Secretary of the CPSU. During the next three years, *Perestroika* came, the law on cooperatives was passed that allowed Soviet citizens to engage in business activities, and people in both countries started to communicate with each other by email and professional teleconferences. Exporting American computer equipment to Eastern Bloc countries was still officially banned, but it reached the USSR and radically changed the Soviet IT market. To solve the shortage problem and organize at least limited business with American IT companies, the International Computer Club was founded in Moscow in 1988.[1]

For the first meeting with American partners in Moscow, the International Computer Club invited Draper, among others. It is unlikely that the Club's management knew that they were dealing with a glorified phone hacker who had served time in prison—most likely, he was perceived as the creator of a modem for Apple. In Moscow, Draper got to know the entire programming community and was so impressed by the similarities between the Soviet and American computer geeks' lifestyles and skill levels that he decided to facilitate and help each other's communication in every way possible. After returning to California, he posted the following message on the USENET network:

> I recently returned from the Soviet Union . . . There is a LOT of amazing changes going on over there right now. It's not the usual rhetoric of Glasnost and Perestroika, it's more than that. I was so inspired as the results the trip, that I'm just about to publish my experiences while in the USSR. It dissolves a LOT of myth about the Soviet Union and covers all the trivia with a Hackers eyes view of the Soviet Union, and Soviet Hackers Lifestyles, which are very MUCH similar to ours. (Draper, USENET, 1988)[2]

USENET, where Draper had posted his message, was the most popular network of the late 1980s: boasting tens of thousands of subscribers, it hosted wide-ranging discussions around literature, science, politics, technology, child-rearing, and shopping. However, USENET subscribers kept well in mind that the internet as a technology was birthed by the military industry. Even more, some USENETters continued to work for secret institutions. This controversy regarding the spirit of freedom and the origins of the internet was reflected in the discussion that followed Draper's announcement of his trip to the USSR.

"Does anyone out there in Net land WANT to add Soviet sites?? I can think of a hundred reasons why!! not to mention what it would do towards World Peace," Draper enthused in a message posted to the computing-themed comp.misc newsgroup. Quite unexpectedly, even for him, this proposal triggered an avalanche of comments. The seemingly technical question of connecting Soviet programmers to the internet got USENETters discussing potential future developments in the Cold War, totalitarianism, democracy, and the importance of the internet itself as an instrument of civil opposition against official policy. Thousands of messages were posted to the network, a truly extraordinary volume of activity by the standards of the age. The Soviet Union-focused discussion went on for several months, migrating from one newsgroup to another until USENET's first USSR-based users were finally discovered.

The very first response to Draper's post was one of horror. The commenter was Alexander J. Denner, a student at MIT (today, Denner is an influential figure in the pharmaceutical industry):

> I do not think this would be a very good idea. Not that the Soviets do not already have access to American networks (ARPANET, etc.). (I am saying that I am sure the KGB intercepts as much internet information as they can.) Although I have nothing against the Russian people, the Soviets are NOT our friends . . . Also, what if a virus from the US leaks into Russia (or a virus from the USSR gets into the US)? (Draper, USENET, 1988)

Symmetrical fears were expressed by Der Tynan, an emigrant from Ireland and a programmer at a small company called Ultrasystems Defense & Space (he later joined Hewlett Packard Enterprise and became a film producer). It wasn't the KGB that worried Tynan: it was American intelligence services—and their capacity to monitor programmers' communications with the USSR:

> Personally, I think it is a good idea to open up links with communist countries. I think we could all learn something. I'd like to see a day when every country on this planet was connected to USENET (or some variant). The problem, as I see it, is not whether it is a good idea, but whether it is legally possible . . . So, I allow a Soviet site to poll my machine (or vice versa), then one day, some unnamed US agency decides that this is a major problem. So, they dispatch half-a-dozen agents, who confiscate every piece of computing gear I own, and revoke my permanent residency status. That's nice. (Draper, USENET, 1988)

Given the number of spy scandals at the time—and the fear stoked by the media—this belief in the power of the special services was only natural. After all, computer networks were initially designed to protect information, and FBI operatives took a serious interest in the development of the internet and social networks, realizing the potential danger they posed and monitoring the bleeding of strategically important information to the East. In the 1970s, when computer technologies had already attained a sufficient level of development, it was the FBI that instigated a prosecution campaign against hackers, and Draper became one of the campaign's first victims.

Surprisingly, this bore no relation whatsoever to the Soviet secret services. The KGB didn't come to regard the Net as a menace until the mid-1990s. Admittedly, the Soviet secret services did make isolated attempts to infiltrate classified American networks even in the 1980s, according to *The Cuckoo's Egg* story (Stoll 1989). However, *telephone* surveillance really preoccupied the attention of security services. The phones of dissidents, foreigners, certain officials, and other "suspicious persons" were tapped, and although the system remained less automated and centralized than its counterpart in East Germany, for example, telephone conversations served as the primary source of *kompromat*, collected with the help of various listening devices (Soldatov and Borogan, 2015).

The USENET community couldn't assume that the KGB would overlook a phenomenon as significant as the internet. They had a clear idea of the USSR as a totalitarian state, and this represented one of the keystone arguments in the discussion—as voiced by the skeptics. Thus, Larry Cipriani, an AT&T employee and "a Libertarian" who was "very realistic and afraid of the Soviets," tried to explain to his colleagues that the same network could perform completely different functions in America and the USSR:

> So, who exactly is going to be reading USENET in the Soviet Union. Joe Dissident? Or a member in good standing of the Communist Party? Who do you think is allowed to have a ham radio in the Soviet Union? Only someone who is ideologically correct, that's who . . . USENET is uncontrollable and anarchic in the free world, I believe it could be controlled in the SU. Every international phone call that connects to the SU is recorded, the same can be done with USENET . . . When the Soviet Union allows free emigration to all citizens then I will believe they have fundamentally changed. Until then, it is a prison, and only a prison. (Draper, USENET 1988)

Hot on Cipriani's heels came other people, guided not only by the notions of democracy and human rights but also by their own experiences of living in socialist countries. Marcel Samek, who founded a company called Media

Logic a year prior to the events in question, described himself as "an American who originally comes from Eastern Europe." He reminded the discussion's other participants that the Soviet Union was a "Marxist-Leninist totalitarian state," and one responsible, among other things, for exporting its totalitarianism. However, the voices of those who feared reprisals from the secret services or wanted no dealings with a totalitarian state were therefore drowned out by a torrent of positive, even rapturous, responses. Mike Trout, an employee at an electronic publishing house, *BRS Information Technologies,* assumed that "two superpowers capable of reducing each other to radioactive slag have two options: push the button or try to develop a better understanding of each other's viewpoints." In his opinion, public access networks "could be the most powerful anti-war weapons the USA has" (Draper USENET 1988)

From the protests against the war in Vietnam to the nuclear disarmament campaigns of the 1970s, the antiwar movement remained at odds with the American government and official ideology. Efforts to re-humanize the enemy, whose image had been dehumanized by official propaganda, constituted an integral component of this movement. Hence the contention—one commonly made during this discussion, and on other alternative U.S. media outlets—that people "on the other side" of the Iron Curtain weren't any different from people "on this side." They are "folks not unlike ourselves," "made of the same stuff we are," and the Net, with its democratic governance system and the possibilities of noncontrolled communication, is an ideal medium for interacting with Soviet colleagues. "If you really want to undermine the Soviet system, introduce something as uncontrollable and anarchic as USENET," wrote Kent Borg, a Boston-based programmer (Draper USENET 1988).

The polarization of viewpoints among USENET users was a hallmark of a changing historical situation. The Cold War was coming to an end, and the internet was a product, a medium, and a symbol of this process. This was well understood by the participants: it was important for them that the progressive values of the internet community overcame the "generic trauma" of the internet—its origins in secret military laboratories; that fear of war overcame fear of secret services and, ultimately, democracy overcame totalitarianism.

Most of the discussion's participants spoke out in favor of engagement with the USSR (the actual number was 89 percent: Draper subsequently totted up the votes). In fact, the prospect of Soviet programmers being connected to USENET had little to do with the panelists' opinions. In the near future, when the first interactions between Western and Soviet programmers did take place on USENET, their respective views of each other were partially modified.

Kremvax Exists! The First Soviet Man in Cyberspace

The discussion around the USSR's USENET debut had barely subsided when one of the groups got its first Soviet contributor. The contributor in question was Andrei Kolesnikov, a Moscow-based employee of the SovAm Teleport ISP, who subsequently played a role in the creation of the *.ru* zone and became director of the Coordination Centre of the Top-Level Domain for Russia. On December 26, 1989, Kolesnikov sent his first message to the moderated telecommunications-themed group *comp.dcom.telecom*, reporting the news that the first direct line of the BBS had been launched in Tallinn (Kolesnikov, USENET 1989a). Pat Tawson, the group's founder and moderator, noted that, since this was the first message ever to be sent from the USSR, he was publishing it along with metadata about its route for the benefit of "curious readers and students" who might not believe in its veracity.

In an interview to *Itogi* magazine in 2012, Kolesnikov explained how he had joined SFMT (the San-Francisco Moscow Teleport) and shared his point of view on the USENET connection. Shortly before that, he had taken a job as an assistant to Schatz, who was looking for a computer technician. By 1988, the SFMT organization had already held hundreds of video communication sessions between groups of American and Soviet citizens, and all major Soviet media, as well as some ministries and scientific institutes, were connected to its channel. Users of the network launched joint projects, discussed problems of cancer treatment, and shared experiences of recovery from alcohol addiction. "There's a lot of room to make new initiatives now," said Schatz in an interview with the *Los Angeles Times* in 1987: "Governments and bureaucracies are at a dead end. Creating new things is not their job . . . The real creativity will come from larger degrees of freedom" (Zweig 1987).

To sustain this creativity with technical means, Schatz hired people both in San Francisco and Moscow. One of them was Kolesnikov, whose task was to understand the technology that Schatz had brought from the United States:

> Joel showed me how email works. Then my brain began to boil: I could not understand in any way how a Moscow apartment in the house in Maliy Afanasievsky Lane—the American's office—was connected by a modem to America. It beeped and squeaked, then a tick appeared on the computer screen, you wrote the letter, gave the command "Send," and—bam!—it was gone instantly. To America! And there it is! It was a real shock. Faxes weren't even that widespread back then . . . Digging into the menu of the computer system, I saw a lot of different functions that I decided to investigate. I had a brain collapse right there. Apart from receiving/sending mail and the address book, there were conferences, so-called newsgroups. Nowadays, everyone is on about social networks, but that idea was already a reality at the end of the 1980s. (Pokataeva 2012)

In USENET Kolesnikov subscribed to several newsgroups on rock music and started to send messages there: "Our newspapers, TV and magazines reported that 'Rock is shit of Capitalism,' but we ignored this—new generation prefers 'capitalist shit' to official 'balalaika music'" (York, USENET, 1989). Certainly, the subscribers in these groups were also shocked. First of all, by the fact that Kolesnikov writes from Moscow, but also by his musical tastes, which were not much different from those of other users: "I swear, you sound like you grew up in Southern California,"—American music lovers replied (Pokataeva 2012).

The hackers' world turned out to be very compact: it soon became clear that Draper and Kolesnikov knew each other. A couple of days later, Towson decided to hold a Christmas marathon of stories about telecommunications. One of the subscribers sent a story about a hacker who could distinguish between the tones specific to different telephone networks. Kolesnikov answered:

> I think I know this sound/recognizer. Probably he was in Moscow, May 1988. Maybe it's my mistake, but I know one from the States who was in jail, because he could open any system using a special sound generator. (Kolesnikov, USENET 1989b)

Kolesnikov and Draper had indeed met in Moscow during a conference of the Moscow Computer Club in 1988, whereupon Draper, deciding to help out his newfound Moscow friends, posted the above-quoted account of his trip to the USSR. In January 1990 he sent his regards to Andrei before turning his attention to a subject of more immediate interest for him:

> I just returned from Berlin . . . I was standing on the wall on New Years Eve partying with 500,000 East and West Germans. Berlin was the place to be on New Year's Eve. And for all my friends out there, I have pieces of the Berlin wall for you! And Andrei . . . A big fat hello to you and all your friends in Moscow. (Draper, USENET 1990)

The next person who saw Kolesnikov's message was Phil Karn, one of the developers of the TCP/IP internet protocol and packet radio:[3]

> I also know that my TCP/IP package for the PC has found its way into the USSR, so it probably won't be long until we see the first Soviet site on the (amateur radio) Internet. Maybe I can persuade them to name one of their machines "kremvax." :-) (Karn, USENET 1989)

However, Karn didn't have to do anything to get a real kremvax in USENET. In August 1990, programmers from the *Demos* cooperative accessed the internet via Finland, the only country with which the USSR had a direct telephone link, and subscribed to Unix-, humor-, and Soviet politics-themed newsgroups. A couple of weeks later, Demos programmer Vadim Antonov hit the humor-themed group with an anecdote. This was a classic late-Soviet joke about Socialism turning up late to a meeting with Capitalism and Communism because he'd been queuing for meat ("What's a queue?" queries Capitalism. "What's *meat*?" enquires Communism) (Antonov, USENET 1990).

It was then that he was finally noticed. By 1990, the "kremvax" hoax had become a hoary old chestnut, so Antonov wasn't immediately believed—and this even though he'd signed off with words "Vadim Antonov / DEMOS, Moscow, USSR / (It is NOT a joke!)." His post met with a response by turns distrustful and delighted at the fact that American users had finally encountered flesh-and-blood denizens of the Soviet Union: "You're really from the USSR? Prove it!"; "These guys from Moscow have a funny address"; "It's a pity their first post was about humor—now we can't tell if it was a joke or not!"; "I can't believe I've actually lived to see this!" (Antonov, USENET 1990).

Although Draper's intense discussion prepared the information field for the reception of Soviet users, news of their appearance on the USENET spread gradually. A comical case involving the discovery of a Soviet presence on USENET occurred in November 1990, when a user with the handle Tatyana Zaslavskaya began contributing posts to a *soc.women* discussion group thread entitled *Masturbation as self-experience*. The user proceeded to describe their own experience of masturbation, but either got their terms mixed up—or else sought to provoke a brouhaha: "My most favored trick is autocunnilingus! Maybe I am a pervert?" Group member Barbara Hlavin reacted both to the spicy content of the message and its provenance:

> Maybe you are a contortionist? Gosh, all my life I look forward to the destruction of the Iron Curtain, so that there can be free communication between the people of the U.S.A. and the people of the Soviet Union. Finally, one day it happens! And what kind of message do I get?? (Hlavin, USENET 1990)

This encounter with an individual from behind the Iron Curtain prompted an immediate interest in Zaslavskaya's identity—users attempted to verify whether the originating server of the sent email was located in the USSR, and also to analyze Zaslavskaya's mistakes in English to understand how typical they were for native Russian speakers. Everything suggested she was the real deal. Soon enough, however, the USENET sleuths discovered that Tatyana Zaslavskaya was actually a male Soviet teen; his cover blown, said teen promptly left the group, never to return to USENET (or at least not under the same handle as before).

The real heroes of USENET were employees of the Demos cooperative and Relcom joint stock company in 1990. It started in 1983 when Unix software was copied from the open server of UC Berkeley and transported to Moscow on a floppy. This represented a violation of CoCom restrictions, but Soviet programmers had, since the early days of cybernetics in the USSR, regarded CoCom as an obstacle that would need to be circumvented to move forward. Unix ultimately found its way into the Kurchatov Institute and the Minavtoprom Institute of Advanced Training, which unveiled a jointly revised version of the system in 1984—just as Beertema's *kremvax* joke was hitting USENET. An operating system called Demos was ready to go by 1988, and the working group received an award from the USSR State Committee on Science and Technology (Soldatov and Borogan 2015). That same year witnessed the implementation of the Law on Cooperatives, which made it possible to establish a private business in cooperative form.[4]

In 1989 some members of the Demos team inaugurated an eponymous cooperative and began selling their operating system and other software products alongside computers (without leaving their workplaces at the Kurchatov Institute). In February 1990, they accessed the USENET via the university account of a post-graduate student in Helsinki. Demos employee Alexei Rudnev recalled this moment as follows:

> And so, I came back from holiday and people told me, look, we've cut ourselves a window to Europe: have you heard about such and such? Here's his articles in the news, and here's some news about Unix, and here's . . . Everyone had the sense that the Iron Curtain had fallen—prior to this, we were sitting there in our cave, our ears occasionally picking up sounds from the outside, but afterwards we found ourselves somehow integrated into the external world with all its sorrows and its joys. (Davidov 1998)

Once the idea of a Soviet presence on USENET finally lost its original strangeness, Western subscribers started showering the Demos people, who proved to be the most conspicuous Soviet users of the service, with questions upon questions. They wanted to know how to connect to various Soviet cities, sent their best regards and expressed interest in the USSR's political situation. The Soviet users, for their part, answered these questions, shared software, renamed their server "kremvax," and could never have suspected that they'd acquire truly global renown in just a few months' time—during the coup attempt in August 1991. The attempted coup d'état by conservative members of the country's top leadership, aimed at preventing the dissolution of the USSR, was accompanied by the imposition of control over television and the press, as well as the shutdown of major communication channels with the West. For the most part, this effort was successful: journalists from Western television networks were barred from covering the events. However, some regional outlets, such as the Ekho Moskvy radio station, continued broadcasting via telephone lines after their transmitters had been turned off (Ganapolsky and Buntman 2015). The internet emerged as one of the few means of transmitting information beyond the borders of the USSR.

The August Putsch: The Dream of Western Internet Users Is Coming True

One of the coup's principal instigators, KGB Chairman Vladimir Kryuchkov, should have known of the internet's existence. According to the memoirs of Valery Bardin, an employee of the Kurchatov Institute, research institute staff, local-level special services operatives had been aware since the late 1980s that communication with the West was escaping their control thanks to new technologies (Vinogradov 2009). The KGB leadership, however, was still relying for information on the tried-and-tested method of phone bugging—and continued to do so during the putsch itself. Perhaps Kryuchkov hadn't been briefed about the internet's importance, or perhaps he'd simply failed to see it as a significant phenomenon; either way, it was the Net that enabled information about the events of August 19–21 to be leaked to the world. A global leak—in every sense.

At least two internet channels were operational in Moscow that August: in addition to the work being done by Demos, staff at the Interfax news agency were also collecting and circulating information. Interfax had become an independent agency shortly before the putsch, opening an office in the United States and connecting to the web via the American provider SprintNet. Staff at the agency's U.S. office received emails from Moscow before immediately faxing them to the press; if the news really couldn't wait, they had the option of phoning the White House directly (Komissar 2009). Interfax reports also circulated among USENET subscribers, and, ironically enough, one of the agency's first articles about the putsch was published by Beertema, the man behind the "*kremvax*" hoax.

Unlike Interfax staff members, Demos and Relcom programmers weren't journalists and had assumed no informational obligations. Yet they soon realized that they had a duty to make use of the global link they themselves had established not long before August's events. According to first-hand accounts published by Andrei Soldatov and Irina Borogan in *The Red Web*, Demos chief Bardin, his colleague Antonov and Relcom head Alexey Soldatov decided, following a discussion of the risks involved, to inform the USENET community about the events unfolding in Moscow (Borogan and Soldatov 2015, 34). For three days they posted quotes from TV news, their own observations of what was happening at the street level, reports from news agencies and Ekho Moskvy, as well as remarks made by web users in various Soviet cities.

At a certain juncture Yeltsin's staff, too, learned of the internet's existence; his people entered the Demos offices in search of a photocopier and posted a message from the president to his supporters on the Net—in other words, sent it straight to the West. The text, crudely transliterated into Roman script (online Cyrillic encodings would come into use only three years later, once a critical mass of Russophone netizens had emerged), read: "A coup attempt has been launched—the president of the USSR has been removed from power."[5] The American media reacted swiftly, and reports from the diminutive Demos office on Ovchinnikovskaya Embankment reached the papers and TV news without any delay. A Demos employee wrote to a USENET correspondent:

> Don't worry, we're OK, though frightened and angry . . . Moscow is full of tanks and military machines—I hate them. They try to close all mass media, they stopped CNN an hour ago, and Soviet TV transmits opera and old movies. But thank Heaven, they don't consider RELCOM mass media or they simply forgot about it. Now we transmit information enough to put us in prison for the rest of our life. (Davis, USENET 1991)

The USENET community mobilized relatively quickly, and thousands of messages were posted to two USSR-themed groups over the course of the three August days. One user, for instance, proposed that all subscribers based in the West send through their email addresses, evidently so that the Soviet side could maintain some sort of link with the world if the internet went down. Another, meanwhile, posted dozens of pages of addresses and phone numbers of U.S. senators so that internet users could write in and demand that the authorities respond to the situation. USENETters' eagerness to help ended up causing congestion throughout Demos's and Relcom's email systems, which were reliant on telephone lines routed via Finland and couldn't deal with heavy traffic. At some point, Antonov even urged his colleagues not to overload the lines with stupid questions so as not to impede the organization of resistance efforts and unwittingly assist "these fascists" (Antonov, USENET 1991).

The events of August 1991 showed that during critical moments, grassroots-level online communication and cooperation really do come out on top over traditional media. At any rate, a private electronic message written by a first-hand witness to events commanded a great deal more trust in the early 1990s—to say nothing of the fact that such information was disseminated instantly. For USENET denizens, communication with eyewitnesses of the coup was more than a useful means of getting up to speed on the news: it was also symptomatic of a new era. History-making events were now unfolding live on air, and anyone could take part in them. The digital utopia was becoming a reality before people's very eyes. This is why the Moscow programmers' civil efforts came to be glorified the moment the coup failed. Larry Press, a USENETter and information systems expert at California State University, had been acquainted with the Muscovites since 1989 when he visited the USSR to attend a computer science conference. During the coup, Press, like many of his fellow USENETters, forwarded on to user groups various messages he'd received directly from colleagues in Moscow. After it was all over, Press went to significant efforts to ensure that the heroism of the Demos staff wouldn't be forgotten: he published accounts of the coup on USENET, collated relevant materials, and initiated the creation of a still-extant Soviet Coup archive (Press 1991, Soviet Coup Archive). Years later, articles about the democratic triumphs of the early internet continue to appear in the Western press, their tone conveyed by titles such as "Before the Twitter revolutions, there was the USENET revolution" and "The first case of international digital activism" (Press 2011, Joyce 2012).

The recollections by the Soviet participants of these events are clear proof of that: against a backdrop of Western euphoria, they're far less dramatic and apolitical. Antonov has dubbed the activism of August 1991 an "advertising campaign for Relcom," while describing his own role in the most modest terms: "I worked as the censor-in-chief—I'd remove the headlines from the eyewitness reports before sending them on to the news department" (Gagin 1999). The tendency to deploy the terms "censorship" and "propaganda" in ironic fashion is conspicuous among Russian internet pioneers, who were coming to grips with a new international domain while using old Soviet lingo.

The glorious days of August 1991 have been referenced in a handful of interviews and memoirs about the history of the internet, but the latter have never assumed major historical importance for the Soviet participants in these events. "James H. Billington, the Librarian of Congress and a Russianist and Slavic studies expert asked me personally for a copy of the email correspondence exchanged during August 1991. I refused to hand it over," wrote *Demos* founder Mikhail Davidov in a 1998 article published in honor of the cooperative's tenth anniversary. "You really should have done," riposted Antononv. "Local TV hassled me several times. They've long memories too" (Davidov 1998). He described his experience of digital activism in eminently prosaic terms.

Soon after the coup, the USSR collapsed, Relcom and Demos went their separate ways, and USENET was inundated by users from the new Russia—users who would now have to undergo the process of integrating into the internet community. That the Soviet and American participants in the events should differ in their respective assessments of August 1991 was only to be expected. Though they were "biologically one species" (as they had been described three years earlier by their American counterparts), close both professionally and interest-wise, these people remained representatives of two different societies; they had divergent expectations as to the end of the Cold War and entertained divergent utopian visions.

Democrats, Liberals, and Marxists: Discussions Between Western and Ex-Soviet Users

The phenomenon of virtual communities, characterized by a specific ethical code, a spirit of volunteering, and an emphasis on cooperation, served as a springboard for a variety of utopias, political utopias among them. *Netizens*, the aforementioned work by the Hauben mother and son, proved crucial in this regard. Though it provided a detailed history of USENET, the book did more than simply recount events; it was, in a sense, a revolutionary study. The authors collated the majority of their data directly from USENET; after conducting user interviews, they published draft versions of chapters, received critiques of their work, and reworked the text—all on the same network. Conducting interactive field research into online culture, they made use of netizens not only in the capacity of information providers but also in that of critics, analysts, and experts. The Haubens' investigation was also driven by a specific mission. Michael believed—and was fully endorsed in this belief by his mother Ronda—that USENET represented a revolutionary new type of community that could enable the old ideas of direct democracy, until then unrealized by any meatspace society, to become a reality. Hauben devoted a significant part of the book to this issue and also explored it in a number of USENET posts and several articles penned for the *Amateur Computerist* magazine (Hauben and Hauben 1997, Hauben 1993). Here, in particular, is what Michael Hauben wrote about the ideas of the nineteenth-century British political philosopher James Mill (father of John Stuart) and their online implementation:

> Today, computer communications networks, such as the Internet, are technical innovations which make moving towards a true participatory democracy more realistic. Democracy is a desirable form of government, but Mill found it impossible to maintain. Mill lists two practical obstacles in his essay ["Government," 1825]. First, he finds it impossible for the whole people to assemble to perform the duties of government. Citizens would have to leave their normal jobs on a regular basis to help govern the community. . . . The . . . development of the Internet . . . and . . . USENET News . . . is an investment in a strong force towards making direct democracy a reality. . . . The Net allows for a meeting which takes place on each person's own time, rather than all at one time. USENET newsgroups are discussion forums where questions are raised, and people can leave comments when convenient, rather than at a particular time and at a particular place. . . . Current USENET newsgroups and mailing lists prove that citizens can both do their daily jobs and participate in discussions that interest them on their schedules. (Hauben 1997, 315)

Approximately at the same time the Haubens were writing the book, USENET erupted into a fiery debate about socialism and capitalism, with American, Canadian, and ex-Soviet USENETters all adding their pennyworth. The debate's instigator was one Felix Kreisel, systems engineer at MIT, founder of the Iskra Research publishing house, member of the International Committee of the Fourth International, and subscriber to *alt.politics.socialism.trotsky*, among other left-wing newsgroups. A USENETter since the mid-1980s, Kreisel had initially confined himself to writing about IT-related topics but became a regular contributor to threads on socialist ideas after 1991. In March 1992, he posted to *talk.politics.soviet* an entire manifesto regarding the restoration of capitalism in ex-Soviet states:

> The collapse of the Soviet Union by no means implies a failure of Marxism. Real Marxists never asserted that socialism or communism could be build [*sic*] in an isolated backward country. Indeed, socialist construction is only possible as a world-wide measure. (Kreisel, USENET 1992)

Some USENETters showed surprise but kept their responses brief. "Is this guy real? Capitalism may not be an ideal system, but Marxism/Communism has shown it's [*sic*] true colours for the most part of this century, and the picture is definitely not very pretty," retorted Gerry Kokodyniak, a doctoral student at the University of Toronto. A far more engaged response came from Sergei Borodin, a graduate of the Moscow Institute of Electronic Technology (MIET) and an employee of the Institute for Nuclear Research in Dubna who was then working as an engineer at the University of Pennsylvania. Like absolutely all Soviet university graduates, Borodin had been forced to read Marx and Lenin during his studies—failing to do so would simply have meant failing to graduate. This online encounter with a "real-life" Marxist in 1992 made quite an impression on him. Similar to Kokodyniyak, he didn't immediately believe that Kreisel was a sincere socialist:

> The first article about marxism I thought was a joke, when I saw the second, I started to think the guy was serious, finally I decided to answer, though it's not my habit to talk about NONEXISTING THINGS. (Borodin, USENET 1992)

He then proceeded to formulate an argument: if Marxism didn't exist, he insisted, Russia would have been among the leading nations of the First World, and Eastern Europe's level of communications development wouldn't be causing it such severe problems. In Kreisel's historical view, the Bolsheviks inherited a laggard Russia because tsarism was incapable of properly administering the country.

Similar debates flared across various USENET newsgroups during the 1991–1994 period when Russian users were still being integrated into the international internet community and communicated in English. The debates all followed a similar pattern: university scholars from the West would broach the question of Marxism's relevance in the wake of the Soviet dissolution, in response to which USENETters of Soviet origin would describe their traumatic experiences of life under totalitarianism. The former, inclined toward leftist political views, contended that there had been no true realization of Marxism in the USSR. The latter, in contrast, may be identified as right-libertarians who believed that any other attempt to establish state control over the economy and press could only result in yet another totalitarian regime.

The USENET debates reached a conclusion of sorts in 1994 when the *comp.misc* newsgroup played host to an exchange between Michael Hauben and Antonov. Things kicked off when Hauben asked other USENETters about how they'd benefited from computer-based communication (Hauben 1994). He took care to stress that, because he was developing a sociology of computer networks, his interest lay primarily in communication between people, and not between people and computers (the latter being a traditional concern in the engineering milieu since the period of time-sharing in the 1960s). Six years before, Draper had sparked a heated dialogue around Soviet access to USENET in this very newsgroup. This time around, too, the discussion touched on Eastern European and Soviet users who "probably didn't have a clue that there was something more in life," but had become more informed thanks to the Web:

> The increased communications afforded by the Net helped to better certain people's communications with the West. . . . I believe (and others agree) that these increased communications established by the presence of the Net helped people in Eastern Europe to make up their mind to change their surroundings. (Hauben, USENET 1994)

Replying to Hauben, Antonov compared how well-informed Soviet citizens were about Western countries and vice versa. The comparison wasn't in favor of the "Americans" (as is typical for the late- and post-Soviet period, the "West" invariably meant the USA):

> From my experience, Soviet people were much better informed about life in Western countries (at least *everybody* with IQ more than of a cabbage knew for sure that socialism is not the best social system around). Which basically explains why the system fell. On the opposite, most Americans I know have quite fantastic ideas about what life in U.S.S.R. was like and often become real surprised when I point out blatant similarities between the functioning of CPSU and Soviet state economy as compared to corporate politics and deeds of American government. Which explains why they allow the system to stand :-). (Hauben, USENET 1994)

Russophone USENETters were part of the first post-Soviet generation of the technical intelligentsia—and, in the words of Alexei Yurchak, part of "the last Soviet one"; it was this generation that spawned the country's first cohort of entrepreneurs. Soviet education institutions for technical sciences produced large numbers of graduates, who constituted a significant proportion of the country's work-capable citizens. In the late Soviet period, moreover, a scientific or technical qualification was a highly effective means of social mobility, second only to a career in the communist party (Yurchak 2002). Unlike the older generation of scientists and engineers, who in the early post-Soviet years lost much of their status and went through a state of crisis as their earlier achievements were devalued and the Soviet system of science funding had collapsed, members of the younger cohort could realize their potential by swapping Russian universities for Western ones, or indeed by swapping scholarship for entrepreneurship. For these people, the terms "nuclear threat," "struggle for peace," and "common good" were associated with Soviet Marxism-Leninism, which was at odds with their value system, predicated on a contempt for collective responsibility and on a cult of individualism (Klumbyte and Sharafutdinova 2012; Yurchak 2006; Kharkhordin 1999). In the early 1990s, right-libertarianism came to underpin official government policy.[6] Many young people were in opposition to these developments, but their voices were drowned out by a sea of approval from supporters.

The networks' first users, both from the United States and the USSR, far from being random "passers-by," were university graduates with access to computers and networks, socially, culturally, and sometimes professionally proximate to one another. It was precisely these conditions that spawned the utopian vision of the online community as a better version of society. This vision existed in several variants: that of *direct democracy*; that of a *cyberspace* unsullied by economic and political problems; that of *digital immortality*. The situation changed dramatically with the advent of mass network usership, a crisis that occurred in the mid-1990s.

The birth in 1993 of USENET's "eternal September" meme may be regarded as its symbolic start. Before then, USENET's users had predominantly been graduate students and university staff—people well acquainted with network technologies and ethics. Newbies would turn up once annually—in September, at the start of the university year. In 1993, the internet service provider America Online (AOL) began offering USENET access to its customers. Cue a vast influx of new users who, on the whole, were not only unfamiliar with the idiosyncrasies of the USENET network but also far removed from university communities. A few months later, a user named Dave Fischer wrote the following: "September 1993 will go down in net history as the September that never ended" (Fischer 1994). Two decades later, in an interview with *Vice*, Fischer described the last years before the internet transitioned from an elite phenomenon to a mass-market one. "My memories of early 90s USENET are of a vibrant, enlightened world of serious discourse," he enthused. "When you're deeply immersed in an elitist clique, it often feels like you're in an open welcoming community. From your perspective, everything's great" (Koebler 2015). When the normal functioning of a relatively closed and established community, complete with its own traditions, ethics, and history, is disrupted by a flood of newcomers, the community responds by construing itself as an elite and sets about waging a symbolic battle against those who don't belong.

In 1993, there were several other key milestones indicating both a blossoming and a crisis of the network communities. At that time the WWW protocol, which enabled the creation of websites with texts and pictures, became widespread, and the first graphic browser Mosaic was developed. *Wired* magazine, the voice of the digerati[7] techno-optimism of the 1990s, was founded. The new magazine gave readers a sense of belonging to an elite club of *future natives*, actively used the romantic image of "cyberspace," and compared the development of the internet to humankind's discovery of fire (Streeter 2011).

This was followed by "Declaration of the Independence of Cyberspace" by John Perry Barlow, an internet activist, poet, and Grateful Dead lyricist, and discussions about "California ideology"—that is, the transformation of California's hippies from techno-utopians bent on achieving universal online communion into an "electronic agora"—linchpins of electronic neoliberalism, owners of commercial internet companies, and champions of right-wing values (Barbrook and Cameron 1995). Many users from the former Soviet Union joined the internet exactly at this time. These were not yet users en masse, which happened a decade later, but no longer a rare few either. For them, Barlow's libertarianism was certainly closer than his left-wing critique: one of the first issues of *Zhurnal.ru*, a magazine about the internet, published a translation of his "Declaration." At the same time, as the WWW protocol became widespread, the USENET ceased to be a common space where American users could discuss things with post-Soviet ones. The internet was no longer a miracle.

6

The Russian Colonization of the American Internet

In 1992 a Finnish user named Antti Karttunen asked in the group *soc.culture.soviet* about Venedikt Erofeyev's *Moscow–Petushki*, a novel he'd recently read in translation (and which had been available only in *samizdat* during the Soviet period). In particular, Karttunen wanted to know how autobiographical the book was, what became of its author, and whether the Petushki station was real or fictional (Karttunen, USENET 1992). And he volunteered an observation of his own, noting that *Moscow–Petushki* was best read when severely hung over. Karttunen's post prompted a lively discussion that was still going strong two weeks later.

At first, Russian USENETters ridiculed the very idea of reading Erofeyev in translation: no foreign-language version of the novel, so they believed, could possibly do justice to the original. At the same time, however, they informed Karttunen that the book was "real literature," and an absolute must-read for anyone wishing to understand the Russian people. Finally, they began to argue among themselves, Karttunen's original question now totally forgotten. Most USENET discussions, Russian and not, progressed along similar lines, regardless of the background of their participants. A specific feature of the Soviet- and Russia-themed newsgroups was that they were often sparked by questions about Russian literature and culture. This chapter will examine the evolution of the Russian internet, from its earliest interactions with non-Russian users to subsequent emancipation of the *runet* and finally the crystallization of the idea of a Russian world.

At this point, the history of the Russian internet, in a certain sense, comes to an end. What follows are various and often effective attempts by the state to control the network, culminating in the introduction of the "sovereign RuNet" into Russian legislation in 2019. This process, without a doubt, remains the responsibility of the contemporary Russian regime. At the same time, it is a logical continuation of the dramatic history of the leftist utopia of universal grassroots communication—from its powerful inception in the 1920s, its revival under new conditions in the late 1950s, to its complete abandonment in the late Soviet 1980s.

What Is Russia: Quest for Identity

The early years of the Russian internet were simultaneously the last years of USENET in its original form. A common space like English-language groups about the USSR and Russia, presupposed dialogue. This meant that Russians had to explain a lot about themselves, their country, history, and views. Sometimes these explanations turned into a kind of a guide to Russia for foreigners struggling to fathom the Russian national character and the realities of Russian life. At the same time, USENETters also embarked upon a "reconfiguration process," involving self-descriptions, analyses of old identities, and pursuits of new ones ("What do we mean by the terms 'Soviet,' 'non-Soviet,' 'anti-Soviet,' and 'Russian'? What role does the cultural background play?"). In this sense, jokes, folklore, and literature were the most obvious springboards toward defining your identity, especially if you happened to live abroad, as was the case with most Russophone netizens prior to 1997–98. Moreover, these attempts at self-definition proved most effective when encountering "others" and explaining to them the possible meanings of "us."

Examples of self-description feature richly in Requests for Discussion (RfDs).[1] In 1995, for instance, a USENETter named Vorobieff argued for the creation of a new group *soc.culture.russian*: "Russian culture—both the classical and the new—is immense, rich and multifaceted. Russian language—the language of Dostoevsky, Bulgakov, Pasternak—is spoken by hundreds of millions of people throughout the world. The vastness of Russian forests, meadows, steppes, deserts and mountains encompasses eleven time zones" (Vorobieff, USENET 1995).

The most popular Russian-language groups of that period contained the word "Soviet" in their names; frequented by users from the former Soviet republics, they hosted discussions around the historical (colonial) legacy of the USSR: the future of the Soviet fleet in Sevastopol, the rights of

Russian-speaking Estonians, the Karabakh conflict, and anti-Semitic policy at the Moscow State University. This sat not at all well with users from Russia, whether emigres abroad or the handful of people within the country who enjoyed internet access in the early 1990s. Other Russian-language groups belonged to the *relcom* hierarchy and were therefore moderated by the Moscow-based company Relcom, a fact that made some subscribers uncomfortable. It was for this reason that the early 1990s—when USENET remained a principal discussion resource—saw constant attempts to inaugurate groups with a "Russian" rather than "Soviet" orientation. For the USENETters behind these attempts, such groups were far more than mere forums; they symbolized a rejection of the Soviet legacy.[2]

As they rationalized the need for new groups, RfD submitters sought to establish what the terms *Russian* and *Soviet* actually meant, but definitions offered for the former were predominantly negative: "non-Soviet," "anti-Soviet," etc. (Particularly prominent throughout such discussions was the term *sovok*. A derivative of "Soviet" and homonymic with *sovok*, "shovel," or "dustpan," it is used to refer disparagingly to mindless propagators of Soviet values.) The question of who exactly shouldered responsibility for the actions of the Soviet regime and for its colonial policies arose again and again. USENETters from other ex-Soviet republics and autonomous regions, as well as those who hailed from "national minorities," regarded bearers of Russian identity as representatives of the Soviet regime. The latter, however, denied responsibility for the Soviet rule; if anything, they saw themselves among its biggest victims. Sergei Viznyuk, a USENETter responsible for an RfD submitted a year before Vorobieff's, offers the following observations:

> Things Russian are not "Soviet," the two have been antagonistic from the first days of communist takeover in 1917. It would not hurt to also remember that Russian history and culture are not limited to the last 70 years of Soviet domination. (Viznyuk, USENET 1994)

For Viznyuk, "things Soviet" were failures, "things Russian" achievements:

> Soviet is the invasion of Hungary in 1956 and Czechoslavakia in 1968. Soviet is massacre in Vilnius in 1990. Soviet is Gulag. Soviet is Brighton Beach. Soviet is *soc.culture.soviet*. Russian is Dostoevsky and Tolstoy. Russian is Andrei Sakharov and Alexander Solzhenitsin. Russian is Bolshoi Theater and

> Tchaikovsky's music. Russian is the August 1991 when Russians withstood the pressure of Soviet regime and broke free from the Soviet Empire. (Viznyuk, USENET 1994)

It is noteworthy, among other things, that, if "things Soviet" were primarily historical atrocities like the Gulag network and the invasions of Hungary and Czechoslovakia, "things Russian," as far as Viznyuk was concerned, existed primarily in the domains of literature and culture (Sakharov and the August 1991 coup attempt being the exceptions). USENETter Alex Belits put Viznyuk's thoughts in a nutshell: "More accurate: 'I'm Russian, and my shit is Soviet.'"

Russian Emigrants Miss Their Libraries: The Raising of Samizdat

"We brought several floppies loaded with texts, including the complete works of Pasternak, over to America with us," Mikhail Verbitsky recalls in an interview about his move to the United States. "We printed the thing out, only to get a load of different symbols: flowers, dollar signs, clubs, spades . . . We had a lot of fun with it, though, because we deciphered it all using frequency analysis. . . . We had a *samizdat* version of Pasternak's works, too, but it would've been silly to take it to America. This was 1990" (Interview, Moscow, 23.03.2016).

Verbitsky—a world-renowned mathematician and a future *enfant terrible* of the Russian internet, who enjoyed shocking his readers with his radical political views and exotic philosophical theories—graduated from Moscow State University in 1990 before going on to do a postgrad degree at Harvard. Verbitsky was part of a large wave of young mathematicians, physicists, biologists, computer scientists, and engineers who left the former Soviet Union en masse in the early 1990s, primarily to save their careers (Biagioli and Lepinay 2019). For them, leaving meant not only interrupted contacts with family and friends, but also the loss of personal libraries that could not be taken with them. Access to the internet partly compensated for the second problem: the exchange of Russian texts became one of the important features of the early network for this group of users. Using university computers with USENET access, they exchanged links to ftp-libraries online.

During the 1991–1994 period, for example, the newsgroups *soc.culture.soviet* and *talk.politics.soviet* were asked to send over lyrics from Russian rock songs, Vladimir Vysotsky's song and poem anthology *Nerve*, novels by the

Strugatsky brothers, as well as jokes, which were particularly in demand. In 1992, the *soc.culture.soviet* newsgroup hosted a lengthy discussion around an anthology entitled *One Thousand and One Russian Jokes*. Subscribers wanted help with unarchiving and converting it; some requested an English translation, while others tried to ascertain the identity of the original collector.

These and other requests for texts in newsgroups included neither classical Russian literature nor texts from the early twentieth century. In this sense, the above-quoted description of Russian as the language of Dostoevsky, Bulgakov, and Pasternak by user Vorobieff marked a cultural heritage already appropriated but that did not correspond to the actual reading list of his comrades. The same list—Vysotsky, Strugatsky, rock lyrics, jokes—approximately corresponded to the literature that was not distributed by official publishing houses but circulated in homemade copies. That is *samizdat*.

Such collections of texts were widespread in the late USSR. First on tapes and then on floppy disks, they were passed from hand to hand and copied, just like classic *samizdat*. Only the content could be different: Bulgakov's *The Master and Margarita* or Pasternak's *Doctor Zhivago* were classics of the literary *samizdat* and circulated mainly in hard copies that were typewritten or photocopied. Meanwhile the novels by the Strugatsky brothers and the lyrics by Vysotsky were distributed in the form of electronic files and printouts. Accordingly, the scale of distribution changed with copying technology: electronic texts were thousands of times more widely circulated.

It's not surprising, given the USSR's immense number of computing centers, engineering-design bureaus, and research institutes, all of them possessing computers, printers, and occasionally book binderies as well.[3] It was these collections that provided the Russian internet with its first stratum of content during the early 1990s. Alexander Artamonov, a former staff member at the Moscow Experimental Computing Centre, describes the process of collecting and storing electronic texts as follows:

> We had a tape reel on a mainframe that was inscribed with the words "Lena and Yana's archive." The reel was home to various items of samizdat: Vysotsky, Galich, Bulgakov, Solzhenitsyn (I think), the *Kama Sutra* (for sure). . . . Lena and Yana were on the Experimental Computing Centre's staff. Tapes were more durable than HDDs, which had a lifespan of a few months at best. This meant that my night shifts as an operator were spent backing up texts and transferring them from disk to tape. On Sundays, meanwhile, we copied

> whatever we could. We had two generations of archives and, if something were to go awry, we'd be able to restore any file for any given day. It was like breathing—we never discussed whether it should be done or not. As soon as these mainframes arrived on the scene, operators would take these blueprints at night, when the higher-ups weren't there, and enter the text: rat-a-tat-tat . . . Electronic samizdat, basically . . . One reel of tape is about twenty megabytes—decent enough when you're dealing with text. (Interview, Moscow, 10.09.2015)

In the Western tradition, the term *samizdat* has until recently had a narrower meaning: it meant mainly dissident literature, often with political content, which was distributed in typewritten copies. In this sense, the electronic *samizdat* that circulated among the employees of the research institutes and later among the first Russian-speaking internet users belongs more to Soviet popular culture than to the political resistance of the Soviet period. Nevertheless, these two *samizdats* are closely related.

In the mid-1970s, when ECMs and ANPDs (that is, computers and printers) began to be mass-produced in the USSR, many texts successfully migrated from the medium of "classic" *samizdat*—printouts or photographic copies of *tamizdat*[4]—to its electronic counterpart. They were then brought over to the US on floppy disks, as in the case of Verbitsky's collection,[5] before eventually making their way onto FTP sites and, later, into various web libraries.

As the media transition from paper to electronic signal came, *samizdat* partially changed its content. On the one hand, it acquired more and more topics and genres of interest to a wide range of readers. Thus, among the texts appeared science fiction, bardic songs, extensive collections of humor and erotica, as well as articles and books on alternative medicine, orientalism, and esotericism.[6] On the other hand, there were practically no texts on political topics such as *The Chronicle of Current Events* or Solzhenitsyn's books, which were characteristic of proper dissident *samizdat*.[7]

Unfortunately, this part of *samizdat* remains practically unexplored, despite its mass popularity. The *Anthology of Samizdat*, for instance, makes no mention of it whatsoever, while Alexei Pyatkovsky in his detailed overview of *samizdat* described it using such labels as "interest-based publications" and "recreational materials" (which, in his opinion, included "pornographic and astrological literature, psychological tests, [and] catalogues for collectors") (Piatkovskii 2012). In his words, the phenomenon's late period (from the mid-1970s to 1986) was characterized by "the erosion of the ideological purity of *samizdat*, which originated as a form of spontaneous protest against state-imposed censorship, and also as a means of fighting for the free dissemination of information." This depreciation of nonpolitical *samizdat* took place even though disseminating works about yoga or sex could land *samizdat* distributors in prison, too: Anatoly Chernyshev, for, example, was jailed following the "Tomsk scribes" case of 1982 (Chernyshev 2014), as were several *samizdatchiks* who reprinted translations of Robert Street's *Modern Sex Techniques* and other sex-related books in Cherkasy in 1974 (*Razmnozhenie* 1974). It was these *samizdat* publications of mass-market works that became the basis for the first Russian online projects.

In the introduction to the *Anthology of Samizdat*, edited by Vyacheslav Igrunov and Mark Barbakadze, Alexander Daniel offered several definitions of *samizdat*. These, significantly, were based not on the *content* of *samizdat* texts, but rather on the manner in which they were *produced and distributed*. First, *samizdat* is "literature that propagates itself during the process of being disseminated by its own readers"; secondly, each new book is not a simply an individual copy within a print run but a full-fledged new edition (Igrunov and Barbakadze 2005, 30). At the same time, Daniel refers to "ANPD printouts" of the Strugatsky brothers' novel *The Ugly Swans*, which were circulated alongside photocopies of publisher's proofs.[8] He calls them "a colorful form of *samizdat*" wherein the technology itself ensured safe storage for the text:

> No one can see with the naked eye what's stored there on the reel—it could be data for the calculations of some automated control system, or it could be Venechka Erofeyev's *Moscow-Petushki*. You come in, mount the tape onto the tape drive, seek out a moment when there're no outsiders in the computer control room, launch the program—and the ANPD starts printing the text. What comes out is a wide, endless paper strip, about fifty centimetres wide, and on it is Berdyayev's *The Origins and Meaning of Russian Communism*. (32)

If the printout, being the characteristic—and technically determined—*samizdat* form, "acquired significance [in the West] as a symbol of the Soviet dissident struggle" (Komaromi 2004, 600), electronic *samizdat* had as much of a recognizable appearance. It was a printer paper with perforated edges; sans serif typeface; exclusive use of uppercase letters only (in most cases). The latter was due to a technical idiosyncrasy of drum printers, whose drums came in three variants: Cyrillic uppercase/lowercase; Latin uppercase/lowercase; Cyrillic uppercase/Latin uppercase. Texts printed on these machines frequently contained English words, so, more often than not, only the third drum was used—switching drums specifically for *samizdat* purposes would have been inconvenient. The covers of books produced in this way usually sported titles printed in large letters consisting of asterisks as drum printers lacked a font size adjustment facility.

Of course, magnetic tapes and ADCP printouts evoked completely different associations. Strugatsky's novels, as well as jokes, yoga manuals, and erotic literature were more often seen in this form. These texts, as well as technical manuals for programmers, circulated on tapes and printouts until the first third of the 1990s, when they all became text files on the internet.

The transition to the online environment sometimes proved difficult for new users, however, and paper *did* mediate between them and electronic documents for some time to come. "Retraining people familiar with *pneumatic post*[9] to use email was an absolute cinch, but folk used to chewing the fat in smoking rooms or bathhouses were far slower on the uptake," remarks Alexey Babiy, the human rights organization International Memorial board member involved in the development of the internet in Krasnoyarsk during the 1990s, of his experiences in upskilling new users.

Everything Is Literature

In the early 1990s, electronic collections of texts became the first content of the Russian internet. Maxim Moshkov's Library—one of the most popular 1990s Russian-language websites still in existence today—began life in a somewhat similar fashion. In 1993, Moshkov was working as a programmer and system administrator at the Mathematics Department of the Russian Academy of Sciences, then one of the few places in Moscow with both email access and its own FTP site. Moshkov recalls in an interview:

> Suddenly we got word that there's this thing called the World Wide Web. The guys from Chernogolovka found it. The Mathematics Institute ought to put a little something up in the window, as it were, so the West could have a look-see. We found virtually the only site that existed at the time—the personal page of the World Wide Web's developer [Tim Berners-Lee]. It had a photo you could download and open in a separate window, as well as a bit of info about him. We took some files from the CERN server and used them—

> copy-pasted and reworked—to create a page for the institute. "Right," our boss said, "all staff members need to have pages of their own." (Interview, Moscow, 25.03.2016)

Berners-Lee's page had a hobbies section as well as a bio, which, in the eyes of the first post-Soviet generation, seemed like a rather unusual way of presenting yourself in a public forum:

> Everyone began creating their own pages. We all bigged ourselves up as best we could. . . . I said in my hobbies section that I had a collection of writings about tourism, rock music and literature, and I uploaded them there. . . . I'd kept these files at the institute, so it was only fitting to do so. (Interview, Moscow, 25.03.2016)

Moshkov's Library has changed little since then. The site that exists today is effectively the hobbies section of a résumé inspired by the personal website of Berners-Lee.

The owners of electronic collections before the internet era themselves often used the word "*samizdat*" ("electronic *samizdat*," "*samizdat* printed on ADCPU," etc.). Because for them, the most important feature of *samizdat* was its free, uncontrolled production and distribution of texts. In online posts and articles from the mid-1990s, Russian authors also thematized the features of *samizdat* inherited from the internet. They described classical *samizdat* as a "magic crystal reflecting the principles of the Net's existence" and regarded the internet as a "universal *samizdat*"; manifestos for a "new Russian *samizdat*" were penned, and the ultimate victory of traditional Russian "literarycentrism" proclaimed (Schmidt 2011, 192–204). At the turn of the millennium, Oleg Novikov wrote:

> At some point, historians of *samizdat* will subject to thorough analysis the situation in our country during the 1990s of the twentieth century. The absence of official censorship and the massive spread of computer technologies have enabled literature lovers to see their works published. (Novikov 2000, cited in Schmidt 2011, 192)

"What is the Internet? The same thing as *samizdat*, only in an American incarnation," asserts a character in Sergei Kuznetsov's *The Crystal Coffin*

(Kuznetsov 2003). Over the course of the novel, the author and his protagonists offer several partial definitions of the internet: it is at once a "promise of the future" and an "investment object," "kitchen-table chit-chat" and "assorted gossip," "a window on the world" and "the idea of equality in its purest form," and, finally, a "sacred space that exists in counterbalance to the offline world." Above all, however, it is a perfected version of *samizdat*: an American network that provides a level of access to existing texts with no precedent in Soviet history, as well as the opportunity to publish one's own.

By eliminating the material properties of *samizdat*—whether typewriter, photocopy, tape, or ADC printout—the internet provided virtually limitless possibilities for replication and distribution. To get the desired text and become a reader, you only needed access to the internet. It was not much more difficult to become an author. Classical *samizdat* also meant that any distributor could add his own texts to the collection of others' texts, which led, for example, some researchers to criticize *samizdat* as a source of graphomania (Belenkin 2012, 21). But only the internet bestowed a truly mass scale on writing in the world of Russian literature.

The Emancipation of the Russian Internet

Back in the time of Russian-speaking USENET groups, the canon of the Russian internet was formed: the first libraries, including collections of jokes and the first literary games, appeared (Gorny 2009; Schmidt 2011). According to Eugene Gorny, a participant in the first online projects and an internet historian, literary games replaced for Russian users the Multi-User Dungeons, or MUDs, which had existed since the days of the ARPANET and were based on the exchange of lines.

As the web protocol spread, new opportunities appeared and Russian-language websites began to emerge. Moshkov calls 1996 the year when he "robbed the internet," boosting the volume of his library from fifteen megabytes to one hundred. 1996 also saw several firsts for the internet in Russia: it was the year of the country's first online literature competition (Teneta), its first dating chat room (Krovatka), its first internet café (Tetris in Saint Petersburg), and its first search engine (Rambler). Domestic internet infrastructure was making great strides, too. Soros's Open Society Foundation announced a major university internetization program, with 33 institutions going online nationwide (Fedotova 2015). Meanwhile, Cityline, one of the first mass-market commercial ISPs, appeared on the scene: as well as providing internet access, it also worked to develop Russian-language content. Finally, the internet arrived in many of Russia's major cities alongside local web projects: city portals, news sites, network services, and so forth.[10] According to data published in 1996 by Vadim Maslov on the Sovinformburo website, there were some 48,000 computers within the .su and .ru zones at the time (Maslov 1996).

The "web culture herald" Zhurnal.ru was also launched in 1996. Several print issues were brought out, but the project soon became online-only. Zhurnal.ru carried reviews and analysis of developments in the world of the Russian internet—now hundreds of sites strong—while also reporting on politics. Verbitsky wrote for the outlet about music, Kuznetsov contributed articles about culture, and, although their political views were diametrically opposed, the Zhurnal.ru forum (alongside others of its ilk) was about the only place in the mid-1990s where they could actually cross paths and engage one another in dialogue. Kuznetsov recalled this state of affairs as follows:

> There was no such thing as public debate in Soviet times, nor did it materialize in post-Soviet Russia. The internet, though, was an exception: it became the only space where public debate could occur. People who read the *Segodnya* [Today] newspaper would never intersect in real life with readers of *Zavtra* [Tomorrow]. . . . The Internet proved to be the first platform capable of facilitating this kind of dialogue. . . . We were on the same subscription list and worked on Zhurnal.ru's first content project together. (Interview, Skype, 26.01.2016)

By 1996, then, the Russian internet was rapidly emancipating itself from the American one—while also being reconceptualized as an independent and self-sufficient phenomenon. In 1997, Raffi Aslanbekov, the author of an online column entitled "Great Uncle's Thoughts," coined the word *Runet* (Aslanbekov 1997). The coinage rapidly gained in popularity across Russian-language forums and columns: the phenomenon of the Russian internet had finally acquired a name of its own. This was the moment when the web ceased to be "American" in the eyes of Russian netizens. This is how Kuznetsov explained these developments:

> In 1996, the year that saw the birth of Teneta, Zhurnal.ru and countless smaller projects, the idea of "let's look at America and do the same stuff Russian-style" finally became the "in" thing. You have to say that we succeeded rather well in

> its implementation—everything that was technologically feasible was replicated in Russia and occasionally even improved. What's more, we created certain stuff that never existed in America at all—and still doesn't. *Zhurnal'nii Zal*,[11] for example: America had nothing comparable. (Kuznetsov 2004)

Around the same time, conflicts began to flare up between emigres outside the country and people living in Russia. In 1994, Relcom moderator Dmitry Peskin addressed a few choice words to the former in a USENET message:

> If you don't want to return, don't return. If you do, do . . . No one's forcibly dragging you back here. *Relax. Take it easy, not east. Make love, play ball, buy your own fully digital record studio*,[12] hurl profanity at Americans and Europeans who understand this interethnic language of communication to an ever greater degree, take offense at the fact that "we" didn't take the country down a road that'd make "you" want to return here (we're to blame, of course, no question). Just don't throw shit at us, OK? Assuming that's not too much of an ask for you . . . Today's barricades now run along cultural boundaries, not geographic ones. (Peskin, USENET 1994)

Ten years later, in a 2004 interview with the Russian Cyberspace project,[13] Leonid Delitsyn described how such discussions sounded to emigres' ears:

> Certain Russia-based netizens have accused us, who live abroad, of influencing the content of the Russian internet. We needed to learn to respect other cultures. We lived far from Russia; we had internet access. . . . There was this tradition, in Russia, of regarding anyone who lived abroad as a spy. We brought in foreign values. . . . In the 1990s, nine out of ten people involved in the development of the Russian internet were based abroad.

Until the mid-2000s, liberation from the influence of emigrants on Russian-language content was impossible for the most prosaic reasons. Although Russia was experiencing record growth in internet access, it was still not enough for emigrants to become a minority among Russian-language users. It was partly due to this geographical and cultural distribution of authors that the Russian internet acquired its unique qualities and became Runet.

"In the Beginning Was the Word . . .": The Russian Internet Writes the Bible

The acknowledgment of the Russian segment of the internet as a distinct, unique, and isolated entity within the global network was accompanied by a proliferation of mythologizing narratives. Like the first participants in the American networks of the 1980s, Russian users discovered a new, ideal space for communication, where the principles of physical space did not work and where the state with its system of control and punishment was absent. "In 1996–1997, Runet was an Adamic world, where, by poking at any object, you could endow said object with a name and rest almost assured that the latter would stick to the former," wrote Kuznetsov in 2000 (Kuznetsov 2004). This notion, eminently cosmic in its implications, was shared by many players of the nascent Russian internet: as pioneers of cyberspace, explorers of an empty, unpopulated, as-yet-nameless domain, they knew their actions were all firsts—and that they would echo in eternity; they were writing the Bible.[14]

"In the beginning was the word. And the word was with the Net. And the word was the Net. . . . This is how the internet Bible ought to begin," wrote Alexander Zhitinsky—an author, critic, founder of the Laurence Sterne Literary Association, and an advocate of the literary *Runet* (Zhitinsky 1997). Zhitinsky describes the creators of the first Russian websites as follows:

> This is the first generation of colonists of the Russian Web, if we regard it as analogous to America's Wild West. The most enterprising individuals have rushed online in pursuit of money and freedom, and their names will remain etched in history as the names of pioneers.

This metaphorization of the internet as the Wild West invokes the romantic image of a colonist, an appropriator of seemingly unoccupied territory. Lurking in the metaphor, however, is an additional meaning, one no doubt intended by the author: the Russians have appropriated American technology, recolonizing, as it were, America itself. The instrument for this Russian colonization of the American network was literature. The American technology proved an ideal repository for the traditions of Soviet and Russian culture, wherein *samizdat* represented just one possible manifestation of a more general phenomenon—"literature-centrism,"[15] or the orientation of Russian culture toward literature.

The internet was "the Word" primarily due to technical conditions: while Russian networks enabled the transmission of compact, text-based files, images took an inordinately long time to download, and video transfer was completely out of the question. But contemporary commentators construed this circumstance as a kind of portent favorable to Russia being "literature-centric." Here is how the philologist Mikhail Epstein describes the specificity, if not to say the "special path," of the Russian internet:

> I believe that when Russia acquires technical mastery over these spaces, she will find in them much that is akin to the traditions of her own culture—namely electronic *sobornost'* [communalism, "all-togetherness"], disregard for private property and narrow specialization, metaphysical inebriety and nomadism, dense forests, wide steppes, "flex, my shoulder! swing, my arm!," and so on and so forth . . . Among the Russian traditions set to find the second wind in electronic networks is its "literature-centric quality," myopic predictions of its demise notwithstanding. A virtual space, after all, is a space completely covered by text, a space itself consisting of text. . . . Everyone learns to be a writer, to transform the objective world into words. (Epstein 1998)

Mikhail Epstein was exactly the kind of émigré whose influence on the content of the Russian internet some of its activists sought to counter. A professor at Emory University with a passion for exploring and mastering digital space, he nevertheless viewed this space as the ideal embodiment of Russian culture. Alongside such intellectual endeavors—in the same Runet, on neighboring platforms—more politically charged topics emerged, which later became part of the right-wing mainstream.

Russkii Mir

"Cold War Revenge: A Counterblow in Virtual Space": such is the title of a "strategic report" written by Efim Ostrovsky in 1996 and presented at the annual session of the Ostrovsky Group (Ostrovsky 2006).[16] In his report, Ostrovsky proposes "to consider anew the phenomenon of the Cold War—a war of ideas in which the role of a strike weapon is played not by bits of metal and kilotons of TNT but rather by signs and meanings."

Officially, the Cold War—and, with it, the Soviet Union—had ended five years before Ostrovsky wrote this text. A significant proportion of post-Soviet intellectuals, however, experienced the 1990s as a defeat: political, economic, and cultural alike. They constructed conceptions of a new Russia and a new "Russianness" atop the rubble of the previous *derzhava* (strong state, superpower) with a view to restoring the Motherland to her former status. In Ostrovsky's eyes, the challenge facing this new Russia was to "achieve mastery over virtual space," by which he understood a system of values and "meanings." In this and subsequent works, Ostrovsky and his associates argued for the necessity of creating a new type of empire, "progressive rather than aggressive" in nature and characterized by researcher Marlene Laruelle as an instrument of cultural "soft power" (Ostrovsky 206; Laruelle 2015). Significantly, "creating" in this case meant designing, assembling, and developing "by means of advertising and propaganda"—the very means typically used to promote commercial products.

Three years later, this idea acquired a stable designation: *The "Russian world."* Ostrovsky's coauthor Petr Shchedrovitsky would go on to formulate it as follows:

> Over the course of the twentieth century, under the influence of tectonic historical shifts, world wars and revolutions, a Russian world took shape on the planet—to wit, a networked structure of major and minor communities who think in and speak Russian. It is no secret that scarcely half the population of the Russian world lives within the territory delineated by the administrative borders of the Russian Federation. . . . The fledgling Russian state can and should seek out the foundations of its stability and relevance within the confines of the Russian world, within a policy of pursuing the constructive development of its global networks. (Shchedrovitsky 2000)

The son of Soviet philosopher Georgy Shchedrovitsky, Petr was actively involved in "methodologism," a movement inaugurated by his father.[17] In the mid-1990s, certain methodologists became core personnel within a new Russian profession of "political technologists." Political technologists might be defined as intellectuals who deploy "technologies of the humanities" in an effort to influence public opinion, usually on behalf of politicians, electoral candidates, incumbent presidents, or government bodies. Individuals operating within this profession worked in different cities and even countries throughout the 1990s, acquitting themselves particularly well in Ukraine, where they were dubbed "foreign masters of influencing mass consciousness" (*Chisto ukrainskii* 2001). However, those closest to the methodologist circle rarely settled for grassroots work (molding public opinion about some local candidate or other, etc.). Their real mission, as they saw it, was to effect transformation on a global scale. The notion of the "Russian world" was one of the notable outgrowths of this movement; as the condensed summation of a philosophy underlying a new, virtual Russian colonization drive, it became immensely popular among Russian national-patriotic movements and migrated into real-world politics soon after a few early publications.[18]

The "Russian world" idea became both an impulse of Russia's neo-colonial policy and a direct extension of the history of the Russian internet—this despite the fact that the people behind it intended to bring about neither the full-scale invasion of Ukraine nor a Russophone netizen community. The concept of "network structure" arrived in Russia together with translations of the works by Manuel Castells, who developed the ideas of the network society and the post-information era (Castells 1996–1998), and who had been directly involved in Soviet and Russian intellectual life since 1984.[19] Castells's works were well known among the theorists of the "Russian world."[20]

Shchedrovitsky, Ostrovsky, and their co-authors employ the terms *network structure* and *global networks* to refer to the decentralized distribution of Russian-speaking people, who are to be found all over the world. Their cultural and language connection to their homeland serves as the basis for a new Russian power in a changed historical situation. The Russian world is not exactly about the Russian internet, but serves as an apt metaphor, nonetheless. Their adherents—for instance, the employees of the Rossiyane[21] Foundation (later renamed "Russian world")—applied the notion of the "Russian world" to political realities and understood its network structure as a "cyberspace," which served to unite "the geopolitical potentials of the Russian parent state and Russian diaspora" (Poloskova and Skrinnik 2003).

The genetic links between Runet and the Russian world can be found in the post-Soviet identity crisis. Like the USENETters who mused on the greatness of Russian culture and literature in the mid-1990s, political technologists regarded as central the question of the country's prospects, the possibility of perpetuating its might and its greatness. In the 1990s, with traditional structures and hierarchies in ruins, the Russian language was left, alongside Russian culture, as the sole resource for doing so. In this sense, the finest incarnation of the "Russian world" proved to be the Russophone netizen community—globally scattered developers of online literature, advancers of "literature-centrism," participants in the processes of "electronic *sobornost'*," custodians of other "Russian cultural traditions," all of which found their second life on the internet.

The systematic migration to the Russian internet of political technologies was made possible by another link between the two domains—namely, by the efforts of Gleb Pavlovsky, a producer and intermediary between the "Russian world" and Runet. In 1995, Pavlovsky inaugurated the Russian Institute together with the philosopher Sergei Chernyshev. The purpose of this organization was "to facilitate the emergence of a Russian cultural self-actualization as well as the establishment of institutions of a new social identity." The Institute's co-founders discussed the notion of Russianhood in a series of letters. Pavlovsky wrote to Chernyshev in 1996:

> There's a difficulty in being Russian. To speak Russian, even to be called Russian, is difficult. . . . The collapse of the USSR, which dragged "things Soviet" into oblivion, failed to restore Russians to their former rights. The challenge of the Russian program is to restore things Russian without quotation marks or pseudonyms. (*Iz delovoi* 1997)

This loss of identity, in his opinion, was directly linked to the collapse of the USSR, which resulted in the emergence of a new word: *rossiyanin* (Russian citizen, as opposed to *russkii*, ethnic Russian). Underscoring the artificialness of this epithet, Pavlovsky invokes the United States by way of comparison:

> Imagine an America whose denizens no longer dare to be called Americans, but only *Americaners* or Americanmen. Our civilization lost its internal pivot and the Rubik's Cube puzzle fell apart. Russianhood wasn't overthrown by force, nor was it suppressed. It was depeopled. (*Iz delovoi* 1997)

Precisely this state of affairs prompted the inauguration of the Russian Institute, "one of the first 'landing operations' mounted by the *global corporation Russia*." This pronouncement about the meanings of Russia and Russianness seethes with frustration—one shared by many intellectuals of the 1990s—at the loss of an old identity and the necessity of pursuing a new one. But it also contains a deliberate reference to *Vekhi* (*Landmarks*),[22] an anthology of essays in which Russian intellectuals of the early twentieth century deliberated on similar questions (*Vekhi* 1994).

Pavlovsky was among the first to grasp the potential of the internet as a means of mass communication. His experience of the dissident and *samizdat* worlds, in which the idea of unrestricted publication played a role of supreme importance, may have been conducive to such a realization. Yet its primary catalyst undoubtedly came on the cusp of the 1980s and 1990s, during which period Pavlovsky served as the director of the Civil Society program of Soros's Cultural Initiative Foundation and was involved in the development of Russian social networks, both offline and on the internet.

In 1995, Pavlovsky inaugurated the Foundation for Effective Politics (FEP), under whose aegis he and his co-authors and fellow political technologists provided informational support to election campaigns. In 1995, the FEP entered into a collaboration with the Congress of Russian Communities,[23] but the two most high-profile campaigns to feature its involvement would take place the following year, when Yeltsin managed to remain in power despite facing an acute loss of confidence among the electorate, and in 2000, when Vladimir Putin assumed the presidency. From 1998 to 2011, Pavlovsky served as an adviser to the head of the Russian Presidential Administration, doing so on a voluntary, nonsalaried basis, yet taking regular part in administration meetings at the Kremlin. Thanks to the successes political technology enjoyed throughout the 1990s, the word *polittekhnologiya* rose to popularity in the post-Soviet Russian language, while Pavlovsky became known as the discipline's "father." (It is worth noting that an important role in the emergence of the discipline was played by Yeltsin's American consultants. Invited to assist in his 1996 election campaign, they imported American-style political PR across the Atlantic. It was the creative reworking, by Pavlovsky and his colleagues, of various American methods that became known as "political technology"—a distinctively Russian form of campaigning predicated on leaks, *kompromat,* and other types of informational manipulation) (Wilson 2005; Krastev 2006).[24]

In 1997, the Russian Institute launched the *Russian Journal*, an online publication which carried analytical essays, book reviews, and articles where methodologists/political technologists discussed the nature of the new Russia and sketched out initiatives in support of the Russian language and culture (it was there, in the late 1990s, that Ostrovsky, Shchedrovitsky, and their associates published a series of pieces exploring the notion of the "Russian world"). The *Russian Journal* didn't function solely as a mouthpiece for political technologists, however—it was, if anything, a hobby pursuit for Pavlovsky, who, in the words of Ivan Davydov, the former head of the FEP's online initiatives department, "had always dreamed of being the editor-in-chief of a magazine" (Interview, Moscow, 27.10.2016). The FEP's principal online endeavors, meanwhile, involved political assignments: launching personal web pages for politicians, building sites with election-related content, or inaugurating entire new online media outfits. These included *Smi.ru* (a media review site); *Litera.ru* (a site designed to become the "literary gateway" to the internet (Litera.ru 1998)); *Lenta.ru*, *Gazeta.ru*, and *Vesti.ru* (a trio of news sites); *vvp.ru*, as in Vladimir Vladmirovich Putin (a site created specifically to host content around the presidential elections); *Kreml.org* (a "political expert network"); and *Strana.ru* (which became renowned for its semi-official interpretations of political events).

While some of these projects were directly commissioned by politicians and political movements, others were created as independent entities, and still others feigned independence even as they fulfilled political assignments. In his book *Reconstruction of Russia: Mass Media and Politics in the Russia of the Nineties* Ivan Zasursky wrote:

> Given the intensity of political intrigue in Russia during the 1990s, it is unsurprising that political technologists were among the first to grasp the possibilities offered by the Internet. The Internet proved a useful weapon for political consultants involved in the information wars—information could be anonymously published online and then cited as a source. The upshot of this was a spread of questionable, inaccurate and illegally obtained data, propelled to general awareness thanks to publications in the press. (Zasursky 2016)

The political leverage that Pavlovsky brought to the internet meant an influx of money, and the subsequent professionalization of the Russian internet—that is, the gradual transformation of leisure, entertainment, and volunteering into a source of regular earnings. In the 1990s, the Russian internet was too small to assume that online literature, news sites, and political initiatives could coexist, independently of one another, within its confines. Distinct online initiatives were often masterminded by the same people, whether erstwhile USENETters or writers of "amateur literature" who had found positions at the *Russian Journal* before migrating to other FEP projects.

Now they found opportunities to write for money, kick-starting an era of professional online journalism and gradually transforming the internet from a marginal medium into a mainstream one.

From the time when telepathy experiments were still part of cybernetics and considered a promising field of future science to the triumph of network-based political technologies, only a couple of decades had passed. The leftist utopia of global human interconnectedness gave way to the right-wing concept of an exclusively "Russian" internet, cybernetics lost all its authority, amateurs became professionals, and only literature remained a cult pursuit among Russian users for some time. However, it now served the powerful post-Soviet ressentiment.

In Lieu of Conclusion

Piotr Voronov, the protagonist of Pavel Dmitriev's historical fantasy *It's Not Too Late*, lives in 2010 and owns a small company that installs computer networks. One day, returning from a client in a car, he gets into an accident and, recovering, finds himself in 1965. That is, at the very time when cybernetics was at its climax, dozens of Soviet research institutes were designing computers, and Glushkov was promoting the idea of an all-union digital network. Possessing information from the future, Voronov sets an ambitious goal to change the country's history: to develop computer technology, build a Soviet computer network, and thus not only save Soviet industry from lagging behind the United States but also to "prevent the collapse of the USSR" in general:

> We need a "big leap" in digital technology. The rationale seems simple. All the progress of the next fifty years of humanity's development as a civilization has, in fact, digital technology at its core . . . How many digital electronic devices do I use every day, not counting my laptop and cell phone? TV, VCR, microwave, air conditioner, clock, refrigerator, electric stove, security alarm, elevator. Even a doorbell with a dozen tunes didn't come without a processor and memory. (Dmitriev 2012–2015)

To avoid the "mistakes" obvious to the protagonist, causing the world to use American technology and the internet, Voronov meets Glushkov and tries to convince him to redesign the OGAS project. Years of his efforts do not lead to the Soviet internet. Nonetheless, Voronov accomplishes his main task: the USSR manages to avoid collapse. Chinese-style socialism emerges in the country, as the novel's author describes it: business is allowed, and flourishes, but the Soviet Union retains its territories and superpower status.

Dmitriev's novel belongs to the historical fiction genre about *popadanets* (the protagonist—*popadaet*—ends up in another time period), popular in Russia in the 2000s and 2010s. It originated on literary websites and self-publishing platforms and existed exclusively online until major Russian publishers noticed its phenomenal popularity. Over twenty years, several dozen novels about *popadanets* were published, with circulation ranging from 3,500 to 6,000 copies (Galina 2019, 55). One of the book series was entitled "*Imperial science fiction*."

Fantasy fiction novels about *popadanets* have in common not only traveling into the past, but also the conservative political program that determines the mission of the protagonist. This post-traumatic literature, as a rule, describes such a past, in which the most painful "historical mistakes" for the author and his audience are corrected: the USSR does not collapse but becomes a world leader.

Two novels written a hundred years apart, Bogdanov's *Red Star* and Dmitriev's *It's Not Too Late*, can be considered the extremes of Soviet science utopia. They present essentially the same concept: socialism armed with network technologies that guarantee the system's stability. Only in the first case, we have an alternative future, as Bogdanov's novel is considered one of the last classic utopias, and the Dmitriev's book tells a story about an alternative past. Between them lies the history of Soviet modernity, from the radical revolutionary techno-utopias reactivated by the scientific and technical revolution in the 1960s to the successful attempts to hack the Iron Curtain, and finally to the traumatic integration of post-Soviet Russia into the global world.

Mikhail Suslov, a researcher of contemporary Russian fiction, considers books about *popadanets* to be conservative utopianism and notes that the revanchist agenda is juxtaposed with "quasi-post-colonial sensibility" and "feelings of disempowerment" in them (Suslov 2016). This combination, due to the collapse of the USSR and the end of the Cold War, was characteristic of that part of the former Soviet citizenry who experienced the loss of their high professional status. Among them were many scientists and engineers who had experienced a dramatic change in their status in the 1990s. At that time, the United States remained the only pole of the world, and huge flows of American products, music, movies, lifestyle, and money, as investment or charity, poured into Russia. The return flow consisted of emigrants, often highly skilled professionals, former employees of research institutes. From the point of view of those who remained, the confrontation between the two superpowers ended in defeat and Russia's humiliating status. That is why Dmitriev's *popadanets* is trying to convince the country's leadership to create the internet, preventing America's victory in the Cold War.

"The *Lost Chance Theory*" is the name given by Roman Abramov, a researcher of the history of Soviet technology, to a popular judgment about the reasons for the collapse of the Soviet system:

> "According to this theory, a few bad strategic decisions were made in the second half of the 1960s, which were fatal to the country's computer industry: it wasn't possible to upgrade the industrial control and production systems, to become a post-industrial society and move to the knowledge economy." This refers to the decision to copy IBM-360 instead of developing Soviet models and the refusal to implement the OGAS project. (Abramov 2017, 64)

The Soviet network projects are still regarded by observers and involved parties as a potential internet that did not take place due to organizational, political, or economic reasons. According to this approach, if cybernetics had provided the Soviet Union with the internet, it would have "won" the Cold War, which meant that it would become a world monopoly. The authors of an article about the history of Soviet computer development quote the words of Boris Babayan, a corresponding member of the Russian Academy of Sciences, in a section entitled "Betrayal":

> I think this was a crucial stage in the evolution of domestic computing technologies. Creative groupings were all broken up, viable projects were shut down and the decision was made to shoehorn everyone into the same "box." From that moment on, everyone had to ape American hardware. . . . After everyone had been forced into a single box, people's creativity dried up. In a manner of speaking, the work was so utterly uncreative that their brains began to wither away. (Sosnovskii and Orlov 2011)

Anatoly Morozov, a member of Glushkov's team, in an interview with the Ukrainian newspaper *Fakty* (*Facts*), speaks directly about the project of an All-Union network as a lost chance for geopolitical superiority:

> If the country's leadership had supported the project back then, we would have avoided the problems that led to the collapse of the economy, and subsequently that of the Soviet Union as well. (Lisnichenko 2011)

What imaginary future exists today? Belief in advanced science that will sooner or later solve most of humanity's problems still drives visionaries, their startups and million-dollar budgets. Only now that the Soviet project is over, the imagined future is left only at one of the two former Cold War poles: Silicon Valley. In fact, this Silicon Valley vision differs little from the techno-utopias of the Soviet cyberneticians: it is about the complete merging of virtual and actual realities, about the synthesis of man and computer—up to and including digital immortality—only now it is called the "technological singularity." One of the iconic futurologists Ray Kurzweil, who was in charge of machine learning and computational linguistics at Google, estimated in his latest book that it will come by 2045 (Kurzweil 2024).

Meanwhile, Russia, at least, in its official narrative, continues to live in a "glorious past" rather than aspiring to a bright future. Advanced technologies in the Russian imaginary have been replaced by pseudo-traditional practices like shamanism. The Iron Curtain has been replaced by the concept of a "sovereign internet." Although the staging of the USSR of the past can never lead to the construction of the exact same USSR, there are some similarities. Just like in the early 1970s, when the internet was small and all its routes could be counted on one's fingers, today there are only a few external traffic exchange hubs and all of them have been put under control by the Russian authorities (Russia 2020, Wilde and Sherman 2022). In the end, what the participants of the first online contacts of the late 1980s did not see in their worst nightmares happened: instead of a cold war, Russia unleashed the most ordinary one.

Despite the temptation to ascribe culpability to internet enthusiasts—post-Soviet Russian philosophers and writers, authors of the Russian World ideology and of the historical fantasy about *popadantsy*—for the current catastrophe, which is the war that Russia is waging in Ukraine, we have to admit that other people are now giving orders and doing the killing. And that the Russian internet in these terms is merely a particular reflection of the history of post-Soviet society. Nevertheless, the historical connection between the attempts to rebuild the power lost during the collapse of the USSR and the current reality cannot be ignored. From the perspective of media archaeology, this can be conceptualized as a return of materiality, which was previously negated by the internet as an electronic medium. Furthermore, the impact is exponentially greater: rather than the distribution of a book or a printed document, the concept of "great culture" is now embodied by murder and robbery carried out by marauding troops. Once, the boundless potential of the internet, celebrated by Russian-speaking users, became the foundation for the concept of the Russian world. Then the internet became too small for the Russian world: it wanted real territories.

ACKNOWLEDGMENTS

This book was made possible primarily thanks to the German Research Foundation (DFG) who supported the research project *Andersdenken digital*, dedicated to the history of Russian internet and conducted in 2015–2018 at the Free University of Berlin (grant SCHM 2378 / 5-1). I would like to express my deepest gratitude to Henrike Schmidt for inviting me to join the project and for her unwavering trust in me as a researcher.

I would like to extend special thanks to the first-generation Russian-speaking internet users who generously shared their experiences, impressions, and reflections from thirty years ago in interviews with me.

I sincerely and with deep respect thank the reviewers, and especially Reader A, who has remained anonymous to me, for their enormous effort in analyzing and critiquing the initial manuscript, which truly helped to improve it. I am also deeply thankful to Igor Reichlin, for his moral support and valuable comments on the English version of the book.

I am fortunate to have scholars of Russian and Soviet history among my friends, to whom I want to express my immense gratitude for their invaluable advice and willingness to discuss my research: Kirill Ospovat, Zinaida Vasilieva, Polina Kolozaridi, and Leonid Yuldashev.

To my crazy and wonderful family, I want to say thank you for being with me all these years and for patiently listening to my stories.

NOTES

Chapter 1. Soviet Power Plus the Digitalization of the Entire Country

1. The Soviet concepts of immortality and, in particular, Vassily Kuprevich's works, are examined in Anya Bernstein's *The Future of Immortality: Remaking Life and Death in Contemporary Russia* (Bernstein 2019).

2. Boris Malinovskij's book was the first study on the history of Soviet computers. Its author, a computer designer in Kiev, collected a great deal of evidence from participants in various Soviet projects. Many of these memoirs cannot be verified. The story about the BBC radio was told to Malinovskij by Bashir Rameev himself. Slava Gerovitch, a researcher of the history of Soviet computers and cybernetics, lists other possible sources of this information: a special double issue of the journal *Advances in Mathematical Sciences* published in 1946 was devoted to "mathematical machinery"; or it could be information collected by intelligence services that conducted industrial espionage—one of the chief priorities of Soviet foreign intelligence (Gerovitch 2001). One way or the other, the first computer project would eventually be initiated by Rameev.

3. The only original Soviet project was the computer *Setun'*, built in 1959 in the design bureau at the Moscow State University. *Setun'* was based not on binary but on ternary logic designed by the Lwów–Warsaw School in 1917. However, *Setun'* did not change the world's computer industry, which still builds computers based on binary logic.

4. The idea of cashless payment itself was not original: as early as 1871, the American company Western Union introduced a system of payment by telegraph (Standage 2007). However, Glushkov's concept of electronic payments was part of his grand utopia of electronic socialism, followed logically by communism. Unlike American companies that introduced electronic payments to stimulate purchases, Glushkov created his system with the idea of doing away with money altogether. At least when his version of electronic socialism is replaced by communism . . .

5. Igor Poletaev was a prominent cyberneticist, author of one of the first books on cybernetics in Russian (Poletaev 1958). Moreover, he was the one who sparked a major discussion about "physicists" and "lyricists" (*fiziki* and *liriki*) in the pages of the *Literaturnaya Gazeta* in 1960 (Bogdanov 2011). Poletaev's son mentioned Malinovsky Jr. as a frequent guest at their parents' house (Poletaev 1998).

6. In Bogdanov's *Red Star*, the Martians carry out blood transfusions to rejuvenate themselves: "You know that in order to increase the viability of cells or organisms, nature constantly supplements one individual with another. Thus, when the vitality of unicellular beings is impaired by a lack of variation in the environment, they fuse together, two becoming one; this is the only way they have of recovering the 'immortality' of their protoplasm. . . . We go even further and perform mutual blood transfusions between human beings, whereby each individual receives from the other a number of elements which can raise his life expectancy" (Bogdanov 1984, 85). The startup Ambrosia, for instance, touts "young blood" rejuvenation treatments, echoing the century-old ideas of Alexander Bogdanov (Ambrosia Plasma 2020). According to Bernstein, though, startups, by transfusing the blood of the young to the old for money in the spirit of vampiric capitalism, have perverted Bogdanov's central idea that positive effects should accrue to both young and old alike (Bernstein 2019, 78). Nevertheless, Bogdanov's theory is still remembered today—for example, his theory of "physiological collectivism" became relevant in connection with the pandemic of COVID-19, as it was found that the blood serum of people who had been infected with the virus eases the disease course (Helbing 2021).

7. Lenin formulated his criticism of Alexander Bogdanov and other proponents of Ernst Mach's philosophy of physics in his 1908 article "Materialism and Empiriocriticism" (Lenin 1977).

8. In articles published in the late 1920s Bogdanov describes not only the technology and organization of blood transfusion, but also its ideological and symbolic significance—the "physiological collectivism" that awaits society if all its members "overcome individualism" and exchange blood (Bogdanov 2003, Krementsov 2011). Bogdanov's ideas are often regarded as an extension of the early twentieth century's neo-religious movements (Polianski 2012). And yet the research carried out at Moscow's Institute of Blood Transfusion, founded by Bogdanov in 1926 (and known today as the National Haematology Research Centre), served to bring blood transfusion firmly into the sphere of modern medicine, so that it came to be seen as no less scientific a process than hypnosis, once regarded as the province of stage magicians. In 1932, after Bogdanov's death from an unsuccessful blood transfusion, the All-Union Institute of Experimental Medicine was founded on the initiative of Gorky who, according to philosopher and writer Mikhail Agurskii, hoped that it would bring closer the moment of the victory of science over nature, and thus make immortality possible (Agurskii 1991). For more on immortality at the turn of the nineteenth and twentieth centuries and in today's Russia, see Bernstein, 2019.

9. In this interview, as well as in Gennadii Maksimovich's book "Conversations with Academician V. Glushkov," released three years later, Glushkov mentions the ACS "Lvov," installed in the late 1960s at the Lvov television factory: "I remember a case that happened back in 1967. I was reporting to the State Committee for Science and Technology on the results of our work. In the meeting room, there was a teleprinter installed, and I suggested to those present to ask the 'Lvov' system via it what was happening at the factory. I remember a question being asked: 'How are things in the third assembly workshop?'—'It is now 11:27 Lvov time,' immediately responded the computer. 'According to the plan, 117 televisions were supposed to be produced on the assembly line by this time. The actual output is 112. To meet the schedule, it is necessary to increase the number of operators at the second workstation from two to three'" (Maksimovich 1978, 64). The only significant difference between the real ACS "Lvov" and the fictional Martian system of computing centers created by Bogdanov 60 years earlier lies in the presence of planning. Bogdanov's system determined its needs on its own and did not require managerial intervention from a Martian. Glushkov's system monitored the execution of a plan previously entered into the system by a human.

10. The idea of expanding the possibilities of the human body with the help of cybernetics was not specific to Soviet scientists. Wiener, the first cyberneticist ever, wrote about the possibility of "traveling by telegraph along with train and airplane travel" and considered the problem of moving the body by electronic means to be temporary and technically solvable (Wiener 1954, 103–4).

Chapter 2. The Technology of the Future Is Telepathy

1. Like other Soviet cyberneticists, Poletayev was inspired by Wiener's book (1948), which was given to him by Bruk (Fet 2004).

2. In the 1910s and 1920s, Vladimir Bekhterev attended telepathy sessions on a regular basis as he was interested in the activities of psychics and telepaths (Bekhterev 2014). This topic did not belong exclusively to Russian science but was relevant to the European neuroscientists and psychologists in the 1920s. Around the same time, Sigmund Freud was also looking at the issue of telepathy. He called it "a kind of psychical counterpart to wireless telegraphy" and assumed that during the telepathic process two people have the same psychic act. According to Freud, the signal may be transmitted by some unidentified physical process (Freud [1922] 1964, 36; Halliday 2007).

3. Igor Mirzalis, one of the Soviet parapsychologists and author of a historical review of world parapsychology, believes that the electromagnetic hypothesis of telepathy was born as early as 1892, when it was expressed by three scientists independently of each other: E. Houston, E. Thomson, and W. Crooks (Plekhanov 2004).

4. There is a theory that Vasiliev continued his research after 1938, but it was classified and supervised by the NKVD and NarKomOborony (People's Commissar of Defense), but it is impossible to verify this, given that the archives of the special services are inaccessible (Rubel et al. 2016, Pervushin 1999, 115, Shalamov 2004).

5. Raphael Kherumian (1903–1983) was a Baku-born artist who emigrated to Paris in 1931. An aficionado of parapsychology, Kherumian worked at the Institut Métapsychique International (IMI). The work of the Institute for the Study of Telepathy served as a blueprint for the American remote viewing research program of the 1960s (Varvoglis and Evrard 2010).

6. In an interview with Martin Ebon, Messadie suggested that "intelligence" about the *Nautilus* was supplied to the editorial team by Jacques Bergier, a regular contributor to the magazine and consultant to the French special services. Born in Odessa, Bergier had played an active role in the French Resistance, been tortured by the Gestapo and spent time at a concentration camp; he died in 1978, shortly before Ebon began his investigation. The declassified CIA documents describe the story of *Nautilus* as a hoax, but the source of information is not specified (CIA 1971).

7. In 1928, the journal *Planovoe khoziaistvo* (Planned Agriculture) published an article by Kazhinsky in which he proposed to solve the drought problem by using electroscopes invented by California engineer William Haight (Kazhinsky 1928). These devices, mounted on 40-meter-tall towers, condensed atmospheric humidity and artificially induced precipitation. According to Kazhinsky's idea, the spread of electroscopes would make it possible to avoid famine in the driest years and "to successfully solve the question of weather management in the broadest state understanding of the meaning of this word."

8. In 1924, Andrei Platonov, as head of agricultural electrification at the Voronezh Governate's Agricultural Department (Gubzemotdel), wrote to the Narkomzem about the resources he needed to continue his work. In particular, he mentioned a tractor, which Voronezh Governorate could not afford to buy. Bernard Kazhinsky, in his position as a specialist for electrification and mechanization of agriculture at the Narkomzem, was in charge of office work, so he first forwarded Platonov's request for a tractor to other services, and next, answered him personally. "Perhaps Platonov had some knowledge of Kazhinsky's ideas when he tried to develop his 'electromagnetic transformer-resonator,' depicted later in the story *The Ether Channel*," write the authors of the commentary edited by Natalia Kornienko (Platonov 2016, 96).

9. According to American intelligence services, who closely watched the progress of Soviet parapsychology, by 1968 there were at least 27 laboratories and institutes in the USSR that specialized in the study of telepathy. Among them, for example, was the Department of Technical Parapsychology at the All-Union Correspondence Engineering Institute; the Section of Technical Parapsychology and Biointroscopy at the Central Board of the Scientific and Technical Society (NTO) of the machine-building industry; laboratories and departments at the Institute of Radio Engineering and Electronics of the USSR Academy of Sciences, at the Institute of Automation and Electrometry of the Siberian Branch of the USSR Academy of Sciences. Among others, an important place on the map of Soviet parapsychology was the Kazakhstan State University in Alma-Ata (present day Almaty), where the biophysicist Victor Inyushin conducted experiments with telepathy and later became the author of the scandalous

"water memory" theory (Van Dyke and Juncosa 1973; *Parapsychology in the USSR* n.d.). According to the authors of the book *Psi-voiny. Zapad i Vostok* (Psi-Wars: East and West), the Institute for Problems of Information Transmission at the USSR Academy of Sciences, "along with cybernetics, computer science, and the development of electronic communication technologies . . . almost from the very beginning opened a direction for the study of information processes in living systems and bioinformatics" (Rubel et al. 2016, 98).

10. According to Andrew Pickering's study, many British cyberneticists came to the new discipline from neurobiology and psychiatry. Perhaps this is why the application of cybernetic methods to physiology was particularly important to them (Pickering 2010, 5). For example, the topic of telepathy was put on the agenda of a Ratio Club meeting in 1951 by John Bates, one of the club's founders (Husbands and Holland 2008, 116; Dewhurst 2018).

11. The article by Sobolev, Kitov, and Lyapunov contained a reference to Gulyaev's article: "It has been established (see Gulyaev 1955) that the processes occurring in closed feedback circuits of living organisms are amenable to mathematical description and by their characteristics approach the processes occurring in complex nonlinear systems of automatic regulation of mechanical devices" (Sobolev et al. 1955, 4; Gulyaev 1955, 7).

12. Information about Kazhinsky's work for Glushkov can be found in a 1973 CIA report (CIA 1973) and in an article by journalist Sergei Krivenkov (Krivenkov 2016). According to other sources, Kazhinsky lived in Moscow until his death in 1962 (Plyusch 1979).

13. Because of disputes within the cybernetics community, the departmental affiliation of the biocybernetics group changed: in 1959 it was a group at the Institute of Mathematics of the Ukrainian SSR Academy of Sciences, in 1961 it was transferred as a department to the Computing Center of the Ukrainian SSR Academy of Sciences, which in the same year, through Glushkov's efforts, became the Institute of Cybernetics.

14. Among others, mathematician and rocket control specialist Evgeny Zolotov (Tver) developed theoretical foundations of telepathy in the field of cybernetics; physiologist, head of the Section of Technical Parapsychology and Biointroscopy at the Central Board of the Scientific and Technical Society of Machine-Making Industry Gennady Sergeev (Leningrad), trying to reproduce the *Nautilus* experiment, built devices capable of detecting a telepathic signal under the water; astrophysicist Nikolai Kozyrev (Pulkovo) created a model of telepathy based on concept of time; head of the Bionics Department of the Institute of Automatics and Telemetry of the Siberian Branch of the USSR Academy of Sciences Perov (Novosibirsk) experimented on rabbits with "communication between sensorially disconnected bioobjects"; physicists Yuri Gulyaev (namesake of Pavel Gulyaev), Eduard Godik, and Yuri Kobzarev (Moscow) studied skin vision and telekinesis; Gennady Plekhanov, head of the bionics laboratory at the Siberian Institute of Physics and Technology at Tomsk State University, studied "direct transmission of information in ants," etc. (Perov 1984, 362; Plekhanov 2004; Kernbach 2013).

Chapter 3. Telepathy—Spacebridge—Internet

1. Murphy conducted transatlantic telepathy experiments with French parapsychologist René Warcollier, director of the International Metaphysical Institute in Paris and a close colleague of Raphael Heroumian—the same one who in 1958 sent a publication about the *Nautilus* submarine experiment to Leonid Vasiliev (see chapter 2).

2. The cooperation of parapsychologists with intelligence services and the military in both the USSR and the United States has its own history. It was because of the commissions by the military and intelligence services that computer science as well as psychology, anthropology, and linguistics were developed during World War II and the first postwar years. At the very beginning of the Cold War, from 1948 to 1950, Margaret Mead studied Russian culture and Russian attitudes toward power on behalf of the RAND Corporation, a private research organization founded by the U.S. Air Force. Her husband Gregory Bateson, an anthropologist and a cybernetics and parapsychology enthusiast, worked on "black propaganda" during World War II, when the social sciences and humanities in America were heavily commissioned by the military and intelligence agencies (Cooper 1947; Price 1998). The CIA's collaboration with Harold Puthoff in the 1970s was a natural continuation of the interaction between science and intelligence agencies, not a qualitatively new stage.

3. In February 2019, the Russian Defense Ministry's magazine *Army Collection* published an article about a training program for "combat telepaths" who can not only read minds at a distance but can also recognize the contents of computers and documents stored in safes (Poroskov 2019).

4. Although Huxley did not speak publicly about psychics or telepathy, his interest in parapsychology and his influence on the development of the discipline were enormous. In the early 1950s, he and his wife organized Tuesday meetings at their home where they conducted hypnosis experiments and discussed paranormal phenomena. As researcher Jake Poller writes, in the mid-1950s, Huxley traveled to visit the famous parapsychologist Andrija Puharich, who conducted experiments with telepaths and clairvoyants. Later, one of the subjects claimed that Huxley also had telepathic abilities. Huxley wrote nothing about telepathy and admitted only to practicing hypnosis (Poller 2019, 83).

5. Karl Nikolayev is the stage name of Karl Nikolayevich Gurvich.

6. According to Lyubov Plekhanova, a former employee of the Institute of Chemical Physics of the USSR Academy of Sciences, Karl Nikolaev was the adoptive father of her colleague Boris Sviridov. In the 1970s, Nikolaev often came to the institute, doing informal demonstrations and lectures on telepathy, and spoke about his biography (Interview, WhatsApp, May 25, 2021).

7. The novel's protagonist, one Darwin Fall, is a researcher of "supernormal powers," paralleling Murphy himself. Fall realizes he's being pursued—and discovers a secret network comprised of scientists, spies, and double agents. Their objective? To put the forces of the occult at the service of history. While on a trip to the USSR, Fall strikes up a friendship with KGB agent Vladimir Kirov, who, like the real-life Karl

Nikolayev, is preoccupied with telepathy and devotes more thought to spiritual transcendence than to his work assignments. Though he gave hundreds of interviews about his travels across the USSR, Michael Murphy never did reveal exactly which elements of the book were fact and which fiction.

8. In the title of this symposium the word "unconscious" had to be replaced by "unconscious psychic activity" due to the disapproval by the party authorities, although the word remained in the four-volume collection of the symposium papers (*Bessoznatel'noe* 1978–1989).

9. Roman Jakobson, Vyacheslav Ivanov, Louis Althusser, Natalia Avtonomova, and others.

10. It is a curious coincidence that the initiator of Djuna's career as a healer of high officials was Nikolai Baibakov, a close associate of Alexei Kosygin and, since 1965, chairman of the Gosplan. In other words, an institution that, according to Glushkov's concept, at that very time was to move to full automation thanks to computer networks (see chapter 2). According to Djuna, after she successfully cured his wife, Baibakov allocated two million dollars from the Gosplan budget for research conducted by the Institute of Radio Engineering and Electronics (Djuna 2015). Of course, there is no deep connection between telepathy and the internet in this fact: it is just that the idea of unknown human potential excited everyone at that time, even active figures of the planned economy.

11. Russell Targ's memoirs mentioned a telepathy session with Djuna, Iosif Goldin, and the Murphys' assistant Anna Kuchev in Moscow in 1984, which Targ said was successful (Targ and Harary, 1984). In the 2000s, Djuna switched from a scientific discourse to an occult one, she began to mention the Assyrian origin of her father and even proclaimed herself an Assyrian queen (Savitskaia 2015). However, in the 1970s and 1980s, her activities remained within the framework of medicine, albeit alternative.

12. Georgi Lozanov was a Bulgarian educator and psychologist who developed in the 1960s the method of suggestion for accelerated language learning. In 1966, under the patronage of Ludmila Zhivkova (daughter of the General Secretary of the Central Committee of the Bulgarian Communist Party), Lozanov founded the Institute of Suggestology, which became famous for its research on the phenomenon of Vanga.

13. In the 1970s and 1980s, many Americans (Jim Hickman estimated them as thousands of people) traveled to the USSR as private visitors to establish contacts with Soviet people. Many members of the first wave of "citizen diplomats" were associated with the Esalen Institute or with the Murphys' circles (Robert Fuller, former provost of Oberlin College and cofounder of *Internews*, Werner Ehrhardt, Fuller's coauthor of *The Hunger Project* and author of popular personal growth seminars and others) (Malcomson 2017; Wagner et al. 1987).

14. The topic of an athlete's reserve (or "ultimate") capabilities brought together physiologists, psychologists, and parapsychologists, providing a natural scientific refuge for those interested in the problem of human potential from a New Age perspective (*Problemy* 1982; Polotsk 1980; Kuznetsov 1979).

15. Since the early 1990s, *Internews* has switched to support of independent television in Russia, and over the course of 20 years has educated and trained staff for many city and regional television companies. Almost all of them were closed or reorganized in the 2010s.

16. Academicians Velikhov and Rauschenbach were on good terms with Goldin; their acquaintance probably dates back to the late 1970s, when the Commission was established. With the help of the academicians, Goldin repeatedly managed to get out of the psychiatric hospital, where he was placed for lack of permanent employment or, as it was called in the Soviet Criminal Code, "idleness." According to Sol Shulman's recollections, Goldin's last diagnosis was: "Obsession with connecting America and Russia via space bridges" (Shulman 2017).

17. Esalen's activities, including the Soviet-American Exchange Program and Joel Schatz's projects, along with the Rockefellers and Soros, were supported by Henry Dakin, an engineer by training, the heir to a toy factory, and a philanthropist. He was interested in parapsychology and conducted experiments himself, and also financed the activities of parapsychologists and civilian diplomats who traveled from the United States to the USSR.

18. Soros disbanded the Cultural Initiative Foundation and founded the Open Society Institute and the International Science Foundation (ISF). In 1993, the ISF financed the construction of the first phase of Moscow's fiber-optic backbone network, and in 1996, the Open Society Institute announced a program for the internetization of universities, which ended in 2001 and brought the internet to 33 universities across Russia.

19. SovAm Teleport, a commercial company, has a complicated history. It was founded in 1990 as a joint venture between San-Francisco Moscow Teleport (SFMT) and VNIIPAS. It provided access to financial and information systems (S.W.I.F.T, MICEX, Reuters, Western Union), databases, corporate network resources, backup systems, etc. In 1992 the British company Cable & Wireless became the third owner of SovAm Teleport. In 1993 SFMT changed its name to GTS (Global TeleSystems). In 1996 GTS became the sole owner of SovAm Teleport and founded a new company, Golden Telecom. After the 1998 crisis, GTS concentrated on European projects and merged all its subsidiaries in the former USSR into one Golden Telecom. In 1999, Golden Telecom bought the internet service provider Glasnet, which by that time had become a commercial company. In 2001, Golden Telecom declared bankruptcy, but existed until the late 2000s, when it was absorbed by Vimpel-Communications.

Chapter 4. User Revolution

1. In *Cyberpunk: Outlaws and Hackers on the Computer Frontier*, Katie Hafner and John Markoff point out that the word *hacker* acquired the meaning of "computer pirate" only after it was appropriated by a new generation in the 1980s (Hafner and Markoff, 1985).

2. The number became symbolic and came to feature in the names of Usenet newsgroups 15–20 years later, when a new generation of hackers subscribed to the network.

3. 18 U.S. Code § 1343—Fraud by wire, radio, or television. This law, which had existed since the late nineteenth century, initially covered only fraud committed using the US Postal Service. In 1952, it was amended to cover wire telecommunications, and eventually came to encompass cybercrime as well, before the anti-hacker Computer Fraud and Abuse Act (CFAA) was enacted in 1986.

4. Because Draper continued producing the blue boxes, and even hoped to make money from them, he was arrested again five years later. Agreeing to cooperate with the FBI, the hacker spent four months in prison, gave up phreaking on his release—and became a computer engineer at Apple. Apple co-founder Steve Wozniak, a fan of Draper's since the days of the *Esquire* splash, had even spent some time selling "blue boxes" on the Berkeley campus. It was Wozniak who drafted Draper into Apple to develop the Charley Board, a forerunner of the modern modem.

5. The interview took place in 1992 but was not published until 2003.

6. In the late 1980s, the Komsomol was rapidly commercialized and often served as an official cover for all sorts of initiatives, whether business-related or otherwise. Following the adoption in 1988 of a Council of Ministers decree entitled "On the facilitation of the commercial activities of the Komsomol," Komsomol business became virtually the principal province of young functionaries. What was nonmainstream and dangerous at the beginning of the decade—and carried a potential prison sentence—became the norm in its closing years.

7. Similarly, one of the most important rules of netiquette in early networks and chats (Usenet, Fido, IRC) was not to post overly lengthy messages that would produce expensive traffic or block mailboxes (Hambridge 1995, Sternberg 2000).

8. Articles about selected cases of "radio hooliganism" were regularly published in the 1970s and early 1980s in *Radio* monthly magazine (Kazanskij 1971, Afon'kin 1973, Tagunov 1976).

9. Radio Mayak was just one component in an extensive cable radio project involving the installation of *radiotochkas* in all Soviet apartments, industrial facilities and institutions. The project was successfully completed by the end of the 1980s.

10. In October 1988, Gene Spafford from the Department of Computer Science at Purdue University posted statistics on the Usenet. According to her estimates, "well over 1 million articles have been posted to the Usenet since its origination in 1979" (Spafford, Usenet, 1988).

11. Initially, ARPANET represented an unattainable ideal for Usenet's creators—as a classified government project, the former commanded vast funding and had been developed by the country's finest minds. Since ARPANET was a closed, military-owned network, the programmers behind Usenet had little understanding of how it worked. In particular, they were convinced that it was a political project, and that it would cost $100,000 to join—hence their initial framing of Usenet as "a poor man's ARPANET" (Hauben and Hauben 1997).

12. In the USSR, the first FidoNet node appeared in 1990 in Novosibirsk. Within a few months, new nodes appeared in Novosibirsk and Chelyabinsk and the Russian (at that time—still RSFSR) domain zone R50 was registered (*Asia Patrysheva* 2019).

13. It is difficult to claim that one hundred percent of post-Soviet FidoNet nodes were located on employer-paid phone lines, since it is impossible to collect information on all nodes. However, from the existing memoirs and interviews I have conducted, the opposite is not yet known.

14. "Academic day" in Soviet research institutes was a present day for its scientific staff. That is, in this case, the one day of the week when the staff of the Presidium of the USSR Academy of Sciences had to come to the office.

15. The novel was published in 1969, when the first version of the ARPANET network was launched, linking two California universities, the Stanford Research Institute and the University of Utah. Dick, who also lived in California, was unaware of the military developments, but he managed to anticipate, if not establish, the ideas that fascinated the generation of "electronic hippies" and cyberpunks that followed him.

16. Unlike Philip K. Dick, William Gibson was already aware of the existence of computer networks, although he claimed not to have used them. Nevertheless, he described a future virtual reality and a computerized reconstruction of human consciousness, coining the terms "cyberspace," "matrix," and "construct."

17. The social sciences have a plethora of terms to designate the processes that unfolded over the course of the 1980s: "second modernity," "postmodernity," "networked society," "globalization," etc. (Beck 1992, 2006; Castells 2000; Giddens 1990). Of particular concern for us here are two issues. The first is the specific thrust of these metamorphoses—namely, a growing societal need for interactivity, which encompassed people's relations with the authorities and transformed the role of the media. The second is the fact that similar, if not identical, processes were taking place not only across the West, in the First World, but also across the countries of the "Eastern Bloc" (Baysha 2014).

Chapter 5. The USSR is Connected to the USENET

1. The history of the club has been researched only by journalists. Some claim that it was founded with the approval of the KGB (Gershkovich et al. 2020), others that it was under the direct control of the Soviet secret services (Tofaniuk 2013).

2. In 2001, the Usenet archive was purchased from Deja News Research Service by Google and published on a Google Groups website.

3. Packet radio technology was integrated into some BBSs, with radio links replacing telephone lines.

4. As private businesses operating within the framework of the socialist system, cooperatives were consistent with Marxist ideology because they were worker-owned organizations, which precluded any "exploitation of man by man." After the enactment of a second law permitting hired labor, some *kooperatory* suddenly became very rich—a state of affairs entirely incompatible with official ideology. A case in point was Artyom Tarasov, the "first Soviet millionaire." Tarasov inaugurated the Tekhnika cooperative in 1989 and pocketed three million roubles. His deputy, whose financial returns were comparable to Tarasov's, was a member of the CPSU, and his party dues amounted to 90,000 roubles—an inconceivable sum for a Soviet person (Dodolev 2011).

5. In original: "PREDPRINQTA POPYTKA GOSUDARSTWENNOGO PEREWOROTA, OTSRANEN OT DOLVNOSTI PREZIDENT SSSR"

6. In a speech marking the three-year anniversary of Russia Day (June 12), when the parliament of the RSFSR declared its sovereignty from the Soviet Union in 1990, Yeltsin praised the "invaluable legacy of the reforms of Peter the Great, Alexander II, Pyotr Stolypin, the legacy of Russian industrialists and entrepreneurs. Ever ours," he continued, "is the free-spirited tradition of Rublev and Pushkin, Tolstoy and Solzhenitsyn; ever ours are the precepts of Academician Andrei Dmitrievich Sakharov. Russians, like other peoples, have an inherent desire for freedom, happiness, prosperity; they desire, too, to possess property, to feel a sense of ownership. We're moving toward democracy and the market precisely because this is the only way to achieve greater freedom and greater prosperity. Our existence is now undergoing a transformation. Freedom—the opportunity to work for oneself, for one's family, for one's future—is gradually gaining ground in Russia" (Den' nezavisimosti 2015).

7. The word "digerati" (from digital and literati) referred to the internet elite and "cyberintellectuals"—people who were at the origins of or have made significant contributions to the history of the internet and internet culture. There is some debate about its invention. According to one version, the word first appeared in an article by John Markoff in *The New York Times* on the future of supercomputers—the word "digerati" referred to professional users of computers and networks (Markoff 1992).

Chapter 6. The Russian Colonization of the American Internet

1. In order to propose a new newsgroup, USENETters are required to submit a formal "Request for Discussion" (RfD). Following a one-month discussion period, during which all users are entitled to put forward arguments for and against the proposal, a "Call for Votes" (CfV) is issued, and the proposal is accepted or rejected as per the vote's result.

2. When discussing new groups from the *culture* hierarchy, the groups' initiators would also advance various arguments in their favor, as required by the "request for discussion" format. Discussions of groups themed around Ukrainian and Belarusian culture featured references to the size of the country or its population: "soc.culture.ukrainian will provide a suitable forum for the discussion of Europe's second largest country" (Rekshynskyj, USENET 1993); "there are over 10 million Belarusians in the Republic of Belarus, plus an additional 3.5 million that are members of the Belarusian diaspora" (Kasaty, USENET 1996). The same argument was advanced in an RfD about the creation of a group themed around the culture of Burma: "Burma is the largest nation of southeast Asia" (Beker, USENET1993). However, they made no mention of the greatness of the national culture, its value, or influence on culture across the world. The discussions of the Ukrainian and Belarusian groups underscored the need for contacts between country and diaspora while also stressing that citizens of other nations must have the opportunity to learn more about the states in question; in the case of the Burma group, a crucial argument in favor of its creation pointed to the ban

on political debate within the country—and, consequently, to the importance of being able to conduct it online.

3. According to a report entitled "Soviet Computer Software and Applications in the 1980s," commissioned by the National Council for Soviet and East European Research, there were some 200,000 computers in the USSR by the late 1980s (Judy and Clough 1989).

4. People who had film-developing and photoprinting equipment at home would make copies of *tamizdat* texts—that is, Russian-language books published abroad; they also photographed foreign books and rare Soviet publications. Photographic *samizdat* were widespread, but books produced in this manner were rather awkward to read due to the particular quality of photo paper.

5. Which, in Verbitsky's words, included works by Alexander Galich, Bulat Okudzhava, Boris Grebenshchikov, Osip Mandelstam, and Boris Pasternak.

6. To get a sense of what range of *samizdat* texts would have been read by people of my generation and older, I conducted a survey on Facebook. Of 58 respondents, a handful mentioned political or dissident *samizdat*, but most said that they'd read *samizdat* of the literary variety alongside esoterica (Hindu mysticism, astrology, the works of Blavatskaya), collections of humor (pornographic jokes included), and works on alternative medicine (yoga, homeopathy, etc.). Lyrics by Vysotsky, Okudzhava, and Galich enjoyed particular popularity amongst my respondents, as did the poems of Brodsky, Tsvetayeva, Gumilyov, and Akhmatova, the poetry and prose of Pasternak, the novels of Bulgakov, and the science fiction of the Strugatsky brothers. My father's library, which I inherited from him, includes editions of Bulgakov's *Master and Margarita* and Pasternak's *Doctor Zhivago*, both of these bound in the workshop of the Institute of Chemical Physics of the Soviet Academy of Sciences, as well as several folders of texts—some typewritten, some photocopied, and some printed on photographic paper. Among them are essays on astrology and oriental studies (the latter predominantly concerning Indian mystical teachings), a Russian translation of the *Kama Sutra*, anonymous pornographic stories, and loose sheets brimming with jokes (humorous toasts, poems, etc.).

7. There were exceptions, however. Vladimir Pribylovsky, an active distributor of uncensored literature, "encountered a computer for the first time in [nineteen] eighty-three—and immediately harnessed it in the service of *samizdat*" (Piatkovskii 2012).

8. *The Ugly Swans* was put into production at the Molodaya Gvardiya [Young Guard] publishing house in 1968, but then removed from print and banned from publication. Hence the highly unusual form of the samizdat text—printed photographs of the galley proofs.

9. *Pneumatic post*—a system of high-speed mail delivery within a single building, usually a large factory or research institute.

10. Over the course of my research, I managed to interview only a handful of people involved in the development of the Russian internet beyond Moscow (namely in Novosibirsk, Irkutsk, and Krasnoyarsk). It may be surmised from these interviews

that large cities with academic centers had gone online by 1993–1994. That said, local content began to be produced only toward the end of the decade (ditto the emergence of local online communities). In recent years, the local history of the internet in Russia has become the focus of active study by researchers from the Internetophile Club in Moscow (Muravyov and Kolozaridi 2020, Yuldashev 2020).

11. Zhurnal'nii Zal (Magazine Reading Room) is an internet library consisting of texts from various "thick" literary magazines, which continue to be published in print form. The project became a possibility, among other reasons, owing to the absence of any copyright policy in Russia of the 1990s.

12. The *italics* are in the English original text.

13. The Russian Cyberspace website and the book *Control + Shift: Public and Private Usages of the Russian Internet* (Schmidt, Teubener, and Konradova 2007) are the fruit of a research project *Virtuelle (Wieder)Vereinigung? Mechanismen kultureller Identitätsbildung im russischsprachigen Internet* (2003–2006). ["Virtual (Re)Unification? Mechanisms of cultural identity formation in the Russian-language Internet"] (2003–2006). The website, which is no longer accessible, hosted interviews with the project's participants.

14. In 1994, in order to improve Russian-language search, colleagues, relatives, and friends of the Yandex founders embarked upon a digitization of the Bible. As Segalovich recalls, a 1990s vintage box marked "Bible: Version 1.0" was to be found in the Yandex office for a long time (Segalovich 2013). For the project's orchestrators, as representatives of the late-Soviet intelligentsia, the choice of text was motivated (their Christian sympathies aside) by its manifest "un-Sovietness." Beyond this explicitly articulated motive, the newly typed up, effectively rewritten, Yandex-indexed Bible symbolically inaugurated the history of a new world—that of the Russian internet.

15. *Literature-centrism* is a concept that has existed in Soviet literary criticism since at least the late 1960s (Dmitrieva 1967, Vorob'eva 2013). After perestroika, it was used in public debates on the "crisis" of Russian culture. According to advocates of this concept, the primary manifestations of this crisis were a decline in the traditional dominance of literature in the Russian cultural life, a concomitant decline in the popularity of reading, and a wholesale transition from verbal genres to "simpler" visual ones (Vezhlian 2016).

16. The Ostrovsky Group, or GOST Strategy Group, is an informal community inaugurated by Efim Ostrovsky in 1994. Consisting predominantly of methodologists and political strategists, it describes itself as "an association of experts working within the techno-humanitarian paradigm" (Ostrovsky 2006).

17. The Moscow Methodological Circle was founded in 1958 by the philosopher Georgy Shchedrovitsky. The Circle's activities were initially confined to seminars devoted to the establishment of the movement's philosophy. Subsequently, however, the methodologists began to stage so-called "games"—brainstorming sessions used to thrash out solutions to particular problems—at city and factory administrations. After 1991, some of the younger methodologists migrated to the fields of political technology, cultural management and public administration. For example, Sergey Kiriyenko, an

erstwhile co-author of Ostrovsky and Shchedrovitsky, became prime minister of Russia and subsequently the head of Rosatom (Pertsev 2016).

18. Originating in the articles of Ostrovsky, Shchedrovitsky, and their colleagues, the concept of the "Russian world" eventually found its way into the speeches of the Russian president. First referenced in Putin's 2001 speech at the Congress of Compatriots, it became the ideological fulcrum of the war in Eastern Ukraine thirteen years later. "The triad of states that are home to the Russian people, and where the Russian language and Russian culture are predominant [that is, Russia, Ukraine and Belarus], constitutes the Russian world," asserted Igor Strelkov (Girkin), the former defense minister of the so-called Donetsk People's Republic, in a 2017 interview with *business-gazeta.ru* (Igor' Strelkov 2017). The concept's originators have repeatedly distanced themselves from its subsequent evolution in the political sphere, insisting that their initial formulations were misunderstood (Russkii Mir 2001).

19. Manuel Castells paid his first visit to the USSR in 1984 and travelled to Russia on numerous occasions during the 1990s. He and his wife Emma Kiselyova, a sociologist from Novosibirsk, have co-written several analyses of how Russia has handled the transition from industrial to information society (Castells and Kiselyova 1995, 2001). Castells also headed an advisory group invited by the Russian government in 1992 to produce a report on the "social and political problems of economic reforms and structural transition in Russia" (Castells 1996–1998, Vol. 1, 144).

20. "The Formation of a Society of Network Structures," a 1996 article by Castells, was published on Russian Archipelago, a website bearing the subtitle "a network project of the Russian world" (Manuel Castells 2018). A critical response to Castells's work from an advocate of the "Russian world" concept was published in the *Sociological Studies* [Sotsiologicheskiye issledovaniya] journal in 1998 (Inozemtsev 1998).

21. The term *rossiyane* refers to citizens of Russia, and stands in distinction to *russkiye*, or ethnic Russians.

22. *Vekhi* was first published in 1909 and would see several new editions but, being the object of harsh criticism from Lenin, was banned from distribution after 1917. In the late Soviet years, *Vekhi* was in circulation as *samizdat*, and in 1990 was once again republished. In the same year, the *Znamya* magazine published an article by Sergei Chernyshev entitled "New Vekhi" (Chernyshev 1990).

23. The Congress of Russian Communities (1993–2003) is a socio-political association of communities in Russia and the former Soviet republics. Its program was distinctly national-patriotic in character.

24. According to the political scientist Ivan Krastev, Western political consultants and Russian political technologists are radically different beasts, despite superficial similarities: "Political consultants in the West (however low one's opinion of them) work with independent media, and their trade is influencing these media," he writes. "Political technologists are experts in manipulating dependent media. Political consultants in the West are experts at winning votes for their candidates; political technologists are also specialists in winning votes, but they take matters one step further—they are also specialists in 'creative counting' of the votes" (Krastev 2006).

WORKS CITED

Abbate J. 2017. "What and Where Is the Internet? (Re)Defining Internet Histories." *Internet Histories* 1 (1–2): 8–14.

Abramov, Roman. 2017. "Sovetskaia inzhenerno-tekhnicheskaia intelligentsiia 1960–80-kh gg.: V poiske granits kollektivnogo soznaniia" [Soviet tech intelligentsia 1960–1980: In search of the limits of collective conscience]. *Vestnik instituta sotsiologii* 8 (1): 115–30.

Abramov, Roman. 2017. "Sovetskie tekhnokraticheskie mifologii kak forma 'teorii upushchennogo shansa': Na primere istorii kibernetiki v SSSR" ("Soviet Technocratic Mythologies as a Form of The Lost Chance Theory: A Case Study of Cybernetics"). *Sociology of Science and Technology* 8 (2): 61–78.

Afon'kin A. 1973. "Mat. chërnomu koroliu" [Checkmate to the black king]. *Radio* (10): 24–25.

Agafonov, Mikhail. 2007. "Sam sebe Gutenberg" ("Self-Help Gutenberg"). Start Copy, April 30. http://www.startcopy.net/lightroom/gutenberg.shtml.

Agurskii, Mikhail. 1991. "Velikii Eretik (Gorky kak religioznyi myslitel')" ["The Great Apostate. Gorky as a Religious Thinker"]. *Voprosy Filosofii* (8): 54–74.

Aksenov, Vasilii, ed. 1998. "Dissidenty o dissidentstve" ["Dissidents on dissent"]. *Znamia* (9): 163–93.

Alan [pseud.]. 2016. "Policy Themes of *Brave New World*: Religion, Public Relations, Drugs, Transhumanism, Evolution Doctrine Implies Inevitability of Developments Instead of Their Being the Result of Planning." Power and Reality. Canadian Liberty, November 27. https://canadianliberty.com/power-reality-journal-issue-6/#Part8.

Aleksandrov, Evgenii, ed. 2015. *V zashchitu nauki [In Defence of Science] Bulletin* (16).

"Alferenko Gennadii Petrovich." n.d. Mezhdunarodnyi ob"edinennyi biograficheskii tsentr. Alferenko, Gennadi Petrovich. International United Biography Center. http://www.biograph.ru/index.php/whoiswho/8-economics/25-alferenko (accessed 1 August 1, 2024).

Andersen, Kurt. 2017. *Fantasyland: How America Went Haywire: A 500-Year History*. Random House.

Andriopoulos, Stefan. 2005. "Psychic Television." *Critical Inquiry* 31 (3). 618–37.

Antonov, Vadim. 1991. "Please Read Before You'll Try to E-Mail to Soviet Union." Message posted to talk.politics.soviet, August 19. Archived at https://groups.google.com/d/msg/talk.politics.soviet/p88NuqqaqX8/ncpH1wouzsAJ.

Antonov, Vadim. 1990. "Computer Joke." Message posted to eunet:jokes, September 1. Archived at https://groups.google.com/d/msg/eunet.jokes/WRbjGhjcYp4/9HizLe8PHbkJ.

Asia Patrysheva. 2019. "Internet—ėto uzhe ne prosto set′. Ėto zhizn′" [The Internet is no longer just a network. It's life]. DataArt, August 29. https://habr.com/ru/companies/dataart/articles/465509/.

Aslanbekov, Raffi. 1997. "Chto Velikii Diadia dumal" [What did the great uncle think]. August 30, 1997. Archived at https://web.archive.org/web/19970730114907/http://www.cityline.ru/uncle/thinks/110697.html.

Balson, David. 1985. *International Computer-Based Conference on Biotechnology: A Case Study*. IDRC.

Banerjee, Anindita. 2011. "Electric Origins: From Modernist Myth to Bolshevik Utopia." In *The Electric Age*, edited by Olivier Asselin, Silvestra Mariniello, and Andrea Oberhuber. University of Ottawa Press.

Barbrook, Richard. 2015. *Internet-revoliutsiia* (*Internet Revolution*). Ad Marginem Press.

Barbrook, Richard, and Andy Cameron. 1995. "Californian Ideology." *Mute* 1 (3). https://www.metamute.org/editorial/articles/californian-ideology.

Baysha, Olga. 2014. *The Mythologies of Capitalism and the End of the Soviet Project*. Lexington Books.

Beck, Ulrich. 1992. *Risk Society: Towards a New Modernity*. Translated by Mark Ritter. SAGE.

Beck, Ulrich. 2006. *The Cosmopolitan Vision*. Translated by Ciaran Cronin. Polity Press.

Beertema, Piet. 1984. "USSR on Usenet." Google Groups (4/1/84). Message posted to eunet.politics, April 1. Archived at https://groups.google.com/forum/?hl=en#!msg/eunet.politics/_WKpffStBPc/JaaDBecKCM8J.

Beker, Brian. 1993. "RFD: soc.culture.burma." Message posted to news.groups, November 16. Archived at https://groups.google.com/g/news.groups/c/KaSoAhUn7xM/m/foccMnf5GeoJ.

Bekhterev, Vladimir. 2014. "Gipnoz. Vnushenie. Telepatiia" [Hypnosis. Induction. Telepathy]. *Almanac MOI*. Vol. 9. Mysl′.

Belenkin, Boris. 2012. "Rukopisnoe" kak "pechatnoe"? "Pechatnoe" kak "rukopisnoe"? ["Handwritten" as "printed"? "Printed" as "handwritten"?] *Zapiski o samizdate*. GPIB Rossii—Mezhdunarodnyĭ Memorial—"Zven′ia." 14–21.

Belkin, Viktor, and Aleksandr Birman. 1964. "Samostoiatel′nost′ predpriiatii i ekonomicheskie stimuly" ["Independence of Enterprises and Economic Incentives"]. *Izvestia*, December.

Bellis, Mary. 2016. "Charles Herzfeld on ARPAnet and Computers." About.com, July 1. Archived at http://archive.is/D63Wa#selection-397.0-401.656.

Belyaev, Alexander. 1947. *Vlastelin mira* (*The Ruler of the World*). Rodina.

Berg, Aksel. 1962. "Nauka velichaishikh vozmozhnostei" ("A Science of The Greatest Possibilities"). *Priroda* 7: 16–22.

Bernstein, Anya. 2019. *The Future of Immortality: Remaking Life and Death in Contemporary Russia*. Princeton University Press.

Biagioli, Mario, and Vincent Antonin Lépinay, eds. 2019. *From Russia with Code: Programming Migrations in Post-Soviet Times*. Duke University Press.

Bogdanov, Aleksandr. 1984. *Red Star: The First Bolshevik Utopia*. Edited by Loren Graham and Richard Stites. Translated by Charles Rougle. Indiana University Press.

Bogdanov, Alexandr. 2003. "O fiziologicheskom kollektivizme" ("On Physiological Collectivism"). *Vesntik MIAB* 2(14). https://ruslit.traumlibrary.net/book/bogdanov-vestnik/bogdanov-vestnik.html.

Bogdanov, Konstantin. 2011. "Fiziki vs liriki. K istorii odnoi pridurkovatoi diskussii" ("Physicists vs Lyricists: On the History of a 'Silly' Discussion"). *Novoe literaturnoe obozrenie* (111): 48–66.

Bondarenko, Valerii. 2017. "Sub'ektivnaia istoriia ASUP 'L'vov' i SKB sistemotekhniki PO 'Elektron' glazami sistemnogo analitika." *O sem'e Dedusenko i sem'iakh, sviazannykh s neiu. Blog administratora saita* ("A Subjective History of ASUP 'L'vov' and System Engineering SKB at PO "Elektron" as Told by a Systems Analyst"). November 4. http://dedusenko.at.ua/blog/subektivnaja_istorija_asup_lvov_i_skb_sistemotekhniki_po_ehlektron_glazami_sistemnogo_analitika/2017-11-04-143.

Borodin, Sergei. 1992. "Capitalist Restoration in the Ex-USSR." Message posted to talk.politics.soviet, December 9. Archived at https://groups.google.com/g/talk.politics.soviet/c/aGIzIbuFxwA/m/gZQ-4O-L8qgJ.

Bruk, Isaak. 1955. "Ob upravliaiushchikh mashinakh" ("On Managing Machines"). *Priroda* 5 (May): 18–26.

Bykov, Rolan. 2011. *Ia pobit nachnu snachala! Dnevniki [I Am Defeated, Let's Start Over! Diary]*. AST: Astrel.

Carlson, Don, and Craig Comstock. 1986. *Citizen Summitry: Keeping the Peace When It Matters Too Much to Be Left to Politicians*. Ark Communications Institute. J. P. Tarcher.

Castells, Manuel, and Emma Kiselyova. 2000. "Rossiia i setevoe obshchestvo. Analiticheskoe issledovanie" ["Russia and The Network Society. Analytical Research"]. *Mir Rossii* (1): 23–51.

Castells, Manuel. 1996–1998. *The Information Age: Economy, Society and Culture*. Blackwell Publishers. 3 vols.

Castells, Manuel, and Gustavo Cardoso, eds. 2005. *The Network Society: From Knowledge to Policy*. Johns Hopkins Center for Transatlantic Relations.

Castells, Manuel, and Emma Kiselyova. 1995. *The Collapse of Soviet Communism: A View from the Information Society*. Figueroa Press.

Castels, Manuel. 2000. *The Rise of The Network Society: The Information Age: Economy, Society and Culture*. John Wiley & Sons.

Central Intelligence Agency. 1972. *Controlled Offensive Behavior—USSR (U)*. FOIA Collection. CIA. https://www.cia.gov/library/readingroom/docs/CIA-RDP96-00792R000600360001-2.pdf.

Central Intelligence Agency. 1973. *Cryptologic Aspects of ESP*. FOIA Collection. CIA. https://www.cia.gov/readingroom/docs/NSA-RDP96X00790R000100030008-7.pdf.

Central Intelligence Agency. 1971. *ICL Computers for the USSR*. 0000969851. FOIA Collection. CIA, January 1. https://www.cia.gov/library/readingroom/docs/DOC_0000969851.pdf.

Central Intelligence Agency. n.d. *Parapsychology in the USSR*. CIA-RDP96-00792R000500210002-8. FOIA Collection. CIA. https://www.cia.gov/readingroom/docs/CIA-RDP96-00792R000500210002-8.pdf.

Central Intelligence Agency. 1985. *Soviet Computer Technology: Little Prospect for Catching Up*. FOIA Collection. CIA. https://www.cia.gov/library/readingroom/docs/CIA-RDP86R00995R000501130001-8.pdf.

Chalidze, Valery. 1977. *Criminal Russia: Essays on Crime in the Soviet Union*. Random House.

Chernyshev, Sergei. 1990. "Novye vekhi" ["New Landmarks"]. *Znamia* (1): 151–66.

"Chernyshev Anatolii Alekseevich." 2014. Tomskii memorial'nyi muzei "Sledstvennaia tiur'ma NKVD." May 5. Video. https://nkvd.tomsk.ru/projects/posledniysvidetel/videovosp/chernyshevaa/.

"Chisto ukrainskii proekt" ["The Very Ukrainian Project"], *Ukrainskaia pravda*, 2001, October 29. https://www.pravda.com.ua/rus/news/2001/10/29/4363697/.

Chugunov, Oleg. 2007. "Predchuvstvie interneta" [" Internet Adventure"]. In *Computerra*, October 31. https://old.computerra.ru/2007/706/337861/.

Clover, Charles. 2016. *Black Wind, White Snow: The Rise of Russia's New Nationalism*. Yale University Press.

Colomina, Beatriz. 2001. "Enclosed by Images: The Eameses' Multimedia Architecture." *Grey Room* (2): 5–29. Archived at http://csis.pace.edu/~marchese/TextImage/colomina_eames.pdf.

"Computerszene 1955." 2020. Heinz Nixdorf Museumsforum, October 23. https://blog.hnf.de/computerszene-1955/.

Condon, Chris. 2001. "Why I'm Called Fuzzyman." Nethistory. An Informal History of BITNET and the Internet. 2001. Archived at http://web.archive.org/web/20090726104009/http://nethistory.dumbentia.com/fuzzy.html.

Cooper, John. 1947. "Anthropology in the United States during 1939–1945." *Journal de la société des américanistes* (36): 1–14.

Davidov, Mikhail. 1998. "Vsia pravda o Demose . . ."/ All the Truth About Demos News.demos.su. December. http://news.demos.su/private/demos.html.

Defense Intelligence Agency. 1978. *Paraphysics R&D—Warsaw Pact (U)*, DST-1810s-202–78, March 30. https://www.dia.mil/FOIA/FOIA-Electronic-Reading-Room/FOIA-Reading-Room-Other-Available-Records/FileId/39972/.

Den' nezavisimosti Rossii, 25 let spustia / Russian Undependence Day 25 Years Later. 2015. Yetsin Tsentr, June 11. https://yeltsin.ru/news/den-nezavisimosti-rossii-25-let-spustya/.

Derrida, Jacque, and Nicholas Royle. 1988. "Telepathy." *Oxford Literary Review* 10 (1/2), Anniversary Issue. Edinburgh University Press, 3–41.

Dewhurst J. 2018. *British Cybernetics: The Routledge Handbook of the Computational Mind*. Routledge.

Dmitriev, Pavel. 2011–2013. "Eshche ne pozdno" ["It's Not Too Late Yet"]. Samizdat. http://samlib.ru/d/dmitriew_p/.

Dmitrieva, N. A. 1967. "Literatura i drugie vidy iskusstva" ["Literature And Other Arts"]. *Kratkaia literaturnaia entsiklopediia*, Vol. 4, 229–44. Sovetskaia entsiklopediia. http://feb-web.ru/feb/kle/kle-abc/ke4/ke4-2292.htm.

Dodolev, Evgenij. 2011. Zamknutyi krug Manezhki / The Never-Ending Circle of Manezhnaya Square. *Moskovskaia pravda*, October 3. http://old.mospravda.ru/issue/2011/03/10/article26559/.

Douglas, Charlotte, ed. 1990. *Khlebnikov Collected Works*. Harvard University Press.

Dragunov, Anthony. n.d. "Fidonet As Is." Vlz.Stoppers.Club. Last modified 1997. http://stoppers.chat.ru/AFIDO.HTM.

Draper, John. 1988. Soviet Access to Usenet. Message posted to news:comp.misc November 13, archived at https://groups.google.com/forum/#!topic/comp.misc/xT5PUC64bfU%5B1-25%5D.

Draper, John. 2014. "I'm the person who showed Steve Jobs The Blue Box." Reddit, September 28. https://www.reddit.com/r/IAmA/comments/2hpje1/im_the_person_who_showed_steve_jobs_the_blue_box/.

Draper, Theodore. 1989. *The Roots of American Communism*. I. R. Dee.

Driscoll, Kevin, and Julien Mailland. 2017. *Minitel: Welcome to the Internet*. MIT Press.

Driscoll, Kevin. 2016. "Social Media's Dial-Up Ancestor: The Bulletin Board System." *IEEE Spectrum* 53 (11): 54–60.

Dudlei, Evgeniia. 1974. "Parapsikhologiia v Sovetskom Soiuze" (Parapsychology in the USSR). *Okkul'tizm i ioga* (*Occultism and yoga*) (57): 19–31.

Ebon, Martin. 1983. *Psychic Warfare: Threat or Illusion*. McGraw-Hill.

Eden, Amnon H., Eric Steinhart, David Pearce, and James H. Moor, eds. 2012. *Singularity Hypotheses*. The Frontiers Collection. Springer-Verlag.

Edwards, Benj. 2022. "My Secret Life as an 11-Year-Old BBS Sysop. Revisiting the Wonder and Betrayal of Online Life Circa 1992." *Arstechnica*, January 12. https://arstechnica.com/information-technology/2022/12/my-secret-life-as-an-11-year-old-bbs-sysop/.

"EFF 30th Anniversary." 2010. Electronic Frontier Foundation. Accessed August 1, 2024. https://www.eff.org/tags/eff30.

Ellman, Michael. 1973. *Planning Problems in the USSR: The Contribution of Mathematical Economics to Their Solution 1960–1971*. Cambridge University Press.

Emmelhainz, Irmgard. 2023. "Authoritarianism and the Cybernetic Episteme, or the Progressive Disappearance of Everything on Earth." *Revista Portuguesa De Psiquiatria E Saúde Mental* 9 (1): 5–8.

Engelbart, Douglas. 1962. "Augmenting Human Intellect: A Conceptual Framework." SRI Summary report. October. Archived at https://www.dougengelbart.org/content/view/138.

Epshtein, Mikhail. 1998. "O virtual'noj slovesnosti" On Virtual Literature *Russkij Zhurnal*, May 26. Archived at https://web.archive.org/web/20000919215450/http://www.russ.ru:8080/journal/netcult/98-06-10/epstyn.htm.

Ettinger, Robert. 1972. *Man into Superman: The Startling Potential of Human Evolution—And How to Be Part of It*. St. Martin's Press.

Ettinger, Robert. 1964. *The Prospect of Immortality*. Doubleday.

Fedotov, Dmitrii. 2012. "Besovskaia sila, chekistskii vodevil' i besslavnyi konets SSSR"/ A Devilish Force, A KGB Vaudeville and Inglourious End of the USSR. Livejournal, July 1. https://double-bind.livejournal.com/59386.html.

Fedotova, Elena. 2015. "Chto fond Sorosa sdelal dlia Rossii"/ ["What the Soros Foundation Has Done for Russia Kommersant"]. November 30. https://www.kommersant.ru/doc/2866188.

Fet, Yakov. 2004. "Igor' Andreevich Poletaev i ego kniga 'Signal'" ["Igor' Andreevich Poletaev and His Book 'Signal'"]. *VIVOS VOCO*. http://vivovoco.astronet.ru/VV/PAPERS/BIO/FET.HTM.

Fet, Yakov, ed. 2007. *Aksel Ivanovich Berg. 1893–1979*. Nauka.

Fischer, Dave. 1994. "longest USENET thread ever." Message posted to alt.folklore.computers, January 26. Archived at https://groups.google.com/g/alt.folklore.computers/c/wF4CpYbWuuA/m/jS6ZOyJd1osJ.

Forte, Robert, ed. 1999. *Outside Looking In: Appreciations, Castigations, and Reminiscences*. Park Street Press.

Foucault, Michel. 1972. *Archaeology of Knowledge*. Routledge.

Freud, Sigmund. 1964. "Dreams and Occultism." *New Introductory Lectures on Psychoanalysis, Standard Edition*. Vol. 22. Hogarth Press.

Freud, Sigmund. 1964. "Dreams and Telepathy." *The Standard Edition of the Complete Psychological Works of Sigmund Freud*, vol. 23 (1920–1922). Hogarth Press, 195–220.

Gaddy, Clifford. 1991. "The Labour Market and the Second Economy in The Soviet Union." *Berkeley-Duke Occasional Papers On the Second Economy In the USSR* (24) (January).

Gagin, Alexandr. 1999. "The Lord of Bugs." Interview with Vadim Antonov. *InterNet* 16. http://www.gagin.ru/internet/14/5.html.

Galina, Maria. 2019. "Ressentiment and Post-traumatic Syndrome in Russian Post-Soviet Speculative Fiction: Two Trends." Edited by Suslov M. and Bodin P.-A. *The Post-Soviet Politics of Utopia: Language, Fiction and Fantasy in Modern Russia*. I.B. Tauris, 39–59.

Ganapol'skii, Matvei, and Sergei Buntman. 2015."Kak glushili 'Ekho' v avguste 1991-go / How Echo Moskvy Was Jammed in August 1991." Broadcast. June 12, 09:47. *Ėkho Moskvy*. https://echo.msk.ru/programs/otgoloski/1565288-echo/.

Gere, Charlie. 2002. *Digital Culture*. Reaktion Books.

Gerovitch, Slava. 2002. *From Newspeak to Cyberspeak. A History of Soviet Cybernetics*. MIT Press.

Gerovitch, Slava. 2008. "InterNyet: Why the Soviet Union Did Not Build a Nationwide Computer Network." *History and Technology. An International Journal* 24 (4): 335–50. https://doi.org/10.1080/07341510802044736.

Gerovitch, Slava. 2001. "'Mathematical Machines' of the Cold War: Soviet Computing, American Cybernetics and Ideological Disputes in the Early 1950s." *Social Studies of Science* 31 (2) (April): 253–87.

Gershkovich, Evan, Pjotr Sauer, and Jake Cordell. 2020. "How Mishustin Rose to the Top: Old Ties, Savvy and a Knack for Systems." *The Moscow Times*, January 27. https://www.themoscowtimes.com/2020/01/27/how-mikhail-mishustin-rose-to-the-top-old-ties-savvy-and-a-knack-for-systems-a69052.

Gibson, William. 1984. *Neuromancer*. Ace.

Giddens, Anthony. 1990. *Consequences of Modernity*. Polity Press.

Gilman, Robert. 1987. "Spacebridges: Linking the People of the World Together with Communications Technology. An Interview with Joseph Goldin." *In Context* (15): 58. Archived at https://www.context.org/iclib/ic15/goldin/.

Glushkov, Viktor. 1990. "Kibernetika i ee primenenie v narodnom khoziaistve" ["Cybernetics and its application in the national economy"]. In *Kibernetika, vychislitel'naia tekhnika, informatika: Izbrannye trudy* (*Cybernetics, Computer Science, Informatics: Selected works*), vol. 3, Naukova dumka.

Goldstein, Joshua, and John Freeman. 1990. *Three-Way Street: Strategic Reciprocity in World Politics*. University of Chicago Press.

Golubev, Alexey. 2020. *The Things of Life: Materiality in Late Soviet Russia*. Cornell University Press.

Golyshko, Aleksandr, and Nikolai Repin. 2002. "O sviazi Internet: V Rossiiu s liubov'iu" ["On Internet Communication: To Russia with Love"]. *Radio* (9): 71–72.

Goodman, Seymour. 2003. "The Origins of Digital Computing in Europe." *Communications of the ACM*, 46 (9): 21–25.

Gorbanevskaïa, Natalia. 2009. "Samizdat et Internet." *Revue Russe* 33 (1): 137–43.

Gordon, Dmitrii. 2015. "Djuna Davitashvili." V gostiakh u Dmitriia Gordona. / Djuna Davitashvili. On a Visit to Dmitrii Gordon. YouTube video, 39:53. January 4. https://www.youtube.com/watch?v=tRoJxCn4YuI.

Gorelik, George. 1983. "Bogdanov's Tektology: Nature, Development and Influences." *Studies in Soviet Thought* 26: 37–57.

Gorelik, George. 1975. "Re-Emergence of Bogdanov's Tektology." *Academy of Management Journal* 18: 345–57.

Gorham, Michael S., Ingunn Lunde, and Martin Paulsen, eds. 2014. *Digital Russia: The Language, Culture and Politics of New Media Communication*. Routledge.

Gorky, Maxim. 1953. "O temakh"/ ["On Issues"]. Collected works, Vol. 27. Художественная литература, 97–109.

Gorny, Eugene. 2009. *A Creative History of the Russian Internet*. VDM Verlag Müller.

Gorny, Eugene. 2008. "More Than Humor: Jokes from Russia as a Mirror of Russian Life." In *Internationalizing Internet Studies: Beyond Anglophone Paradigms*, edited by Gerard Goggin and Mark McLelland. Routledge.

Gorny, Eugene. 2009. *The Virtual Persona as a Creative Genre on the Russian Internet*. DVM Verlag Dr. Muller.

Greenfield, Adam. 2006. *Everyware: The Dawning Age of Ubiquitous Computing*. New Riders Publishing, 2006.

Greenstein, Shane. 2000. "Commercialization of the Internet: The Interaction of Public Policy and Private Choices or Why Introducing the Market Worked so Well." *Innovation Policy and the Economy* 1: 151–86. https://www.jstor.org/stable/25056144.

Grekova, Tatiana and Iurii Golikov. 2011. *Meditsinskii Peterburg*. Health Care of Petersburg. Folio-Press.

Grier, David Alan, and Mary Campbell. 2000. "A Social History of Bitnet and Listserv, 1985–1991." *IEEE Annals of the History of Computing* 22 (2): 32–41.

Gromov, Andreĭ, and Oleg Kuzin. 1990. *Neformaly: kto est' kto?* [Neformaly: Who Is Who?]. Mysl'.

Gulyaev, Pavel. 1955. "Chto takoe biofizika" ["What is biophysics"]. *Nauka i zhizn' (Science and Life)* (1): 7–13.

Gusejnov, Gasan. 2000. "Zametki k antropologii russkogo interneta: Osobennosti jazyka i literatury setevykh ljudej" ["Remarks on the Anthropology of Russian Internet: Specifics of Language and Literature of Net People."] *Novoe literaturnoe obozrenie* 43. Archived at http://magazines.russ.ru/nlo/2000/43/main8.html.

Gusman, Yulii. 2007. "Pervyi kosmicheskii telemost: istoriia iz pervykh ust." ["The First Space Television Bridge: A First-Hand Historical Account"]. *RIA Novosti*, October 29. https://ria.ru/20071029/85788741.html.

Hafner, Katie, Lyon, Matthew. 1996. *Where Wizards Stay Up Late. The Origins of the Internet*. Simon & Schuster.

Hafner, Katie. 2001. "A Paternity Dispute Divides Net Pioneers." *New York Times*, November 8.

Hafner, Katie. 1997. "The Epic Saga of The Well." *Wired*, January 5. https://www.wired.com/1997/05/ff-well/.

Hafner Katie, Markoff, John. 1991. *Cyberpunk: Outlaws and Hackers on the Computer Frontier*. Simon & Schuster.

Hagemeister, Michael. 2012. "Konstantin Tsiolkovskii and the Occult Roots of Soviet Space Travel." In *The New Age of Russia. Occult and Esoteric Dimensions*, edited by Birgit Menzel, Michael Hagemeister, and Bernice Glatzer Rosenthal. Verlag Otto Sagner.

Hagemeister, Michael. 1997. "Russian Cosmism in the 1920s and Today." In *The Occult in Russian and Soviet Culture*, edited by Bernice Glatzer Rosenthal. Cornell University Press.

Hahn, Harley. 1994. *Internet Yellow Pages*. Osborne/McGraw-Hill.

Halliday, Samuel. 2007. *Science and Technology in the Age of Hawthorne, Melville, Twain, and James: Thinking and Writing Electricity*. Palgrave Macmillan.

Hambridge S. 1995. *Netiquette Guidelines*, FYI 28, RFC 1855. https://www.rfc-editor.org/info/rfc1855.

Hauben, Michael, and Rona Hauben. 1997. *Netizens: On the History and Impact of Usenet and the Internet*. IEEE Computer Society Press.

Hauben, Michael. 1993. "Common Sense. The Net and Netizens: The Impact the Net has on People's Lives." *The Amateur Computerist* 5 (3/4): 11–13. Archived at http://www.ais.org/~jrh/acn/ACN5-3-4.pdf accessed August 1, 2024.

Hauben, Michael. 1994. "Interested in Thoughts on the Computer as a Communications Device." Message posted to comp.misc, March 29. Archived at https://groups.google.com/g/comp.misc/c/zG3vuUYt5Do/m/jSy8f4ODojgJ.

Helbing, Felix. 2021. "New Lease on Life for Physiological Collectivism? Reading Bogdanov in the Time of COVID." University of Pittsburgh blog, June 24. https://aseees.org/wp-content/uploads/2015/02/June-2021.pdf.

Hlavin, Barbara. 1990. "Masturbation as Self Experience." Message posted to soc:-women, November 15. Archived at https://groups.google.com/d/msg/soc.women/MArDJqXDr3c/TEZvKsiZUDsJ.

Hochschild, Adam. 1986. "Slow-Scan to Moscow." *Mother Jones* 11 (4). Archived at https://www.motherjones.com/politics/1986/06/slow-scan-moscow/.

Householder, Alston S. 1955. "Digital Computers in Eastern Europe," *Computers and Automation* (12): 8. http://bitsavers.informatik.uni-stuttgart.de/magazines/Computers_And_Automation/195512.pdf.

Humphrys, Mark. n.d. "The Internet in the 1980s." School of Computing. Dublin City University. Accessed August 1, 2024. http://computing.dcu.ie/~humphrys/net.80s.html.

Husbands, Phil, and Owen Holland. 2008. "The Ratio Club: A Hub of British Cybernetics." In *The Mechanical Mind in History*, edited by Phil Husbands, Owen Holland, and Michael Wheeler. MIT Press.

"Igor' Strelkov: 'Novyi 1991 god dlia Rossii v toi ili inoi forme uzhe neizbezhen'" (Igor Strelkov: The New 1991 in This or That Form Is Inevitable for Russia). 2017. *Business Online*, January 17. https://www.business-gazeta.ru/article/334586.

Igrunov, Viacheslav, Barbakadze, Mark. 2005. "Antologiia samizdata. Nepodtsenzurnaia literatura v SSSR 1950-e–1980-e gg." ["The Samizdat Anthology. Uncensored Literature in the USSR in 1950–1980s"]. In 3 vols. Mezhdunarodnyi institut gumanitarno-politicheskikh issledovanii.

In Memoriam: J. C. R. Licklider 1915–1990. 1990. Systems Research Center. https://web.stanford.edu/dept/SUL/library/extra4/sloan/mousesite/Secondary/Licklider.pdf.

Inozemtsev V. L. 1998. "Vozvrashchenie k istokam ili proryv v budushchee?" ["Back to the Roots or A Breakthrough to Future?"]. *Sotsiologicheskie issledovaniia* (8): 140–47.

Istoriia vychislitel'noi tekhniki v Rossii, stranakh byvshego SSSR i SEV. ["A History of Computing Technology in Russia, ex-USSR Countries, and COMECON"]. n.d. International Conference. https://www.sorucom.org/.

Ivanov, Nikolai. 2004. "Amerikantsy na nashu aktivnost' s samogo nachala koso smotreli" ["Americans Were Cautious About Activity from the Very Beginning"]. *Istoriia interneta v Rossii* (10). Archived at https://web.archive.org/web/20081120125411/http://www.nethistory.ru/memories/1080505501.html.

Ivanova, Ekaterina. 2014. "Sergei Lebedev: predmety i dokumenty" ["Sergei Lebedev: Subjects and Documents"]. *Politekh*, March 13. https://polymus.ru/ru/news/blogs/channels/8116-rossiyskie-deyateli-nauki-i-tehniki/8360/. Accessed August 13, 2020.

"Iz delovoi perepiski Gleba Pavlovskogo i Sergeia Chernysheva." (From the Business Correspondence of Gleb Pavlovsky and Sergey Chernyshev). 1997. *Russkii zhurnal*, July 14, archived at http://old.russ.ru/journal/dsp/97-07-14/pav-che.htm.

Jason Scott. 2005. "BBS: The Documentary." *Archive.org*, https://archive.org/details/BBS.The.Documentary.

Jim Hickman's Reflections of Stanley Krippner. 2019. New Thinking Allowed with Jeffrey Mishlove. June 9. https://www.youtube.com/watch?v=lzpFGDqGY3E.

Joyce, Mary. 2012. "From the Tank Turret to Usenet: First International Case of Digital Activism?" *Meta-activism.org*, October 10. http://www.meta-activism.org/2012/10/usenet-vs-the-tanks-first-international-case-of-digital-activism/.

Judy, Richard W., and Robert W. Clough. n.d. "Soviet Computer Software and Applications in the 1980s. June 1989." Hudson Institute. Archived at https://web.archive.org/web/20170828112726/https:/www.ucis.pitt.edu/nceeer/1989-801-5-2-Judy.pdf.

Kalugin, Oleg. 2003. "'Svjatoj' apostol Oleg" ["Holy Apostle Oleg"]. Interview by Anna Brojdo. *Argumenty i Fakty. Dolgozhitel* (8). http://www.aif.ru/archive/1678871.

Kaminskii K. 2020. *Ėlektroroman Andreia Platonova* (*Andrei Platonov's electro-novel*). Novoe literaturnoe obozrenie.

Karn, Phil R. 1990. "'First' BBS in USSR." Message posted to comp:dcom.telecom, January 1. Archived at https://groups.google.com/d/msg/comp.dcom.telecom/Fj5jlUctiio/DaJjWgmk2jYJ.

Karttunen, Antti. 1992. "Venedikt Erofejev: Moskva—Petushki." Message posted to soc.culture.soviet, November 3. Archived at https://groups.google.com/g/soc.culture.soviet/c/OkslMjCX46g/m/rz8eYCN4J2kJ.

Kasaty, Peter. 1996. "RFD: soc.culture.belarus moderated." Message posted to soc.culture.baltics, April 8. Archived at https://groups.google.com/g/soc.culture.baltics/c/u-nhXTFbXTE/m/FWzzxeM1umEJ.

Kazanskii, Ivan. 1971. "Radiokhuliganstvo pered sudom" ["Radio Hooligans on Trial"]. *Radio* (6): 25–26.

Kazantsev, A. 1957. "Nabliudeniia za radiosignalami s iskusstvennogo sputnika Zemli i ikh nauchnoe znachenie" ["Observations of radio signals from an artificial Earth satellite and their scientific significance"]. *Radio* (6): 17–19.

Kazhinskiy, Bernard. 1963. "Biological Radio Communications." Defence Documentation Center for Scientific and Technical Information. Cameron Station. Alexandria, Virginia, April 1. https://apps.dtic.mil/dtic/tr/fulltext/u2/415676.pdf.

Kazhinsky, Bernard. 1962. *Biologicheskaia radiosviaz'* (*Biological radiocommunication*). Academy of Sciences' Publishing House.

Kazhinsky, Bernard. 1928. "Iskusstvennoe regulirovanie pogody pri pomoshchi ėlektrichestva" ["Artificial weather regulation by electricity"]. *Planovoe khoziaistvo* (3): 231–41.

Kelly, Kevin. 1994. *Out of Control. The New Biology of Machines, Social Systems and the Economic World.* Addison-Wesley.

Kelly, Kevin. 2010. *What Technology Wants.* Penguin Group US. Kindle Edition.

Kelly, Kevin. 2002. "God Is the Machine." *Wired*, January 12. https://www.wired.com/2002/12/holytech/?pg=1&topic=&topic_set=.

Kernbach, Serge. 2013. *Unconventional Research in USSR and Russia: Short Overview.* December 5. https://arxiv.org/pdf/1312.1148.pdf.

Kharkhordin, Oleg. 1999. *The Collective and the Individual in Russia: A Study of Practices.* University of California Press.

Khiltunen, Valerii. n.d. https://web.archive.org/web/20220314000915/https://www.hvar.ru/services_99.php.

Khiltunen, Valerii. 2008. "Aksel' Ivanovich, chelovek derzhavnyi" ["Aksel Ivanovich the Statesman"]. *Studiia Khvara*, January 30. http://www.hvar.ru/services_99_1306.php.

Khlebnikov, Velimir. 1990. *The King of Time.* Edited by Charlotte Douglas. Translated by Paul Schmidt. Harvard University Press.

.Khodakov, Viktor. 2010. *Nauchnye shkoly komp'iuterostroeniia: istoriia otechestvennoi vychislitel'noi tekhniki* (*Scientific Schools of Computer Science: History of Homeland Computer Engineering*). Oldi-Plius.

Kitov, Anatolij. 1956. *Elektronnye tsifrovye mashiny* (Electronic Digital Machines). Sovetskoe Radio.

Kitov, Vladimir, and Valerii Shilov, eds. 2020. *Anatolii Ivanovich Kitov.* Maks Press.

Klein, Peter G. 2006. "Government Did Invent the Internet, But the Market Made It Glorious." Mises Institute, June 12. https://mises.org/library/government-did-invent-internet-market-made-it-glorious.

Klumbyte, Neringa, and Gulnaz Sharafutdinova. 2012. *Soviet Society in the Era of Late Socialism, 1964–1985.* Lexington Books.

Klyosov, Anatole. 2010. *Internet. Zametki nauchnogo sotrudnika* [Internet. Essays of a Researcher]. MGU.

Klyosov, Anatole. 1985. "V modu vkhodiat telekonferentsii" ["Teleconferences Are Becoming a Trend"]. *Nauka v SSSR* (6): 84–89.

Knauth, Geoffrey.1988. "John Draper's note re: USSR & joint ventures in software." Message posted to news.admin, November 10. Archived at https://groups.google.com/g/news.admin/c/fmBl_WQT9Kk/m/OhgUvcJsk28J.

Koebler, Jason. 2015. "It's September, Forever." *Vice*, September 30. https://motherboard.vice.com/en_us/article/nze8nb/its-september-forever.

Kogan, Ippolit. 1967. "Informatsionnyi analiz eksperimentov telepaticheskoi sviazi" ["Informational analysis of telepathic communication experiments"], *Radiotekhnika* 22 (1).

Kogan, Ippolit. 1969. "The Information Theory Aspect of Telepathy." Translated by Firmin Joseph Krieger. RAND Corporation. Accessed August 1, 2024. https://www.rand.org/pubs/papers/P4145.html.

"Kogda poiavilsia samyi pepvyi uzel v SSSR?" 2005. Sbornik chasto zadavaemykh voprosov (ChAVO) konferentsii FIDONET.HISTORY. ("When Did the First Hub in the USSR Appear?" A Digest of the FIDONET.HISTORY conference FAQ). March 11. Archived at https://web.archive.org/web/20080529081718/http://www.debryansk.ru/~pvp/fhfaq/03NFT5RQ.html.

Kolesnikov, Andreĭ. 1989. "Calling the BBS in Tallinn, Estonia." Message posted to comp:dcom.telecom, December 26. Archived at https://groups.google.com/d/msg/comp.dcom.telecom/eTV9-YGR-js/Kz56By7jhu4J.

Kolesnikov, Andrei. 1989. "Hi-Rise Joe." Message posted to comp:dcom.telecom, December 29. Archived at https://groups.google.com/d/msg/comp.dcom.telecom/I-YFpnaI6e4/dEjUQMtGfGUJ.

Kolmogorov, Andreii. 1968. "Avtomaty i zhizn'" ["Automata and life"]. *Kibernetika ozhidaemaia i kibernetika neozhidannaia* (*Cybernetics expected and cybernetics unexpected*), edited by Aksel Berg and Ernest Kolman. Nauka, 12–30.

Kolozaridi, Polina, and Dmitry Muravyov. 2020. "The Narratives We Inherit: The Local and Global in Tomsk's Internet History." *Internet Histories. Digital Technology, Culture and Society* 4: 49–65.

Komaromi, Ann. n.d. "About Samizdat." Soviet Samizdat Periodicals. Uncensored Texts of the Late Soviet Era. https://samizdat.library.utoronto.ca/content/about-samizdat.

Komaromi, Ann. 2008. "Samizdat as Extra-Gutenberg Phenomenon." *Poetics Today* 29 (4): , 629–67.

Komaromi, Ann. 2004. "The Material Existence of Soviet Samizdat Author(s)." *Slavic Review* 63 (3) (Autumn), 597–618.

Kotel'nikov, Vladimir. 2011. *Sud'ba, okhvativshaia vek* [*A fate that spans the century*]. Vol. 2, Fizmatlit.

Kozyrev, Mikhail. 2012. *Podpol'nye millionery: Vsia pravda o chastnom biznese v SSSR* [Underground Billionaires: The Whole Truth About Private Business in the USSR.] Eksmo.

Krastev, Ivan. 2006. "Democracy's 'Doubles.'" *Journal of Democracy* 17 (2): April 52–62.

Kreisel, Felix. 1992. "Capitalist restoration in the ex-USSR." Message posted to talk.politics.soviet, March 17. Archived at https://groups.google.com/g/talk.politics.soviet/c/XYssa85TtQE/m/iQNNaq6mmAoJ.

Krementsov, Nikolai. 2011. *A Martian Stranded on Earth: Alexander Bogdanov, Blood Transfusions, and Proletarian Science*. University of Chicago Press.

Krementsov, Nikolai. 2014. *Revolutionary Experiments: The Quest for Immortality in Bolshevik Science and Fiction.* Oxford University Press.

Kreps, Evgenij. 1989. *O prozhitom i perezhitom* / On Moscow: Nauka. http://www.infran.ru/vovenko/60years_ww2/kreps_memo1.htm.

Kripal, Jeffrey J. 2007. *Esalen: America and the Religion of No Religion.* University of Chicago Press.

Krippner, Stanley. 1978. "Psychophysiology, Converging Operations, and Alterations in Consciousness." *Bessoznatel'noye. Priroda. Funktsii. Metody issledovaniia,* Vol. I. Tbilisi: Metsniereba, 658–67.

Krivenkov, Sergeii. 2016. "Dezinformaciia" ["Disinformation"]. *Sekretnye materialy 20 veka (20th Century X-Files),* no. 6 (444). https://xfile.ru/x-files/secrets_of_special_services/dezinformatsiya/?sphrase_id=1264797.

Kryshtanovskaia O. V. 1989. *Inzhenery. Stanovlenie i razvitie professional'noi gruppy* [Engineers. Development and Formation of the Professional Group]. Nauka.

K tainam podsoznaniia (*To the mysteries of the subconscious mind*). 1980. *Tekhnika—molodezhi* (*Technology for Youth*) (3): 47–54.

Kukulin, Ilya. 2007. "Al'ternativnoe sotsial'noe proektirovanie v sovetskom obshchestve" ["Alternative Social Design in Soviet Society."] *Novoe literaturnoe obozrenie,* Vol. 6. 169–201.

Kulikova, Nadezhda. 2017. "Glavnyi po anekdotam: istoriia legendarnogo proekta Anekdot.ru" ["The Main Joker: A History of the Legendary Project Anekdot.ru"]. *biz360,* December 6. https://biz360.ru/materials/glavnyy-po-anekdotam-istoriya-legendarnogo-proekta-anekdot-ru/.

Kurzweil, Ray. 1999. *The Age of Spiritual Machines.* Penguin.

Kurzweil, Ray. 2005. *The Singularity Is Near: When Humans Transcend Biology.* Viking.

Kurzweil, Ray. 2024. *The Singularity is Nearer.* Penguin.

Kuteinikov, Aleksei. 2011. *Proekt Obshchegosudarstvennoi Avtomatizirovannoi Sistemy upravleniia sovetskoi ekonomikoi (OGAS) i problemy ego realizatsii v 1960–1980-kh gg* [The Project of the National Automated Control System of the Soviet Economy (NACS) and the Problems of its Implementation in the 1960–1980s]. Diss. . . . Cand. Hist. Sc. http://www.hist.msu.ru/Science/Disser/Kuteinikov.pdf.

Kuteinikov, Aleksej, and Valerii Shilov. 2011. "ASU dlja SSSR: Pis'mo A. I. Kitova N. S. Khrushchevu, 1959 goda" ["ASU for the USSR: Letter from A. Kitov to N. Khrushchev, 1959"]. *Voprosy istorii estestvoznanija i tehniki* 32 (3): 45–52.

Kutikov, Aleksandr. n.d. *Mashina vremeni* (*Time machine*). http://www.mashina-vremeni.com/solnaya/ak/akbio.html.

Kuznetsov, Sergei. 2003. *Grob khrustal'nyi* [The Crystal Coffin]. Amfora.

Kuznetsov, Sergei. 2004. *Oshchupyvaia slona* [Palpating an Elephant]. Novoe literaturnoe obozrenie.

Kuznetsov, Sergei. 1999. "Rozhdenie Igry, smert' Avtora i virtual'noe pis'mo" ["The Birth of Game, the Death of the Author, and Virtual Writing"]. *Inostrannaia literatura,* no 10. Archived at https://magazines.gorky.media/inostran/1999/10/rozhdenie-igry-smert-avtora-i-virtualnoe-pismo.html.

Kuznetsov, Vladimir. 1979. "Antropomaksimologiia nauka o vozmozhnostiakh cheloveka" ["Anthropomaximology is the science of human capabilities"]. *Nauka i zhizn' (Science and Life)*, no. 12, 112–16.

Landsberg, Greg. 1994. "Another iambic nonsense thread." Message posted to soc.culture.soviet, March 16. Archived at https://groups.google.com/g/soc.culture.soviet/c/bVnvB7bClbU/m/Ty9E_z-Vk6MJ.

Langevin, Michael Peter, and Richard Daab. 1990. "Michael Murphy. A Natural History of the Future." *Magical Blend Monthly* (25): 62–65, 110.

Laruelle, Marlene. 2015. "The 'Russian World': Russia's Soft Power and Geopolitical Imagination." Center on Global Interests. https://globalinterests.org/2015/05/26/the-russian-world-russias-soft-power-and-geopolitical-imagination/.

Laskow, Sarah. 2015. "How a Famed New Age Retreat Center Helped End the Cold War." *Alta Obscura*, December 8. https://www.atlasobscura.com/articles/how-a-famed-new-age-retreat-center-helped-end-the-cold-war.

Lavington, Simon. 2011. *Moving Targets: Elliott-Automation and the Dawn of the Computer Age in Britain, 1947–67*. Springer Science & Business Media.

Lavrov, Dmitrii. 2014. "Obraz Elektricheskogo sveta kak otrazhenie sovetskoi ideologii v lakovoi miniatiure Palekha" ["The Image of Electric Light as a Reflection of Soviet Ideology in Palekh Lacquer Miniatures"]. *Bulletin of SPbSU*. Ser. 2. (4): 107–12.

Lebedev, Artemij. 1996. "Latyn', mat' jeje tak . . ." / Screw the Latin Tema.ru. http://www.tema.ru/rrr/ruslat/.

Leibov, Roman. 2003. "Besedy s Dmitriem Maninym o poezii, teorii informatsii i ljubvi" ["Talking to Dmitry Manin About Poetry, Information Theory, and Love"]. *Russkii Zhurnal*, May 20. http://old.russ.ru/netcult/20030520.html.

Lemon Alaina. 2017. *Technologies of Intuition. Cold War Circles and Telepathic Rays*. University of California Press.

Lenin, Vladimir. 1977. *Collected Works* (45 volumes, 4th printing). Progress Publishers. https:// www.marxists.org/archive/lenin/works/cw/index.htm.

Lialina, Olia. 2005. "A Vernacular Web. The Indigenous and The Barbarians." http://art.teleportacia.org/observation/vernacular/.

Lisnichenko, Irina. 2012. "Akademik Glushkov pervym predskazal vvedenie elektronnykh deneg" ["Academician Glushkov Was the First to Predict E-Money"]. *Fakty. Ukraina*, January 31. http://fakty.ua/145868-chlen-korrespondent-nan-ukrainy-anatolij-morozov-akademik-glushkov-pervym-predskazal-vvedenie-elektronnyh-deneg.

Litera.ru. 1998 Archived at https://web.archive.org/web/19980530054954/http://www.litera.ru/literamain.htm.

Litvinova, Elena. 2017. "Sergei Lebedev. Bitva za superkomp'iuter" ["Sergei Lebedev. A Battle for the Supercomputer"]. *Rodina* 6 (617): 75–79.

Long, Steve. 1977. "Captain Crunch: Super Phone Phreak." *High Times*, June 1977, 50.

Loshak, Andrei. 2019. "InterNYET: A History of the Russian Internet. Episode #1." YouTube video, 36:15. September 5. https://youtu.be/hdngdbzayHA.

Lukasik, Stephen. 2011. "Why the Arpanet Was Built." *IEEE Annals of the History of Computing* 33 (3): 4–21. https://ieeexplore.ieee.org/document/5432117/?reload=true.

Lurje, Lev. 2009. "Leningradskii telefonnyi efir" ["Phone Air in Leningrad"]. TV show. *5-tv.ru*, April 25. http://www.5-tv.ru/video/502204/.

Maksimovich, Gennadii. 1978. *Besedy s akademikom V.Glushkovym* [Conversations with Academician V. Glushkov]. Molodaia gvardiia.

Maksimovich, Gennadij. 1975. "Kibernetika XXI veka" ["Cybernetics of the 21st Century"]. *Fantastika, 1973–1974*. Ed. Vitalij Bugrov. Molodaia Gvardiia, 241–64.

Malcomson, Scott. 2017. "War Games." *Carnegy Reporter*, Dec 8, 2017. https://medium.com/carnegie-reporter/war-games-29fe413f1818.

Malinovskii, Alexandr. 2000. *Tektologiia. Teoriia sistem. Teoreticheskaia biologiia* [Tektology. Theory of Systems]. Theoretical Biology. URSS.

Malinovskii, Boris. 1995. *Istoriia vychislitel'noi tekhniki v litsakh* ["A History of Computing Technology"]. Persons Kyiv: Firma KIT, PTOO "A.S.K."

"Manuel Castells." Russkii arkhipelag, last updated 2018. http://www.archipelag.ru/authors/castells/.

Manin, Dmitry. 1997. "Zadushit li kommertsiia utopiiu" ["Will Business Choke Off Utopia?"] *Zhurnal.ru*, No 1 (4). Archived at https://web.archive.org/web/19970525083322/http://www.zhurnal.ru/4/verbit.htm.

Markoff, John. 1992. "Business Technology; Pools of Memory, Waves of Dispute." *New York Times*, January 29, 1992.

Markoff, John. 1989. "Soviet Computing: An Inside View." *New York Times*. March 25.

Maslov, Vadim. n.d. "Russkaia Set': Istorii" ["The Russian Net: Stories"]. Last modified 1996. http://www.kovrik.com/sib/internet/RussNetStoryShort.html.

Maslov, Vadim. n.d. "SovInformBureau." Last modified July 22, 1999. http://www.kovrik.com/sib/.

Maslov, Vadim. 1995. "Guide to Russian Internet Sources." Message posted to soc.culture.soviet, February 5. Archived at https://groups.google.com/g/soc.culture.soviet/c/oQaTtyXvmwg/m/LeLYgVf-6WYJ.

May, Edwin C., and Sonali Bhatt Marwaha, eds. 2018–19. *The Star Gate Archives: Reports of the United States Government Sponsored Psi Program, 1972–1995*. 4 vols. McFarland.

"May Ivanych Muxin." N.M.Zh.D. 1996—***. April 2, 1996. https://www.tema.ru/rrr/ruslat/may.html.

McLuhan, Marshall. 1969. "The Playboy-Interview." *Playboy*, March 1969.

Menzel, Birgit, Michael Hagemeister, and Bernice Glatzer Rosenthal. 2012. *The New Age of Russia: Occult and Esoteric Dimensions*. Verlag Otto Sagner.

Menzel, Birgit. 2019. "New Age Diplomacy: The Role of the Esalen Institute in Ending the Cold War." New Age in Russia, 11/12/2019. https://newageru.hypotheses.org/1903.

"Michael Murphy." 1976. *New Yorker*, May 1, 48.

Milner, Greg. 2009. *Perfecting Sound Forever: An Aural History of Recorded Music*. Faber and Faber.

Mitchell, Edgar, and Stanley Krippner. 2016. *Telepathy (Psychic Exploration)*. Cosimo Books. Kindle.

Mitnick, Kevin, and William Simon. 2003. *The Art of Deception: Controlling the Human Element of Security*. Wiley.

More, Max, and Ray Kurzweil. 2002. "Max More and Ray Kurzweil on the Singularity." Kurzweil Accelerating Intelligence. February 26, 2002. https://www.kurzweilai.net/max-more-and-ray-kurzweil-on-the-singularity-2.

More, Max. 1990. "Transhumanism: Toward a Futurist Philosophy." *Extpory* (6): 6–12. Archived at https://web.archive.org/web/20051029125153/http://www.maxmore.com/transhum.htm.

Moss, Thelma. 2015. *Psychic Research in the Soviet Union*. Cosimo Classics. eBook.

Mumford, Michael D., Andrew M. Rose, and David A. Goslin. 1995. "An Evaluation of Remote Viewing: Research and Applications." The American Institutes for Research, September 29. http://www.lfr.org/lfr/csl/library/airreport.pdf (accessed August 01, 2024).

Murphy, Michael. 1982. *An End to Ordinary History*. Tarcherperigree.

Natale, Simone. 2011. "A Cosmology of Invisible Fluids: Wireless, X-Rays, and Psychical Research Around 1900." *Canadian Journal of Communication* 36 (2), 163–75.

Natale, Simone, and Gabriele Balbi. 2014. "Media and the Imaginary in History: The Role of the Fantastic in Different Stages of Media Change." *Media History* 20: 203–18.

Natale, Simone. 2012. "Understanding Media Archaeology." *Canadian Journal of Communication* 37: 523–27.

Natale, Simone, and Diana Pasulka, eds. 2019. *Believing in Bits: Digital Media and the Supernatural*. Oxford University Press.

Naughton, John. 2016. "The Evolution of the Internet: From Military Experiment to General Purpose Technology." *Journal of Cyber Policy* 1 (1): 5–28.

nitoc [pseud.]. 2012. "shtuchnyi Brodskii" ["Exceptional Brodsky"]. Soviet life, Livejournal, August 30. https://soviet-life.livejournal.com/1582482.html.

Novak, Matt. 2012. "Tripping Through the Cold War: Drug Warfare in the Retrofuture." Smithsonianmag.com, May 18. https://www.smithsonianmag.com/history/tripping-through-the-cold-war-drug-warfare-in-the-retrofuture-100014010/#SgWugticsJC8VpC6.99.

Oborona [pseud.]. April 4, 2008. https://air-spb.ucoz.ru/forum/5-14-237-16-1209912696.

"Oral-History: Yury Gulyaev." 2017. Interviewed by Victor Plessky and Clemens Ruppel for the IEEE History Center. Engineering and Technology History Wiki. October 31. https://ethw.org/Oral-History:Yury_Gulyaev.

Ostrander, Sheila, and Lynn Schroeder. 1970. *Psychic Discoveries Behind the Iron Curtain*. Prentice-Hall.

Ostrovskii, Efim. 2006. "Revansh v kholodnoi voine." Gumanitarnyi portal, August 15. https://gtmarket.ru/laboratory/expertize/2006/2238.

Oushakine, Serguei. 2001. "The Terrifying Mimicry of Samizdat." *Public Culture* 13 (2): , 191–214.

Pantell, Richard, and Harold Puthoff. 1969. *Fundamentals of Quantum Electronics.* Wiley.

Parisi, Valentina, ed. 2015. *Samizdat. Between Practices and Representations. Lecture Series at Open Society Archives, Budapest, February–June 2013.* IAS Publications no. 1, Central European University, Institute of Advanced Study, Budapest.

Perov, V. P. 1984. "Postanovka issledovanii nalichiia sviazi mezhdu sensorno-razobshchennymi bioob'ektami" ["Setting up studies of the presence of connectivity between sensory-disjointed biobjects"], *Ėlektromagnitnye polia v biosfere (Electromagnetic fields in the biosphere).* Vol. 1, Nauka, 302–12.

Pertsev, Andrei. 2016. "Kremlevskii mechtatel': kto formiroval mirovozzrenie Kirienko" ["The Kremlin Dreamer: Who Shaped Kirienko's Mindset"]. Carnegie Moscow Center, October 26. https://carnegie.ru/commentary/64928.

Peskin, Eugene. 1994. "IRC: #scs channel." Message posted to relcom.talk, March 31. Archived at https://groups.google.com/g/relcom.talk/c/GFFnLGJIIFg/m/VrSGU5Ooil8J.

Peters, Benjamin. 2016. *How Not to Network a Nation. The Uneasy History of the Soviet Internet.* MIT Press.

Peters, John Durham. 1999. *Speaking into the Air: A History of the Idea of Communication.* University of Chicago Press.

Petersen, Keith. 1985. "INTERVIEW.WLC—An interview with Ward Christensen." Message posted to net.micro.cpm, April 24. Archived at https://groups.google.com/g/net.micro.cpm/c/KhxLm6GqE2k/m/qO1hNCB6RoAJ.

Piatkovskii, Aleksei. 2012. "Ocherk istorii samizdata" ["Essay on the history of the Samizdat"]. Gefter.ru. August 8. http://gefter.ru/archive/5757.

Pickering A. 2010. *The Cybernetic Brain. Sketches of Another Future.* University of Chicago Press.

Pinch, Trevor, and Harry Collins. 1984. "Private Science and Public Knowledge: The Committee for the Scientific Investigation of the Claims of the Paranormal and Its Use of the Literature." *Social Studies of Science* 14 (4): 521–46.

Pis'ma inzhenera, kandidata tekhnicheskikh nauk Kazhinskogo Bernarda Bernardovicha k K.Ė. Tsiolkovskomu (Letters of engineer, candidate of technical sciences Kazhinskii Bernard Bernardovich to K.E. Tsiolkovsky). n.d. Archives of K. E. Tsiolkovsky, op. 5, d. 265. http://www.ras.ru/ktsiolkovskyarchive/5_actview.aspx?id=1285.

Platonov, Andrei. 2016. *Ia prozhil zhizn': Pis'ma 1920–1950 godov [I've lived my life: Letters from the 1950s and 1960s]*, Elena Shubina's Publishing Haus.

Platonov, Andrei. 2004. *Sochineniya* (Collected papers). Vol. 1/2.

Platonov, Andrei. 1991. "A Technical Novel: Bread and Reading." *Index on Censorship* 20 (8): 38–50. August 1. https://doi.org/10.1080/03064229108535179.

Plekhanov, Gennadii. 2004. *Tainy telepatii, "Fenomen umnogo Gansa" [Secrets of Telepathy. "The Clever Hans Phenomenon"].* Veche.

Plyushch, Leonid. 1979. *Na karnavale istorii [At the carnival of history].* Overseas Publications Interchange. https://www.sakharov-center.ru/asfcd/auth/?t=book&num=2056.

"Poetry & Prose archives of SCS/SCR." *De.Lit.Zyne*. Last modified June 4, 1996. http://teneta.rinet.ru/DeLitZyne/LITERATURE/.

Pokataeva, Elena. 2012. "Internet kak predchuvstvie" ["Internet As Premonition"]. *Itogi*, No. 1 (812), January 1 50–54. Archived at http://www.itogi.ru/exclus/2012/1/173518.html.

Poletaev, Andrei. 1998. "Voennaia kibernetika," ili Fragment istorii otechestvennoi "lzhenauki" ["Military Cybernetics," or An Essay on the History of National False Science]. *Ocherki istorii informatiki v Rossii*. edited by Dmitrii Pospelov and Yakov Fet. OIGGM SO RAN, 515–30.

Poletaev, Igor. 1958. *Signal*. Radio.

Polianski, Igor. 2012. "Between Hegel and Haeckel. Monistic Worldview, Marxist Philosophy, and Biomedicine in Russia and the Soviet Union." In *Monism: Science, Philosophy, Religion, and the History of a Worldview*, edited by Todd H. Weir. Palgrave Macmillan.

Poller, Jake. 2019. *Aldous Huxley and Alternative Spirituality*. Aries Book Series "Texts and Studies in Western Esoterism," vol. 27. Brill.

Poloskova, Tat'iana, and Vitalii Skrinnik. 2003. *Russkii Mir: Mify i Realii*. Moskovskii Fond "Rossiiane."

Polotsk, Ilan. 1980. "Otodvinut' bar'er: Beseda s chlenom Komissii po kompleksnomu izucheniiu cheloveka Nauchnogo soveta po kibernetike AN SSSR I.B. Charkovskim" ["Pushing Back the Barrier: A Conversation with I.B. Charkovsky, Member of the Commission for the Complex Study of Man of the Scientific Council on Cybernetics of the USSR Academy of Sciences"]. *Sovetskaia molodezh'*. Riga, April 27.

Poroskov N. 2019. "Supersoldat dlia voin budushchego" ["A Super Soldier for the Wars of the Future"]. *Armeiskii vestnik* (February): 86–91. http://sc.mil.ru/files/morf/military/archive/AS_02_2019.pdf.

Possamai, Adam. 2005. *Religion and Popular Culture: A Hyper-real Testament*. Peter Lang.

Pototsky, Dan. 2014. "Anatole Klyosov: The Original Soviet Internet Geek." *Russia Beyond*, April 7, 2014. https://www.rbth.com/science_and_tech/2014/04/07/anatole_klyosov_the_original_soviet_internet_geek_35713.html.

Povarov G. "Norbert Viner i ego 'Kibernetika.'" 1968. In Norbert Viener, *Kibernetika ili upravlenie i svjaz' v zhivotnom i mashine* [Cybernetics or Control and Communication in The Animal and the Machine]. Sovetskoe radio, S. 24.

Pozner, Vladimir. 2012. "Proshchanie s illiuziiami" ["A Farewell to Delusions"]. Astrel.

Prangishvili, A. S., A. E. Sherozia, and F. V. Bassin, eds. 1978–1989. *Bessoznatel'noe. Priroda. Funktsii. Metody issledovaniia* [The Unconscious. Nature. Functions. Methods of research]. 4 vols. Metsniereba Publishing House.

Press, Larry. 1991. "Wide-Area Collaboration." *Communications of the ACM* 34 (12). http://som.csudh.edu/fac/lpress/articles/relcom.pdf.

Press, Larry. 2011. "Before the Twitter Revolutions, There Was the Usenet Revolution." *CIS 471: Internet applications and technology and their implications for individuals, organizations and society*. January 29, 2011. http://cis471.blogspot.de/2011/01/before-twitter-revolutions-there-was.html.

"Pressa v obshchestve (1959–2000). Otsenki zhurnalistov i sotsiologov. Dokumenty"/ Mass Media and Society (1959—2000). Opinions of Journalists and Sociologists. 2000. *Biblioteka Moskovskoĭ shkoly politicheskikh issledovanii*. Vol. 23. http://www.evartist.narod.ru/text25/001.htm.

Price, David. 1998. "Gregory Bateson and the OSS: World War II and Bateson's Assessment of Applied Anthropology." *Human Organization* (4): 379–84.

Problemy rezervnykh vozmozhnostei cheloveka [*Problems of Human Reserve Capacity*]. 1982. Collection of works. Edited by V. V. Kuznetsov. VNIIFK.

Puthoff, Harold, and Russel Targ. 1976. "A Perceptual Channel for Information Transfer over Kilometer Distances: Historical Perspective and Recent Research." *Proceedings of the IEEE* 64 (3): 329–54.

Puthoff, Harold, and Russel Targ. 1974. "Psychic Research and Modern Physics." Mitchell, E. (Ed.), *Psychic Exploration: A Challenge for Science*. Putnam's, 1974.

Puthoff, Harold. 1996. "CIA-Initiated Remote Viewing at Stanford Research Institute." *Journal of Scientific Exploration* 10 (1): 63–76.

Putin, Vladimir. 2001. "Vystuplenie na otkrytii Kongressa sootechestvennikov" ["An Opening Address at a Congress of Compatriots"]. Transcript. http://kremlin.ru/events/president/transcripts/21359.

Raushenbach, Boris. 2003. *Prazdnye mysli: ocherki, stat'i, vospominaniia* [Idle Thoughts: Essays, Articles, Memoirs]. Gareeva. Agraf.

"Razmnozhenie i rasprostranenie seksual'no-pornograficheskikh materialov" ["Multiplication and Distribution of Sexual and Pornographic Features"]. 1974. KGB report. Copy of archival document published by Eduard Andriushchenko (@kgbfiles_rus). Telegram posting, July 9, 2020. https://t.me/kgbfiles_rus/1765.

Rekshynskyj, Bohdan. 1993. "RFD: soc.culture.ukrainian." Message posted to news.groups, March 26. Archived at https://groups.google.com/g/news.groups/c/wGuudOocK-g/m/XzblYcKGUMYJ.

Revich, Vsevolod. 1971. "Predvidenija sbyvajutsja" ["Adventures are coming true"]. *Khimiya i Zhizn'* (Chemistry and Life) (2): 41–42.

Rheingold, Howard. 1993. *The Virtual Community*. Addison-Wesley Longman. Electronic Version. http://rheingold.com/vc/book/intro.html (accessed August 13, 2020).

Rindzevičiūtė, Eglė. 2016. *The Power of Systems. How Policy Sciences Opened Up the Cold War World*. Cornell University Press.

Rogachev, Jurij. 1998. *Vychislitel'naia tekhnika ot M-1 do M-13 (1950—1990)* ["Computing Technology From M-1 To M-13"]. NIIVK.

Rotenberg, Vadim. n.d. "Triumf bessoznatel'nogo" ["Triumph of the Unconscious"]. *Sait psikhofiziologa Vadima Rotenberga* (*Website of psychophysiologist Vadim Rotenberg*). http://www.vsrotenberg.rjews.com/1m.html#.YO3uxmT7SL0.

Rubel, Viktor, Aleksei Savin, and Boris Ratnikov. 2016. *Psi-voiny: Zapad i Vostok. Istoriia v svidetel'stvakh ochevidtsev* [Psy-Wars: West and East. History as Told by Witnesses]. Postum.

Rubel, Viktor. 2010. *Tainye psi-voiny Rossii i Ameriki: ot Vtoroi mirovoi do nashikh dnei* ["Secret Psy-Wars Between Russia and the States: From the Second World War Until Now."] AST.

"Russkii Mir: vosstanovlenie konteksta" (Russian World: Recovery of Context). 2001. Russkii arkhipelag, September. http://www.archipelag.ru/ru_mir/history/history01/shedrovitsky-russmir/.

Ryan, Johnny. *A History of the Internet and the Digital Future*. London: Reaktion Books, 2010.

Safronov, Aleksei. 2019. "Avtomatizirovannaia sistema planovykh raschetov Gosplana SSSR kak neobkhodimyi shag na puti k obshchegosudarstvennoi avtomatizirovannoi sisteme ucheta i obrabotki informatsii (OGAS)" ["The Gosplan Automated Planning System as a Necessary Step Toward the Nationwide Automated Data Processing and Control System (NACS)"]. *Russian Journal of Economic History* 15 (4): 395–409.

Safronov, Aleksei. 2019. *Pionery tsifrovizatsii*. 60. Analiticheskii tsentr pri Pravitel'stvo Rossiiskoi Federatsii.

Samohin, V. P., and K. V. Meshherinova. 2018. "Akademik Sergej Alekseevich Lebedev." *Mashinostroenie i komp'juternye tehnologii* (6): S. 18–88.

"Samouvazhenie, balet i grazhdanskoe obshchestvo" ["Self-respect, ballet and civil society"]. 2014. *Kontinent-Sibir' Online* April 25. https://ksonline.ru/stats/-/id/3040/.

Sarfatti, Jack. 1992, 1995. "Sarfatti's Illuminati: In the Thick of It!" *MindNet Journal* 2 (2A). Archived at http://www.whale.to/b/sarfatti.html.

Savitskaia, Svetlana. 2015. *Djuna: Odinochestvo solntsa* [*Djuna: A solitude of the Sun*]. Eksmo.

Sazikov, Aleksei. 2016. "Ekran Elin" [The Elin Screen]. *Livejournal*, February 2. https://sazikov.livejournal.com/1957.html.

Sazikov, Aleksei. 2014. "'Global'nyi teatr' Iosifa Gol'dina" ["Iosif Goldin's Global Theatre"]. *Teatr. Zhivopis'. Kino. Muzyka. Ezhekvartal'nyi al'manakh GITIS*, 183–93.

Schatz, Joel. 1987. "Perceptions of a Seasoned American Traveler to the Soviet Union." *In Context* (15). Archived at https://www.context.org/iclib/ic15/schatz/.

Schmidt, Henrike, Katy Teubener, and Natalja Konradova. 2006. *Control + Shift. Public and Private Usages of the Russian Internet*. BOD-Verlag.

Schmidt, Henrike. 2011. *Russische Literatur im Internet: Zwischen digitaler Folklore und politischer Propaganda*. Transcript.

Sconce, Jeffrey. 2000. *Haunted Media: Electronic Presence from Telegraphy to Television*. Duke University Press.

Segalovich, Ilya. 2013. "Kak sozdat' kompaniiu—mirovogo lidera?" ["How to Launch a Global Leading Business"]. YouTube video, 1:52. July 25. https://www.youtube.com/watch?v=sby-SvPBuXM.

Setrov M. 1967. "Ob obshhih jelementah tektologii A. Bogdanova, kibernetiki i teorii sistem" ["On general elements of Bogdanov's tektology, Cybernetics and Systems Theory"]. *Uch. zap. kafedr obshhestvennyh nauk vuzov Leningrada. Filosofija* (8): 59.

Shachtman, Noah. 2012. "How Pacific Island Missile Tests Helped Launch the Internet." *Internet Hall Of Fame*, August 27. https://www.internethalloffame.org//blog/2012/08/27/how-pacific-island-missile-tests-helped-launch-internet.

Shchedrovitskii, Petr. 2000. "Russkii mir i Transnatsional'noe russkoe" ["The Russian World and the Transnational Russian"]. Русский журнал, March 2. Archived at http://old.russ.ru/politics/meta/20000302_schedr.html.

Schmidt, Henrike, Katy Teubener, and Natalia Konradova, eds. 2006. *Control + Schift: Public and Private Usage of the Russian Internet*, Books on Demand, 156–76.

Shubin, Aleksandr. 2006. *Predannaia demokratiia: SSSR i neformaly [Democracy Betrayed: The USSR and Neformaly] (1986–1989)*. Evropa.

Shulgin, Alexei. 1996. "Art, Power, and Communication." V2_ Lab for the Unstable media. October 7. https://v2.nl/archive/articles/art-power-and-communication.

Shulman, Sol. 2017. "Polet bumeranga" ["A Boomerang Flight"]. September 20. https://solshulman.wordpress.com/2017/09/20/polet-bumeranga/.

Shura_Balaganov [pseud.]. 2008. "Da khvatit purgu gnat'" ["Don't Give Me This Crap"]. Forum Leningradskogo Efira (Leningrad *Efir* Forum), May 5, 07:08. https://air-spb.ucoz.ru/forum/5-14-352-16-1209956885.

Shure, Caitlin. 2018. "Brain Waves, A Cultural History: Oscillations of Neuroscience, Technology, Telepathy, and Transcendence." PhD diss., Columbia University. https://doi.org/info:doi/.

Smolyak, Olga. 2014. "'Working for Yourself': Resource Theft at a Factory in the Late Soviet Era. Summary." *Laboratorium Russian Review of Social Research*, 6 (2): 21–57.

Snider, Suzanne. 2003. "Est, Werner Erhard, And the Corporatization of Self-Help." McSweeney's Internet Tendency. March 5. https://www.mcsweeneys.net/articles/est-werner-erhard-and-the-corporatization-of-self-help-2003.

Sobolev, Sergei, Anatolii Kitov, and Aleksei Lyapunov. 1955. "Osnovnye cherty kibernetiki." *Voprosy filosofii*, no. 4, 136–48.

Sobolev, Sergei, Anatolii Kitov, and Aleksei Lyapunov. 1955. "Osnovnye cherty kibernetiki." *Voprosy filosofii*, no. 4, 136–48.

Sokolov-Mitrich, Dmitrii. 2014. *Yandex.Kniga* [*Yandex.Book*]. Mann, Ivanov i Ferber. https://www.litres.ru/dmitriy-sokolov-mitrich/yandeks-kniga/chitat-onlayn/.

Soros, George. 1995. *Soros about Soros. Staying Ahead of the Curve*. Wiley.

Sosnovskii, Vladimir, and Anton Orlov. 2011. "Sovetskaia vychislitel'naia tekhnika. Istoriia vzleta i zabveniia" ["Soviet Computing Technology. A History of Rise and Oblivion"]. Russkii proekt, April 4. http://www.rusproject.org/analysis/analysis_2/sovetskie_komputery.

Yadov, V. A., ed. 1977. *Sotsial'no-psikhologicheskii portret inzhenera. Po materialam obsledovaniia inzhenerov leningradskikh proektno-konstruktorskikh organizatsii* [Socio Psychological Depiction of an Engineer. Based on a Study of Engineers of Leningrad Planning and Design Organisations] Mysl'.

Soviet Coup Archive. n.d. Accessed August 01, 2024. http://collapse.su/.

Spafford, Gene. 1988. "Some interesting news stats." Message posted to news.misc, news.admin, October 24. Archived at https://tech-insider.org/internet/research/1988/1024.htm.

Standage T. 2007. *The Victorian Internet: The Remarkable Story of the Telegraph And the Nineteenth Century's On-line Pioneers*. Walker.

Stern, Nancy. 1980. "Herman Goldstine Interview." The Center for the History of Information Processing. August 11. Charles Babbage Institute, University of Minnesota. http://conservancy.umn.edu/bitstream/11299/107333/1/oh018hhg.pdf.

Sternberg, Janet. 2000. "Virtual Misbehavior: Breaking Rules of Conduct in Online Environments." *Proc. of the Media Ecology Association*, Fordham University, June 16–17.

Stoiukhina, Natalia, and Vladimir Mazilov. 2014. "Neizvestnye s"ezdy: Vtoroi psikhonevrologicheskii" / Unknown Congresses: The Second Psychological. *Iaroslavskii pedagogicheskii vestnik* 4 (1): 277–86.

Streeter, Thomas. 2011. *The Net Effect: Romanticism, Capitalism, and the Internet*. NYU Press.

Stuckey, William K. 1979. "Official Circles: Psi on Capitol Hill." *Omni* 1 (10): 24–25.

Sukhanov, Lev. 1992. *Tri goda s Borisom El'tsinym* (*Three years with Boris Yeltsin*). Bara.

Suslov, Mikhail. 2016. "Of Planets and Trenches: Imperial Science Fiction in Contemporary Russia." *The Russian Review* (September): 562–78. https://doi.org/10.1111/russ.12102.

Suslov, Mikhail, and Per-Arne Bodin, eds. 2019. *The Post-Soviet Politics of Utopia: Language, Fiction and Fantasy in Modern Russia*. I.B. Tauris.

Synerj [pseud.]. 2008. "O spirali vremeni, telefonnom efire, neformal'noi gazete, besplatnom syre, i moskovskom SUPe" ["About Spiral of Time, Phone Air, Informal Newspaper and Moscow SUP"]. *Livejournal.com*, March 3. http://synerj.livejournal.com/53071.html.

Tagunov O. 1976. Rasplata za radiokhuliganstvo [A Reckoning for Radio Hooliganism]. *Radio* (7): 63.

Takhtadzhjan, Armen. 1971. "Tektologija: Istorija i Problemy" ["Tectology: History and Problems"]. In *Sistemnye issledovanija*. "Nauka," 205.

Taratorin, Aleksandr. 1997. *Nevydumannaia istoriia ekstrasensov v Rossii*. Santa-Klara.

Targ, Russel, and Jane Katra. 1998. *Miracles of Mind: Exploring Nonlocal Consciousness and Spiritual Healing*. New World Library.

Targ, Russel, and Harold Puthoff. 1974. "Information Transfer Under Condition of Sensory Shielding." *Nature* 251, October 18, 602–7.

Targ, Russell, and Keith Harary. 1984. *The Mind Race: Understanding and Using Psychic Abilities*. Villard Books.

"Telemost nad bezdnoi" [Space Bridge Over an Abyss]. 2012. *Ogonek* 35 (5242), (September): 36. Archived at https://www.kommersant.ru/doc/2009494.

Telesin, Yulius. 1986. *Tysiacha i odin izbrannyi sovetskii politicheskii anekdot* [1001 Selected Soviet Political Jokes]. Ermitazh.

Teltsch, Kathleen. 1988. "U.S.-Style Philanthropy Gains in the Soviet Union." *New York Times*, September 25, 12.

Teneta. n.d. Konkurs russkoi setevoi literatury [Teneta. Russian Net Literature competition]. Last modified 2003. http://teneta.rinet.ru/.

The History of Track Two. n.d. Timeline. *An Institute for Citizen Diplomacy*. https://www.trackii.com/timeline.

"The KGB Performs That Old Red Magic." 1977. *Washington Post*, August 10.

Thomson, Virginia, Dulce Murphy, and Carol Miskel. 2020. "Forty Years Later, Track Two Continues to Expand Its Global Reach." *Esalen.org*, August 20. https://www.esalen.org/post/forty-years-later-track-two-continues-to-expand-its-global-reach.

Tiktin, Sergei, and Dora Shturman. 1985. *Sovetskii Soiuz v zerkale politicheskogo anekdota* [The Soviet Union Reflected Through Political Jokes]. Overseas Publications Interchange Ltd.

Tofaniuk, Elena. 2013. "Kak fond Aleksandra Galitskogo stal liderom venchurnogo rynka" ["How the Alexander Galitsky Fund became the leader of the venture capital market"]. *Forbes*, 2013. https://www.forbes.ru/finansy/investitsii/247848-kak-fond-aleksandra-galitskogo-stal-liderom-venchurnogo-rynka.

Tolstoy, Alexey N. 1945. *Road to Calvary*. Translated by Edith Bone, Hutchinson International Authors Ltd.

Trinkner, Bradley. 2014. "Bolshevik voices: radio broadcasting in the Soviet Union, 1917–1991." *Theses and Dissertations, 545*. Rowan Digital Works. https://rdw.rowan.edu/etd/545.

Turner, Fred. 2000. *From Counterculture to Cyberculture. Stewart Brand, the Whole Earth Network, and the Rise of Digital Utopianism*. University of Chicago Press.

Vakhnin, V. 1957. "Iskusstvennye sputniki Zemli" ["Artificial Earth satellites"]. *Radio* 6: 14–17.

Van Dyke, P. T., and M. L. Juncosa. 1973. *Paranormal Phenomena—Briefing on a Net Assessment Study. A Working Note Prepared for Advanced Research Project Agency*.

Varvoglis, Mario, and Renaud Evrard. 2010. "Institut Métapsychique International." *Mindfield: The Bulletin of the Parapsychological Association* 2 (3): 10–11.

Vasiliev, Leonid. 1963. *Experiments in Mental Suggestion*. Institute for the Study of Mental Images.

Vasiliev, Leonid. 1965. *Mysterious Phenomena of the Human Psyche*. Translated by Sonia Volochova. University Books.

Vasiliev, Mikhail, and Sergei Gushchev. 1963. *Reportazh iz XXI veka* (*Reporting from the XXI Century*). Sovetskaia Rossiia.

Vasiliev Leonid, Guliaev P. I., Poletaev I. A. 1995. "Telepaticheskaia sviaz'" ["Telepathic Connection"]. In *Parapsikhologiia i psikhofizika* (*Parapsychology and Psychophysics*) no. 2. C.3–8.

Vaughan, A. 1971. "Interview: Montague Ullman, MD." *Psychic* 2, no. 6, June.

Vekhi: Landmarks. A Collection of Articles About the Russian Intelligentsia. 1994. Translated by Marshall S. Shatz and Judith E. Zimmerman. M. E. Sharp.

Velikhov, Evgeny. 2010. *Moi put': Ia na valenkakh poedu v 35-i god: Vospominaniia* ["My Way: I Will Drive to 1935 in My Felt Snow Boots"]. ACT.

Velminski W. 2017. *Homo Sovieticus. Brain Waves, Mind Control, and Telepathic Destiny*. Translated by Erik Butler. MIT Press.

Verbitsky, Mikhail. 1993. "Mein Kampf and freedom." Message posted to soc.culture.soviet, June 9. Archived at https://groups.google.com/g/soc.culture.soviet/c/NEFmK1bnP8c/m/q7JWo58A4h8J.

Verbitsky, Mikhail. 1997. "Gigantomakhiia: informatsionnaia voina" ["Gigantomachy: An Information War"]. *Zhurnal.ru* (4). Archived at https://web.archive.org/web/19970525083322/http://www.zhurnal.ru/4/verbit.htm.

Vezhlian, Evgeniia. 2016. "'Opredelenie situatsii': fakty k razmyshleniiu" Defining the Situation: Facts to Reflect Upon. Interview with Mark Lipovetskii. Gefter.ru. October 17. http://gefter.ru/archive/19743.

Videmann, Vladimir. 2019. *Zapreshchennyi Soiuz. Khippi, mistiki, dissident* [A Union Forbidden: Hippies, Mystics, Dissidents]. RIPOL Klassik; Pal'mira.

Vilenskaia, Larisa. 1985. "Chudesa i tragedii chernogo iashchika. Chto proiskhodit s parapsikhologiei v SSSR" ["Miracles and Tragedies of the Black Box. What is Happening to Parapsychology in the USSR"]. *Grani*, no. 138, Frankfurt am Main.

Vinogradov, Mikhail. 2009. "Ot Rozhdestva Runeta" ["AD Runet"]. *The New Times*, Vol. 6, February 16, 2009. https://newtimes.ru/articles/detail/2972/.

Vinokurov, Igor, Gurtovoi, Georgii. 1993. *Psikhotronnaia voina, ot mifov—k realiiam* [*Psychotronic warfare, from myths to realities*]. Misteriia.

Viznyuk, Sergei. 1994. "RFD: soc.culture.russia." Message posted to soc.culture.soviet, July 10. Archived at https://groups.google.com/g/soc.culture.soviet/c/Yvoq5Z1AKYA/m/O2g_4AVNrcoJ.

Vorob'eva, A. A. 2013. "Literatura vlasti i vlast' literatury: k voprosu o funktsiiakh literaturotsentrizma v sovetskoi kul'ture" ["Literature of Power and Power of Literature: On Functions of Literature-Centrism in Soviet Culture"]. *Molodezh' i nauka*. Krasnoiarsk: Sibirskii federal'nyi un-t. https://core.ac.uk/download/pdf/38641661.pdf.

Vorobieff. 1995. "RFD: soc.culture.russian." Message posted to news.groups, January 9. Archived at https://groups.google.com/g/news.groups/c/wUUqed_KrBE/m/mgF4Y9TRIqkJ.

Wagner, Gale, Michael Shuman, and Lila Forest. 1987. "Citizen Diplomacy. What It Is, How It Began, and Where It's Going." *In Context* (Winter). Archived at https://www.context.org/iclib/ic15/shuman/.

Wells, H. G. 1921. *Russia in the Shadows*. George H. Doran. https://gutenberg.net.au/ebooks06/0602371h.html.

Wiener, Norbert. 1954. *The Human Use of Human Beings: Cybernetics and Society*. Doubleday.

Williams, Hayley. 2015. "The Hacker Who Inspired Apple: John 'Captain Crunch' Draper." *Lifehacker*, November 17. https://www.lifehacker.com.au/2015/11/the-hacker-who-inspired-apple-john-captain-crunch-draper/.

Wilson, Andrew. 2005. "Virtual Politics: 'Political Technology' and the Corruption of Post-Soviet Democracy," *Johnson's Russia List*. Email newsletter, December 21. Archived at http://www.russialist.org/archives/9324-5.php.

Winston, Brian. 1998. *Media, Technology and Society: A History; From the Telegraph to the Internet*. Routledge.

Wood, Jim. 2014. "Michael Murphy." *Marin Magazine*, July 28. https://marinmagazine.com/conversation/michael-murphy/.

Yagodinskii, Viktor. 1989. "Marsianin zabroshennyj na Zemlju. O A. Bogdanove (1873–1928) i ego utopijah" ["A Martian Stranded on Earth: On A. Bogdanov (1873–1928) and his Utopias"]. In *V mire fantastiki*. Molodaja gvardija.

Yakovlev, Alexandr. 2005. *Sumerki* [Twilight]. Materik.

Yuldashev, Leonid. 2020. "Tonét—rekonstruktsiia odnoi istorii" ["The Tonet: Reconstruction of a History"]. *Neprikosnovennyi zapas* 2 (130): 72–94.

Yurchak, Alexei. 2002. "Entrepreneurial Governmentality in Postsocialist Russia: A Cultural Investigation of Business Practices." In *The New Entrepreneurs of Europe and Asia*. M. E. Sharpe.

"Za kulisami tain prirody. Interv'iu s I. M. Koganom" [Behind the Scenes of the Mysteries of Nature. An Interview with I.M. Kogan]. 1988. *Vecherniaia Moskva*, October 29. Archived at http://www.kogan-im.com/books/articles/19881029.php.

Zabotin, Vladimir, and Nina Shlippenbakh. 1968. "Biologicheskaia sviaz'" deistvuet" ["The biological connection works"]. *Tekhnika—molodezhi* (*Technology for Youth*) (12): 14–15.

Zakharchenko, Vasilii. 1975. *Razgovor s ėlektricheskim mozgom* [*Talking to the electric brain*]. Detskaia literatura.

Zasurskii, Ivan. 2016. *Media and Power in Post-Soviet Russia*. Routledge.

"Zerkalo dlia chelovechestva" ["A Mirror for Humankind"]. 1987. *Znanie—sila* 1 (175), (January) 20–27.

Zhitinskii, Aleksandr. 1997. *Zheltye stranitsy Internet 1997: Otdykh i razvlecheniia* [Internet Yellow Pages: Leisure and Entertainment]. Piter. Archived at https://web.archive.org/web/20190415090721/http://www.macca.ru/item.php?id=943.

Zielinski, Siegfried. 2006. *Deep Time of the Media: Toward an Archaeology of Hearing and Seeing by Technical Means*. MIT Press.

Zweig, Connie. 1987. "S.F.-Moscow Teleport—Electronic Détente." *Los Angeles Times*, December 9.

INDEX